The Homilies of St. John Chrysostom

Concerning the Statues

The Homilies of St. John Chrysostom

Concerning the Statues

The Homilies of St. John Chrysostom
Concerning the Statues

© Lighthouse Publishing 2025

Written by: St. Chrysostom (347-407 AD)
Translated by: REV. W. R. W. STEPHENS, M.A., (1839-1902)
Updated into Modern U.S English: A.M. Overett (b.1960)

All rights reserved. Without limiting the rights under copyright reserved above, no part of this publication may be reproduced, stored in a retrieval system, or transmitted, in any form or by any means (electronic, mechanical, photocopying, recording or otherwise), without the prior written permission of the copyright owner of this book.

Published by
Lighthouse Publishing
SAN 257-4330
228 Freedom Parkway
Hoschton, GA 30548
United States of America

www.lighthousechristianpublishing.com

HOMILIES OF ST. JOHN CHRYSOSTOM, ARCHBISHOP OF CONSTANTINOPLE, ADDRESSED TO THE PEOPLE OF ANTIOCH, CONCERNING THE STATUES.

Homily I.

The Argument.

This Homily was delivered in the Old Church of Antioch, while St. Chrysostom was yet a Presbyter, upon that saying of the Apostle, 1 Tim. v. 23, "Drink a little wine for thy stomach's sake, and thy often infirmities."

1. Ye have heard the Apostolic voice, that trumpet from heaven, that spiritual lyre! For even as a trumpet sounding a fearful and warlike note, it both dismays the enemy, and arouses the dejected spirits on its own side, and filling them with great boldness, renders those who attend to it invincible against the devil! And again, as a lyre, that gently soothes with soul-captivating melody, it puts to slumber the disquietudes of perverse thoughts; and thus, with pleasure, instils into us much profit. You have heard then today the Apostle discoursing to Timothy of divers necessary matters! For he wrote to him as to the laying on of hands, saying, "Lay hands suddenly on no man, neither be partaker of other men's sins." And he explained the grievous danger of such a transgression, by showing that so men will undergo the punishment of the sins perpetrated by others, in common with them, because they confer the power on their wickedness by the laying on of hands. Presently again he says, "Use a little wine for thy stomach's sake, and thine often infirmities." Today

also he has discoursed to us concerning the subjection of servants, and the madness of misers, as well as on the arrogance of the rich, and on various other matters.

2. Since then it is impossible to go through every part, what part of the words rehearsed would you have us select for the subject of our address to your charity? For as in a meadow, I perceive in what has been read a great diversity of flowers; a multiplicity of roses and violets, and of lilies not a few; and everywhere the various and copious fruit of the Spirit is scattered around, as well as an abundant fragrance. Yea, rather the reading of the divine Scriptures is not a meadow only, but a paradise; for the flowers here have not a mere fragrance only, but fruit too, capable of nourishing the soul. What part then of the things rehearsed do you desire that we bring before you this day? Do you wish what seems the more insignificant, and easy for anyone to understand, to be that which we should handle at present? To me, indeed, this seems proper, and I doubt not you will concur in this opinion. What then is this that might seem plainer than anything else? What but that, which seems so easy, and obvious for anyone to say? Well! What is that? "Use a little wine for thy stomach's sake, and thine often infirmities." Well then, let us employ the whole of our discourse upon this subject; and this we would do, not for the love of praise, nor because we study to exhibit powers of oratory (for the things about to be spoken are not our own, but such as the grace of the Holy Spirit may inspire); but in order that we may stir up those hearers who are too listless, and may convince them of the greatness of the treasure of the holy Scriptures; and that it is neither safe, nor free from peril, to run through them hastily. For if indeed a text so simple and obvious as this one, which seems to the multitude to

contain nothing that need be insisted on, should appear to afford us the means of abundant riches, and openings toward the highest wisdom, much rather will those others, which at once manifest their native wealth, satisfy those who attend to them with their infinite treasures. Assuredly then, we ought not hastily to pass by even those sentences of Scripture which are thought to be plain; for these also have proceeded from the grace of the Spirit; but this grace is never small, nor mean, but great and admirable, and worthy the munificence of the Giver.

3. Let us not therefore listen carelessly; since even they who roast the metallic earth, when they have thrown it into the furnace, not only take up the masses of gold, but also collect the small particles with the utmost care. Inasmuch, then, as we likewise have to roast the gold drawn from the Apostolic mines, not by casting it into the furnace, but by depositing it in the thoughts of your souls; not lighting an earthly flame, but kindling the fire of the Spirit, let us collect the little particles with diligence. For if the saying be brief, yet is its virtue great. For pearls too have their proper market, not owing to the size of the substance, but the beauty of their nature. Even so is it with the reading of the divine Scriptures; for worldly instruction rolls forth its trifles in abundance, and deluges its hearers with a torrent of vain babblings, but dismisses them empty-handed, and without having gathered any profit great or small. Not so however is it with the grace of the Spirit, but, on the contrary, by means of small sentences, it implants divine wisdom in all who give heed, and one sentence often times affords to those who receive it a sufficient source of provision for the whole journey of life.

4. Since then its riches are so great, let us arouse ourselves, and receive that which is spoken with a watchful mind; for I am preparing to plunge our discussion to an extreme depth. The admonition itself hath no doubt seemed beside the purpose, and superfluous to many: and they are apt to talk much in this way, "Was Timothy of himself not able to judge what it was needful to make use of, and did he wait to learn this of his teacher. And then did the teacher not only give directions, but also set them down in writing, graving it there as on a column of brass in his Epistle to him? And was he not ashamed to give directions about things of this nature, when writing in a public manner, to his disciple?" For this end then, that thou may learn that the admonition, so far from being beside the purpose, was a necessary and highly profitable one; and that the thing proceeded not from Paul, but from the grace of the Spirit, viz, that this should have been (I say) not a spoken precept, but one deposited in letters, and to be handed down to all future generations through the Epistle, I shall proceed at once to the proof.

5. For besides the subjects which have been mentioned, there is another, about which some are no less perplexed, enquiring within themselves on what account God permitted a man possessing such confidence towards Him, whose bones and relics expelled demons, to fall into such a state of infirmity; for it is not merely that he was sick, but constantly, and for a length of time; and by these recurring and prolonged infirmities he was not permitted to have even a brief respite. "How does this appear," it may be asked? From the very words of Paul, for he does not say, on account of the "infirmity," but on account of the "infirmities;" and not merely "infirmities," but he clearly speaks of these as being constant, when he says

"thine often infirmities." Let those then attend to this, whoever they are, who being given over to a lingering sickness are querulous and dejected under it.

6. But the subject of enquiry is not only, that being a holy man he was sick, and sick so continually, but that he was at the same time entrusted with the public affairs of the world. For if he had been one of those who have retreated to the tops of mountains; who have fixed their cells in solitude, and who have chosen that life which is free from all business, the matter now enquired into were no such difficulty; but that one thrust forward in the throng, and in whose hands the care of so many Churches was placed, and who superintended whole cities and nations; nay, the world at large, with so much alacrity and diligence, should be subjected to the straitening of infirmities! This it is which most of all may bewilder one who does not duly consider it. Because, even if not for himself, yet for others at least, it was necessary he should have health. "He was the best general," says the objector. "The war was waged by him, not only against the unbeliever, but against demons, and against the devil himself. All the enemy contended with much vehemence, scattering the forces, and capturing prisoners; but this man was able to bring back myriads to the truth, and yet he was sick! For if," he says, "no other injury to the cause had come of this sickness, yet this alone was sufficient to discourage and relax the faithful. If soldiers, when they see their general detained in bed, become discouraged and slack for the fight, much rather was it probable that the faithful should betray somewhat of human nature, when they saw that teacher, who had wrought so many signs, in continual sickness and suffering of body."

7. But this is not all. These sceptics propose yet a further enquiry, by asking for what reason Timothy neither healed himself, nor was healed by his instructor, when he was reduced to this state. Whilst the Apostles raised the dead, cast out devils, and conquered death with abundant ease, they could not even restore the body of one sick man! Although with respect to other bodies, both during their own lives and after death, they manifested such extraordinary power, they did not restore a stomach that had lost its vigor! And what is more than this, Paul is not ashamed, and does not blush, after the many and great signs which he had displayed even by a simple word; yet, in writing to Timothy, to bid him take refuge in the healing virtue of wine drinking. Not that to drink wine is shameful. God forbid! For such precepts belong to heretics; but the matter of astonishment is, that he accounted it no disgrace not to be able, without this kind of assistance, to set one member right when it was disordered. Nevertheless, he was so far from being ashamed of this, that he has made it manifest to all posterity. You see then to what a depth we have brought down the subject, and how that which seemed to be little, is full of innumerable questions. Well then, let us proceed to the solution; for we have explored the question thus deep, in order that, having excited your attention, we might lay up the explanation in a safe storehouse.

8. But before I proceed to solve these questions, permit me to say something of the virtue of Timothy, and of the loving care of Paul. For what was ever more tender hearted than this man, who being so far distant, and encircled with so many cares, exercised so much consideration for the health of his disciple's stomach, and wrote with exact attention about the correction of his

disorder? And what could equal the virtue of Timothy? He so despised luxury, and derided the sumptuous table, as to fall into sickness from excessive austerity, and intense fasting. For that he was not naturally so infirm a person, but had overthrown the strength of his stomach by fasting and water drinking; you may hear Paul himself carefully making this plain. For he does not simply say, "use a little wine;" but having said before, "Drink no longer water," he then brings forward his counsel as to the drinking of wine. And this expression "no longer" was a manifest proof, that till then he had drunk water, and on that account was become infirm. Who then would not wonder at his divine wisdom and strictness? He laid hold on the very heavens, and sprang to the highest point of virtue. And his Teacher testifies this, when he thus speaks, "I have sent unto you Timothy, who is my beloved and faithful son in the Lord;" and when Paul calls him "a son," and a "faithful and beloved son," these words are sufficient to show that he possessed every kind of virtue. For the judgments of the saints are not given according to favor or enmity, but are free from all prejudice. Timothy would not have been so enviable, if he had been Paul's son naturally, as he was now admirable, inasmuch as having no connection with him according to the flesh, he introduced himself by the relationship of piety into the Apostle's adoption; preserving the marks of his spiritual wisdom with exactness in all things. For even as a young bullock linked to a bull, so he drew the yoke along with him, to whatever part of the world he went: and did not draw it the less on account of his youth, but his ready will made him emulate the labors of his teacher. And of this, Paul himself was again a witness when he said, "Let no man despise him, for he works the work of the Lord as I also do." See you how he bears witness, that the ardor of Timothy was the very counterpart of his own?

9. Furthermore, in order that he might not be thought to have said these things out of favor or kindness, he makes his hearers themselves to be witnesses of the virtue of his son, when he says, "But ye know the proof of him, that, as a son with a father, so he hath served with me in the Gospel;" that is, "ye have had experience of his virtue, and of his approved soul." At the same time, however, that he had reached to this height of good works, he did not thereby grow confident; but was full of anxiety and fear, therefore also he fasted rigidly, and was not affected as many are, who, when they have kept themselves to it but ten, or perhaps twenty months, straightway give up the matter altogether. He, I say, was in no wise thus affected, nor did he say anything like this to himself. "What further need have I of fasting? I have gotten the mastery of myself; I have overcome my lusts; I have mortified my body; I have affrighted demons; I have driven away the devil; I have raised the dead; I have cleansed lepers; I am become terrible to the adverse powers; what further need have I of fasting, or to seek safety from that quarter?" Anything like this he did not say, he did not think of; but, in proportion as he abounded with innumerable good works, so much the more did he fear and tremble. And he learnt this spiritual wisdom from his preceptor; for even he, after he had been rapt into the third heaven, and transported to paradise; and had heard unutterable words; and taken part in such mysteries; and traversed the whole world, like some winged being, when he wrote to the Corinthians, said, I fear "lest by any means having preached to others, I myself should be a castaway." And if Paul was afraid after so many signal

good works; he who was able to say, "The world is crucified unto me, and I unto the world;" much more does it become us to fear; and the rather in proportion as we have stored up numerous good works. For then the devil becomes fiercer; then he is more savage, when he beholds us regulating our lives with carefulness! When he sees the cargo of virtue stowed together, and the lading become heavy, then he is in haste to accomplish a more grievous shipwreck! For the insignificant and abject man, although he may be supplanted and fall, brings not so great an injury to the common cause. But the man who has been standing most conspicuously as it were on some eminence of virtue, and who is one manifestly seen and known of all men, and admired of all; when he is assaulted and falls, causes great ruin and loss. Not only because he falls from this elevation but makes many of those who look up to him more negligent. And as it is in the body, some other limb may be destroyed without there being any great damage, but if the eyes be deprived of sight, or the head be seriously injured, the whole body is rendered useless; so also we must say of the saints, and of those who have performed the highest good works; when such are extinguished, when they contract any stain, they bring upon all the rest of the body a universal and intolerable injury!

10. Timothy then, being aware of all these things, fortified himself on every side; for he knew that youth is an age of difficulty; that it is unstable; easily deceived; very apt to slip; and requires an exceedingly strong bridle. It is indeed a sort of combustible pile easily catching anything from without, and quickly kindled; and for that reason he took care to smother it on all sides; and strove to abate the flame in every way. The steed that was

unmanageable and restive he curbed with much vehemence, until he had tamed him of his wanton tricks; until he had made him docile; and delivered him under entire control, into the hands of that reason which is the charioteer. "Let the body," says he, "be infirm; but let not the soul be infirm; let the flesh be bridled; but let not the race of the spirit towards heaven be checked." But moreover, one might especially wonder at the man for this, that being thus diseased, and struggling with such an infirmity, he did not become indifferent to God's business, but flew everywhere faster than those who have sound and vigorous constitutions; now to Ephesus; now to Corinth; often to Macedonia and Italy; appearing everywhere, by land and by sea, with the Teacher, sharing in everything his struggles and continuous dangers; while the spiritual wisdom of his soul was not put to shame by his bodily infirmity. Such a thing is zeal for God! Such lightness of wing does it impart! For as with those who possess well-regulated and sound constitutions, strength is of no avail, if the soul is abject, slothful, and stupid; so with those who are reduced to extreme weakness, no hurt arises from their infirmity, if the soul be noble and well awake.

    11. The admonition however, and the counsel, such as it is, appears to some to give authority for drinking wine too freely. But this is not so. If indeed we closely investigate this very saying, it rather amounts to a recommendation of abstinence. For just consider that Paul did not at first, nor at the outset give this counsel. But when he saw that all strength was overthrown, then he gave it; and even then not simply, but with a certain prior limitation. He does not say merely, "Use wine," but "a little" wine; not because Timothy needed this admonition

and advice, but because we need it. On this account, in writing to him, he prescribes the measure and limit of wine-drinking for us; bidding him drink just so much as would correct disorder; as would bring health to the body, but not another disease. For the immoderate drinking of wine produces not fewer diseases of body and of soul, than much drinking of water, but many more, and more severe; bringing in as it does upon the mind the war of the passions, and a tempest of perverse thoughts, besides reducing the firmness of the body to a relaxed and flaccid condition. For the nature of land that is long disturbed by a superabundance of water, is not thereby so much dissolved, as the force of the human frame is enfeebled, relaxed, and reduced to a state of exhaustion, by the continual swilling of wine. Let us guard then against a want of moderation on either side, and let us take care of the health of the body, at the same time that we prune away its luxurious propensities. For wine was given us of God, not that we might be drunken, but that we might be sober; that we might be glad, not that we get ourselves pain. "Wine," it says, "makes glad the heart of man," but thou makes it matter for sadness; since those who are inebriated are sullen beyond measure, and great darkness over-spreads their thoughts. It is the best medicine, when it has the best moderation to direct it. The passage before us is useful also against heretics, who speak evil of God's creatures; for if it had been among the number of things forbidden, Paul would not have permitted it, nor would have said it was to be used. And not only against the heretics, but against the simple ones among our brethren, who when they see any persons disgracing themselves from drunkenness, instead of reproving such, blame the fruit given them by God, and say, "Let there be no wine."

We should say then in answer to such, "Let there be no drunkenness; for wine is the work of God, but drunkenness is the work of the devil. Wine makes not drunkenness; but intemperance produces it. Do not accuse that which is the workmanship of God, but accuse the madness of a fellow mortal. But thou, while omitting to reprove and correct the sinner, treats thy Benefactor with contempt!"

12. When, therefore, we hear men saying such things, we should stop their mouths; for it is not the use of wine, but the want of moderation which produces drunkenness, Drunkenness! That root of all evils. Wine was given to restore the body's weakness, not to overturn the soul's strength; to remove the sickness of the flesh, not to destroy the health of the spirit. Do not then, by using the gift of God immoderately, afford a handle to the foolish and the impudent. For what is a more wretched thing than drunkenness! The drunken man is a living corpse. Drunkenness is a demon self-chosen, a disease without excuse, an overthrow that admits of no apology; a common shame to our kind. The drunken man is not only useless in our assemblies; not only in public and private affairs; but the bare sight of him is the most disgusting of all things, his breath being stench. The belching, and gaping, and speech of the intoxicated, are at once unpleasant and offensive, and are utterly abhorrent to those who see and converse with them; and the crown of these evils is, that this disease makes heaven inaccessible to drunkards, and does not suffer them to win eternal blessedness: for besides the shame attending those who labor under this disease here, a grievous punishment is also awaiting them there! Let us cut off then this evil habit, and let us hear Paul saying, "Use a little wine." For

even this little he permits him on account of his infirmity; so that if infirmity had not troubled him, he would not have forced his disciple to allow himself even a small quantity, since it is fitting that we should always mete out even the needful meat and drink, which are given us, by occasions and necessities; and by no means go beyond our need, nor do anything unmeaningly and to no purpose.

13. But since we have now learnt the tender care of Paul, and the virtue of Timothy, come and let us, in the next place, turn our discourse to the actual solution of those questions. What then are the questions? For it is necessary again to mention them, that the solution of them may be plainer. For what reason then did God permit that such a saint, and one entrusted with the management of so many matters, should fall into a state of disease; and that neither Timothy himself nor his teacher had strength to correct the disorder, but needed that assistance which was to be had by drinking wine? Such, indeed, were the questions proposed. But it is needful to bring forward a precise solution; so that if any should fall not only into the like sickness and disease, but into poverty, and hunger, and bonds, and torments, and discomfitures, and calumnies, and into all those evils which belong to the present life, although they were great and wonderful saints, you may still be able to find, even for their case, in the things which are to-day to be advanced, an exact and very clear reply to those who are disposed to find fault. For ye have heard many asking such questions, as, "Why ever is it that such an one, a moderate and meek man, comes to be dragged daily before the seat of judgment by another who is lawless and wicked, and to suffer evils without number, and God permits this? For what reason

again was another man, upon false accusation, unjustly put to death?" "Such a man," says the objector, "was drowned; another was thrown down a precipice; and we might speak of many saints, as well in our own days as in the days of our forefathers, who have suffered divers and chequered tribulations." To the end, therefore, that we may see the reason of these things, and that we ourselves may not be disturbed, nor overlook the case of others who thus meet with a stumbling-block, we should attend with earnest heed to the reasons now about to be advanced.

14. For of the diversified and manifold affliction which befalls the saints, I have reasons eight in number to declare unto your love. Therefore let all direct themselves to me with the strictest attention, knowing that there will be no pardon nor excuse left us hereafter for stumbling at the things which happen, if after all, when there are so many reasons, we are just as much perplexed and disturbed as if there were not one to be found.

The first reason then is, that God permits them to suffer evil, that they may not too easily be exalted into presumption, by the greatness of their good works and miracles.

The second, that others may not have a greater opinion of them than belongs to human nature, and take them to be gods and not men.

The third, that the power of God may be made manifest, in prevailing, and overcoming, and advancing the word preached, through the efficacy of men who are infirm and in bonds.

The fourth, that the endurance of these themselves may become more striking, serving God, as they do, not for a reward; but showing even such right-mindedness as to give proof of their undiminished good will towards Him after so many evils.

The fifth, that our minds may be wise concerning the doctrine of a resurrection. For when thou sees a just man, and one abounding in virtue, suffering ten thousand evils, and thus departing the present life, thou art altogether compelled, though unwillingly, to think somewhat of the future judgment; for if men do not suffer those who have labored for themselves, to depart without wages and recompense; much more cannot God design, that those who have so greatly labored should be sent away uncrowned. But if He cannot intend to deprive those of the recompense of their labors eventually, there must needs be a time, after the end of the life here, in which they will receive the recompense of their present labors.

The sixth, that all who fall into adversity may have a sufficient consolation and alleviation, by looking at such persons, and remembering what sufferings have befallen them.

The seventh, that when we exhort you to the virtue of such persons, and we say to every one of you, "Imitate Paul, emulate Peter," ye may not, on account of the surpassing character of their good works, slothfully shrink from such an imitation of them, as deeming them to have been partakers of a different nature.

The eighth, that when it is necessary to call any blessed, or the reverse, we may learn whom we ought to account happy, and whom unhappy and wretched.

These then are the reasons; but it is necessary to establish them all from the Scriptures, and to show with exactness that all that has been said on this subject is not an invention of human reasoning, but the very sentence of the Scriptures. For thus will what we say be at once more deserving of credit, and sink the deeper into your minds.

15. That tribulation then is profitable to the saints, that they may exercise moderation and lowliness, and that they may not be puffed up by their miracles and good works, and that God permits it for this end; we may hear David the prophet, and Paul saying the same. The former says, "It is good for me, Lord, that I have been in trouble, that I might learn thy statutes:" and the latter having said, "I was caught up into the third heaven, and" transported to Paradise, goes on to say, "And lest I should be exalted above measure through the abundance of the revelations, there was given me a thorn in the flesh, the messenger of Satan to buffet me." What can be clearer than this? "That I might not be exalted above measure," for this reason, says he, God permitted "the messengers of Satan to buffet me;" by messengers of Satan, indeed, he means not particular demons, but men ministering for the devil, the unbelievers, the tyrants, the heathens, who perseveringly molested, and unceasingly worried him. And what he says is just this: "God was able to repress these persecutions and successive tribulations; but since I had been caught up into the third heaven, and transported to Paradise, lest through the abundance of these revelations I might be lifted up and think much of myself, he permitted these persecutions, and suffered these messengers of Satan to buffet me with persecutions and afflictions, that I might not be too much exalted." For although Paul and Peter, and all that are like them, be holy and wonderful men, as indeed they are, yet they are but men, and require much caution lest they should be too easily exalted; and as saints more than others. For nothing is so apt to exalt to presumption as a conscience full of good works, and a

soul that lives in confidence. To the end, therefore, that these might suffer nothing of this kind, God permitted that there should be temptations and tribulations; these being powerful to keep them down, and to persuade to the exercise of moderation in all things.

16. That this very particular also contributes much to the showing forth of God's power, you may learn even from the same Apostle, who told us the former. In order that you may not say, (what indeed unbelievers think), that God in permitting this, is some infirm being, and suffers such persons to be continually afflicted, from not being able to deliver His own from dangers: this very thing, I say, observe how Paul has demonstrated by means of these events, showing not only that the events were far from accusing Him of weakness, but that they proved His power more strikingly to all. For having said, "There was given me a thorn in the flesh; a messenger of Satan to buffet me," and having thus signified his repeated trials, he goes on to add, "For this thing I besought the Lord thrice, that it might depart from me; and He said unto me, My grace is sufficient for thee, for My strength is perfected in weakness." "My power," He means, "is seen then when ye are in weakness; and yet through you, who seem to grow weak, the word preached is magnified, and is sown in all quarters." When therefore he was led to the dungeon, after having received a great number of stripes, he took prisoner the keeper of the prison. His feet were in the stocks, and his hands in the chain; and the prison shook at midnight while they were singing hymns. See you, how His power was perfected in weakness? If Paul had been at large, and had shaken that building, the thing would not have been so wonderful. "For this reason," He says, "remain bound; and the walls shall be shaken on

every side, and the prisoners shall be loosed; in order that My power may appear the greater, when through thee, confined and in fetters, all that are in bonds shall be loosed." This very circumstance then it was which at the time astounded the keeper of the prison, that being so forcibly confined, he, through prayer alone, prevailed to shake the foundations, and throw open the doors of the prison, and to unbind all the prisoners. Nor is this the only occasion. But with Peter too, and Paul himself, as well as the other disciples, one may see this occurring constantly; and in the midst of persecution, the grace of God ever flourishing, and appearing by the side of the tribulations, and thus proclaiming His power. Wherefore He says, "My grace is sufficient for thee, for My strength is perfected in weakness."

17. But to show that many would be too often ready to imagine things of them above human nature, unless they saw them enduring such afflictions, hear how Paul was afraid on this very point; "For though I would desire to glory, I shall not be a fool, but now I forbear, lest any man should think of me above that which he sees me to be, or that he hears of me." But what is it that he means? I am able, he declares, to speak of far greater miracles; but I am unwilling; lest the magnitude of the miracles should raise too high a notion of me among men. For this reason Peter also, when they had restored the lame man, and all were wondering at them, in order to restrain the people, and persuade them that they had exhibited nothing of this power of themselves, or from their native strength, says, "Why look ye so earnestly on us, as though by our own power or holiness we had made this man to walk?" And again at Lystra, the people were not only filled with astonishment, but led forth bulls, after

crowning them with garlands, and were preparing to offer sacrifice to Paul and Barnabas. Observe the malice of the Devil. By those very same persons through whom the Lord was at work, to purge out ungodliness from the world, by the same did that enemy try to introduce it, again persuading them to take men for gods; which was what he had done in former times. And this is especially that which introduced the principle and root of idolatry. For many after having had success in wars, and set up trophies, and built cities, and done divers other benefits of this kind to the people of those times, came to be esteemed gods by the multitude, and were honored with temples, and altars; and the whole catalogue of the Grecian gods is made up of such men. That this, therefore, may not be done towards the Saints, God permitted them constantly to be banished,—to be scourged,—to fall into diseases; that the abundance of bodily infirmity, and the multiplicity of those temptations, might convince those who were then with them, both that they were men, who wrought such wonders, and that they contributed nothing of their own power; but that it was mere grace, that wrought through them all these miracles. For if they took men for gods, who had done but mean and vile things, much rather would they have thought these to be such, had they suffered nothing proper to humanity, when they performed miracles, such as no one had ever before seen or heard of. For if when they were scourged, thrown down precipices, imprisoned, banished, and placed in peril every day, there were, notwithstanding, some who fell into this impious opinion, how much rather would they have been thus regarded, had they endured nothing which belongs to human nature!

18. This then is the third cause of affliction; and the fourth is, that the saints might not be supposed to serve God from a hope of present prosperity. For many of those who live in debauchery, when blamed as they often are by many, and invited to the labors of virtue; and when they hear the saints commended for their cheerfulness under great hardships, attack their character on this ground; and not men only, but the devil himself hath taken up this suspicion. For when Job was surrounded with great wealth, and enjoyed much opulence, that wicked demon, being reproached by God on his account, and having nothing to say; when he could neither answer the accusations against himself, nor impugn the virtue of this just man; took refuge at once in this defense, speaking thus, "Doth Job fear thee for naught? Hast thou not made a hedge about him on all sides?" "For reward then," says he, "that man is virtuous, enjoying thereby so much opulence." What then did God? Being desirous to show, that it was not for reward that his saints serve Him, He stripped him of all his opulence; gave him over to poverty; and permitted him to fall into grievous disease. Afterwards reproving him, that he had suspected thus without cause, He says, "He yet holds fast his integrity; to no purpose didst thou move me to destroy his substance." For it is a sufficient reward, and compensation to the saints, that they are serving God; since this indeed to the lover is reward enough, to love the object of his love; and he seeks nothing besides, nor accounts anything greater than this. And if such be the case with regard to a man, much more in relation to God; which therefore that God might demonstrate, He gave more than the devil asked; for the latter said, "Put forth thine hand, and touch him;" but God said not thus, but, "I deliver him unto thee." For

just as in the contests of the outer world, the combatants that are vigorous, and in high condition of body, are not so well discerned, when they are enwrapt all around with the garment soaked in oil; but when casting this aside, they are brought forward unclothed into the arena; then above all they strike the spectators on every side with astonishment at the proportion of their limbs, there being no longer anything to conceal them; so also was it with Job. When he was enveloped in all that wealth, it was not visible to the many, what a man he was. But when, like the wrestler, that strips off his garment, he threw it aside, and came naked to the conflicts of piety, thus unclothed, he astonished all who saw him; so that the very theatre of angels shouted at beholding his fortitude of soul, and applauded him as he won his crown! For, as I have already observed, he was not so well seen of men, when clad in all that wealth, as when, casting it away like a garment, he exhibited himself naked as it were in a theatre, in the midst of the world, and all admired his vigor of soul, evidenced as this was not only by his being stripped of all things, but by the conflict, and by his patience in respect of his infirmity. And as I said before, God Himself did not smite him; in order that the devil might not again say, "Thou hast spared him, and hast not inflicted so great a trial as was necessary:" but he gave to the adversary the destruction of his cattle, and power over his flesh. "I am sure," says He, "of this wrestler; therefore I do not forbid thee to impose on him whatever struggles thou desires." But as those who are well skilled in the sports of the palæstra, and have reason to rely on their art and bodily strength, often do not seize their antagonists upright, nor take an equal advantage, but suffer them to take them by the middle, that they may make a more splendid conquest; so also God gave to the devil to take this saint by the waist, that when he had overcome, after an attack so greatly to his disadvantage, and stretched his adversary on the ground, his crown might be so much the more glorious!

19. It is tried gold! Try it as thou desires; examine it as thou wishes, thou wilt not find in it any dross. This shows us not only the fortitude of others, but also brings much farther consolation; for what says Christ, "Blessed are ye when men shall revile you and persecute you, and shall say all manner of evil against you falsely for my sake. Rejoice and be exceeding glad, for great is your reward in heaven: for in like manner did their fathers unto the prophets." Again, Paul writing to the Macedonians in his desire to console them, says, "For ye, brethren, became followers of the churches of God which are in Judea. For ye also have suffered like things of your own countrymen, even as they have of the Jews." And again, he consoles the Hebrews in like manner, reckoning up all the just who had lived in furnaces; in pits; in deserts; in mountains; in caves; in hunger; and in poverty. For communion of suffering brings some consolation to the fallen.

20. But that this also introduces arguments for the resurrection, hear the same Paul again, saying, "If after the manner of men I have fought with beasts at Ephesus, what shall it profit me if the dead are not raised." And further, "If in this life only we have hope, we are of all men the most miserable." We suffer, he tells us, innumerable evils during the present life; if then there is no other life to be hoped for, what can be more wretched than our condition? Hence it is evident that our affairs are not bounded within the limits of this present state; and

this becomes manifest from our trials. For God could never suffer those who have endured so many and so great evils, and who have spent all the present life in trials and dangers without number, to be without a recompense of far greater gifts; and if he could not suffer this, it is certain that he has prepared another, a better and brighter life, in which he will crown those who have wrestled in the cause of godliness, and proclaim their praises in the presence of the whole world. So that when you see a just man straitened and afflicted; and in sickness, and in poverty, as well as innumerable other woes, till he ends this present life; say to thyself, that if there were no resurrection and judgment, God would not have permitted one, who endured such great evils for His sake, to depart hence without enjoying any good thing; from whence it is evident, that for such He has prepared another life, and one which is sweeter and much more endurable. For if it were not so, then he would not suffer many of the wicked to luxuriate through the present life; and many of the just to remain in ten thousand ills: but since there is provided another life, in which he is about to recompense every man according to his deserts; one for his wickedness, another for his virtue; on that account he forbears, while he sees the former enduring evil, and the latter living in luxury.

21. And that other reason too I will endeavor to bring forward from the Scriptures. But what was it? It was, that we might not say, when exhorted to the same virtue, that they were partakers of another nature, or were not men. On this account, a certain one speaking of the great Elias, says, "Elias was a man of like passions with us." Do you perceive, that he shows from a communion of suffering, that he was the same kind of man that we are?

And again, "I too am a man of like passions with you." And this guarantees a community of nature.

22. But that you may learn that this also teaches us to consider those blessed whom we ought to consider blessed, is evident from hence. For when you hear Paul saying, "Even unto this present hour we both hunger, and thirst, and are naked, and are buffeted, and have no certain dwelling place." And again; "Whom the Lord loves he chastened, and scourged every son whom he receives;" it is certain that it is not those who are enjoying quietness, but those who are in affliction for God's sake, and who are in tribulation, whom we must applaud, emulating those who live virtuously, and cultivate piety. For so speaks the prophet: "Their right hand is a right hand of iniquity. Their daughters beautified, ornamented after the similitude of a temple. Their garners full, bursting from one into another; their sheep fruitful; abundant in their streets; their oxen fat. There is no breaking down of the fence, nor passage through; nor clamor in their streets. They call the people blessed whose affairs are in this state." But what dost thou say, O prophet? "Blessed," says he, "the people whose God is the Lord;" not the people affluent in wealth, but one adorned with godliness; that people, says he, I esteem happy, although they suffer innumerable hardships!

23. But if it were necessary to add a ninth reason, we might say, that this tribulation makes those who are troubled more approved; "For tribulation worked patience; and patience, probation; and probation, hope; and hope makes not ashamed." Do you see that the probation, which comes of tribulation, fixes in us the hope of the good things to come, and that the abiding in trials causes us to have a good hope of the future? So that I did

not say rashly, that these tribulations themselves mark out to us hopes of a resurrection, and make those who are tried the better; for, he says, "as gold is tried in a furnace, so an acceptable man in the furnace of humiliation."

24. There is besides a tenth reason to mention; and what is it, but the one I have before frequently referred to? Viz. that if we have any spots, we thus put them away. And the patriarch, making this matter plain, said to the rich man, "Lazarus hath received his evil things," hence "he is comforted." And besides this, we may find another reason, which is to this effect; that our crowns and rewards are thus increased. For in proportion as tribulations are more intense, so also are the rewards augmented; yea, even far more: "for the sufferings of the present time," it is said, "are not worthy to be compared to the glory that shall be revealed in us." Thus many then being the reasons which we have to advance for the afflictions of the saints, let us not take our trials amiss, or be distressed, or disturbed on account of them; but both ourselves discipline our own souls, and teach others to do the same.

25. And if, O beloved, thou sees a man living in virtue, keeping fast hold of spiritual wisdom, pleasing God, yet suffering innumerable ills, do not stumble! And although thou sees any one devoting himself to spiritual affairs, and about to achieve something useful, yet presently supplanted, be not discouraged! For I know there are many who ofttimes propose a question to this effect: "Such a one," say they, "was performing a pilgrimage to some Martyr's shrine; and whilst conveying money to the poor, met with a shipwreck, and lost all. Another man, in doing the like, fell among robbers, and scarcely saved his life, leaving the place in a state of

nudity." What then should we say? Why that in neither of these cases need one be sad. For if the one met with a shipwreck, yet he hath the fruit of his righteousness complete inasmuch as he fulfilled all his own part. He collected the money together, he stowed it away, he took it with him, he departed on his pilgrimage; but the shipwreck that followed was not of his own will. "But why did God permit it?" In order that he might make the man approved. "But," says one, "the poor were deprived of the money." Thou dost not so care for the poor, as the God who made them? For if they were deprived of these things, He is able to provide a greater supply of wealth for them from another quarter.

26. Let us not then call Him to account for what He does; but let us give Him glory in all things. For it is not lightly and to no purpose that He often permits such events. But beside that He does not overlook those that would have enjoyed comfort from such wealth; and instead of it, affords them some other supply of sustenance; He also makes him who suffers the shipwreck more approved, and provides him a greater reward; inasmuch as the giving thanks to God, when one falls into such calamities, is a far greater matter than giving alms. For not what we give in alms only, but whatever we have been deprived of by others, and borne it with fortitude; this too brings us much fruit. And that you may learn, that the latter is indeed the greater thing, I will make it evident from what befell Job. He, when a possessor of wealth, opened his house to the poor, and whatever he had he bestowed; but he was not so illustrious when he opened his house to the poor, as when, upon hearing that his house had fallen down, he did not take it impatiently. He was not illustrious when he clad the naked with the fleece

of his flock, as he was illustrious and renowned when he heard that the fire had fallen, and consumed all his flocks, and yet gave thanks. Before, he was a lover of man; now, he was a lover of Wisdom. Before, he had compassion on the poor; but now he gave thanks to the Lord! And he did not say to himself, "Why is it that this hath happened? The flocks are consumed from which thousands of the poor were supported; and if I was unworthy to enjoy such plenty, at least He should have spared me for the sake of the partakers."

27. Nothing of this sort did Job utter, no nor think, because he knew that God was dispensing all things for good. That you may learn, moreover, that he gave a heavier blow to the devil after this, when, being stripped of all things, he gave thanks, than when, being in possession of them, he gave alms; observe, that when he was in possession, the devil could utter a certain suspicion, and however false, he yet could utter it: "Doth Job serve thee for naught?" But when he had taken all, and stripped him of everything, and the man yet retained the same good will towards God, from that time his shameless mouth was stopped, and had nothing further to allege. For the just man was more illustrious than in his former state. For to bear nobly and thankfully the privation of all things, is a far greater thing than it was to give alms whilst living in affluence; and it has been accordingly demonstrated in the case of this just man. Before, there was much benignity to his fellow-servants; now, there was exceeding love shown towards the Lord!

28. And I do not lengthen out this discourse without purpose; forasmuch as there are many, who, often whilst engaged in works of mercy, as supporting widows, have been spoiled of all their substance. Some again, by

the accident of some fire, have lost their all; some have met with shipwreck; others, by false information and injuries of that sort, though they have done many alms-deeds, have fallen into the extremes of poverty, sickness, and disease, and have obtained no help from anyone. Lest we should say then, as many often do, "No man knows anything;" what has just been said may suffice to remove all perplexity on this point. Suppose it is objected that "such a one, after having done many alms-deeds, has lost all?" And what if he had lost all? If he gives thanks for this loss, he will draw down much greater favor from God! And he will not receive twofold, as Job did, but a hundredfold in the life to come. But if here he does endure evil, the very circumstance of his sustaining all with fortitude will bring him a greater treasure; for God permits him to fall from plenty to poverty, for the purpose of calling him thus to the more frequent exercises, and greater conflicts. Hath it happened as is often the case, that the fire seizing upon thy house, hath burnt it up and devoured all thy substance? Remember what happened to Job; give thanks to the Lord, who though he was able to forbid, did not forbid it; and thou wilt receive as great a reward as if thou has deposited all thy wealth in the hands of the poor! But dost thou spend thy days in poverty and hunger, and in the midst of a thousand dangers? Remember Lazarus who had to buffet with disease, and poverty, and desolateness, and those other innumerable trials; and that after so high a degree of virtue! Remember the Apostles, who lived in hunger, and thirst, and nakedness; the prophets, the patriarchs, the just men, and you will find all these not among the rich or luxurious, but among the poor, the afflicted, and the distressed!

29. Saying these things to thyself, give thanks unto the Lord, that he hath made thee to be of this part, not hating thee, but loving thee greatly; since He would not have permitted those men either to suffer thus, if he had not exceedingly loved them, because He made them more illustrious by these evils. There is nothing so good as thanksgiving; even as there is nothing worse than blasphemy. We should not wonder that when we become intent upon spiritual things, we suffer much that is grievous. For as thieves do not dig through and assiduously keep watch there, where there is hay, and chaff, and straw, but where there is gold and silver; so also the devil besets those especially who are engaged in spiritual matters. Where virtue is, there are many snares! Where alms-giving is, there is envy! But we have one weapon which is the best, and sufficient to repel all such engines as these; in everything to give thanks to God. Tell me, did not Abel, when offering the first fruits to God, fall by the hand of his brother? But yet God permitted it, not hating one who had honored him, but loving him greatly; and beside that which came of that excellent sacrifice, providing him another crown by martyrdom. Moses wished to protect a certain one who was injured, and he was put into the extremest peril, and banished his country. This too God permitted, that thou might learn the patience of the saints. For if, foreknowing that we should suffer nothing of a grievous kind, we then put our hands to the work of religion, we should not seem to be doing anything great, as having such a pledge of safety. But as it is, those who do such things are the more to be wondered at, even for this; because, though they foresee dangers, and punishments, and deaths, and ten thousand evils, still

they did not desist from those good works, nor become less zealous from the expectation of terrors.

30. As, therefore, the Three Children said, "There is a God in heaven, who is able to deliver us; and if not, let it be known unto thee, O king, that we will not serve thy gods, and that we will not worship the golden image which thou hast set up." Do thou also, when about to perform any duty to God, look forward to manifold dangers, manifold punishments, manifold deaths; and be not surprised, nor be disturbed, if such things happen. For it is said, "My Son, if thou come to serve the Lord, prepare thy soul for temptation." For surely no one choosing to fight, expects to carry off the crown without wounds! And thou, therefore, who hast undertaken to wage a complete combat with the devil, think not to pursue a life without danger, and full of luxury! God hath not pledged to thee His recompense and His promise here; but everything that is splendid for thee in the future life! Be glad and rejoice then, if when thou hast thyself done any good action, thou receive the contrary, or if thou see another suffering this; inasmuch as this becomes to thee the source of a higher recompense! Do not be downcast: nor give up thy zeal, nor become the more torpid; but rather press onward with more eagerness; since even the Apostles, when they preached, although scourged, stoned, and constant inmates of the prisons, did not only after deliverance from dangers, but also in those very dangers, announce with greater forwardness the message of Truth. Paul is to be seen in prison, yea, even in chains, instructing and initiating: and moreover doing the very same in a court of justice, in shipwreck, in tempest, and in a thousand dangers. Do thou too imitate these saints, and cease not from good works, so long as thou art able; and

although thou sees the devil thwarting thee ten thousand times, never fall back! Thou perchance, bearing with thee thy wealth, hast met with shipwreck; but Paul carrying the word, far more precious than all wealth, was going to Rome, and was wrecked; and sustained innumerable hardships. And this he himself signified, when he said, "Many times we desired to come unto you, but Satan hindered us." And God permitted it; thus revealing the more abundantly His power, and showing that the multitude of things which the devil did, or prevented from being done, neither lessened nor interrupted the preaching of the Gospel. On this account Paul gave God thanks in all things; and knowing that he was himself thereby rendered more approved, he exhibited his exceeding forwardness on every occasion, letting none of these impediments prevent him!

31. As often then as we are frustrated in spiritual works, so often let us again take them in hand; and let us not say, "for what reason did God permit these impediments?" for He permitted them to this end, that He might show thy alacrity much more to others, and thy great love; this being the special mark of one that loves, never to desist from those things which are approved by him whom he loves. The man, indeed, who is flaccid and listless, will fall back from the first shock; but he who is energetic and alert, although he be hindered a thousand times, will devote himself so much the more to the things of God; fulfilling all as far as he is able; and in everything giving thanks. This then let us do! Thanksgiving is a great treasure; large wealth; a good that cannot be taken away; a powerful weapon! Even as blasphemy increases our present mishap; and makes us lose much more beside than we have lost already. Hast thou lost money? If thou hast

been thankful, thou hast gained thy soul; and obtained greater wealth; having acquired a greater measure of the favor of God. But if thou blasphemes, thou hast, besides this, lost thine own safety; and hast not regained possession of thy wealth; yea and thy soul, which thou has, thou hast sacrificed!

32. But since our discourse has now turned to the subject of blasphemy, I desire to ask one favor of you all, in return for this my address, and speaking with you; which is, that you will correct on my behalf the blasphemers of this city. And should you hear anyone in the public thoroughfare, or in the midst of the forum, blaspheming God; go up to him and rebuke him; and should it be necessary to inflict blows, spare not to do so. Smite him on the face; strike his mouth; sanctify thy hand with the blow, and if any should accuse thee, and drag thee to the place of justice, follow them thither; and when the judge on the bench calls thee to account, say boldly that the man blasphemed the King of angels! For if it be necessary to punish those who blaspheme an earthly king, much more so those who insult God. It is a common crime, a public injury; and it is lawful for everyone who is willing, to bring forward an accusation. Let the Jews and Greeks learn, that the Christians are the saviors of the city; that they are its guardians, its patrons, and its teachers. Let the dissolute and the perverse also learn this; that they must fear the servants of God too; that if at any time they are inclined to utter such a thing, they may look round every way at each other, and tremble even at their own shadows, anxious lest perchance a Christian, having heard what they said, should spring upon them and sharply chastise them. Have you not heard what John did? He saw a man that was a tyrant overthrowing the laws of

marriage; and with boldness, he proclaimed in the midst of the forum, "It is not lawful for thee to have thy brother Philip's wife." But I urge thee on, not against a prince or a judge; nor against the marriage ordinance outraged; nor in behalf of fellow-servants insulted. But I require thee to castigate an equal, for insolence against the Lord. Truly, if I had said unto thee, punish and correct those kings or judges who transgress the laws, would you not say that I was mad? But John forsooth acted thus. So that even this is not too much for us. Now then, at least, correct a fellow-servant; an equal; and although it should be necessary to die, do not shrink from chastising a brother. This is thy martyrdom, since John was also a martyr. And although he was not commanded to sacrifice, nor to worship an idol, yet for the sacred laws that were despised, he laid down his head. Do thou too then contend, even to the death, for the truth, and God will fight for thee! And make me not this cold reply. "What matters it to me? I have nothing in common with him." With the devil alone we have nothing in common, but with all men we have many things in common; for they partake of the same nature with us; they inhabit the same earth, and they are nourished with the same food; they have the same Lord; they have received the same laws, and are invited to the same blessings with ourselves. Let us not say then, that we have nothing in common with them; for this is a satanic speech; a diabolical inhumanity. Therefore let us not give utterance to such words, but exhibit such a tender care as becomes brethren!

33. This indeed I, for my part, engage with the strictest certainty, and pledge myself to you all, that if all you who are present will but choose to take in hand the safety of the inhabitants of this city, we shall speedily

have it amended throughout. And this, even although but the least part of the city is here; the least as to multitude, but the chief part as it respects piety. Let us take in hand the safety of our brethren! One man inflamed with zeal is sufficient to reform a whole community! But when not merely one, or two, or three, but so great a multitude are able to take on them the care of the neglected, it is in no other way but by our own supineness, and not from our want of strength, that the majority perish and fall. Is it not indeed absurd? When we happen to see a fight taking place in the forum, we go into the midst of it, and reconcile the combatants! But why do I speak of a fight? If, perchance, we see an ass fallen down, we all make haste to stretch out a hand to raise him up. Yet we neglect our perishing brethren! The blasphemer is an ass; unable to bear the burden of his anger, he has fallen. Come forward and raise him up, both by words and by deeds; and both by meekness and by vehemence; let the medicine be various. And if we thus administer our own part, and take pains for the safety of our neighbors, we shall soon become objects of desire and affection to the very persons who have the benefit of our correction; and what is more than all, we shall enjoy those good things which are laid up in store. Which God grant that we may all obtain, by the grace and mercy of our Lord Jesus Christ; through whom and with whom, to the Father with the Holy Ghost, be glory and power and honor, both now and always, and forever and ever. Amen.

Homily II.

Spoken in Antioch in the Old Church, as it was called, while he was a presbyter, on the subject of the calamity that had befallen the city in consequence of the tumult connected with the overthrow of the Statues of the Emperor Theodosius, the Great and Pious. And on the saying of the Apostle, "Charge them that are rich that they be not high-minded," 1 Timothy vi. 17. And against covetousness.

1. What shall I say, or what shall I speak of? The present season is one for tears, and not for words; for lamentation, not for discourse; for prayer, not for preaching. Such is the magnitude of the deeds daringly done; so incurable is the wound, so deep the blow, even beyond the power of all treatment, and craving assistance from above. Thus it was that Job, when he had lost all, sat himself down upon a dunghill; and his friends heard of it, and came, and seeing him, while yet afar off, they rent their garments, and sprinkled themselves with ashes, and made great lamentation. The same thing now ought all the cities around to do, to come to our city and to lament with all sympathy what has befallen us. He then sat down on his dunghill; she is now seated in the midst of a great snare. For even as the devil then leaped violently the flocks, and herds, and all the substance of the just man, so now hath he raged against this whole city. But then, as well as now, God permitted it; then, indeed, that he might make the just man more illustrious by the greatness of his trials; and now, that he may make us more sober-minded by the extremity of this tribulation. Suffer me to mourn over our present state. We have been silent seven days,

even as the friends of Job were. Suffer me to open my mouth to-day, and to bewail this common calamity.

2. Who, beloved, hath bewitched us? Who hath envied us? Whence hath all this change come over us? Nothing was more dignified than our city! Now, never was anything more pitiable! The populace so well ordered and quiet, yea, even like a tractable and well tamed steed, always submissive to the hands of its rulers, hath now so suddenly started off with us, as to have wrought such evils, as one can hardly dare to mention. I mourn now and lament, not for the greatness of that wrath which is to be expected, but for the extravagance of the frenzy which has been manifested! For although the Emperor should not be provoked, or in anger, although he were neither to punish, nor take vengeance; how, I pray, are we to bear the shame of all that has been done? I find the word of instruction broken off by lamentation; scarcely am I able to open my mouth, to part my lips, to move my tongue, or to utter a syllable! So, even like a curb, the weight of grief checks my tongue, and keeps back what I would say.

3. Aforetime there was nothing happier than our city; nothing more melancholy than it is now become. As bees buzzing around their hive, so before this the inhabitants every day flitted about the forum, and all pronounced us happy in being so numerous. But behold now, this hive hath become solitary! For even as smoke does those bees, so fear hath driven away our swarms; and what the prophet says, bewailing Jerusalem, we may fitly say now, "Our city is become 'like a terebinth that hath lost its leaves, and as a garden that hath no water.'" For in like manner as a garden when its irrigation fails, exhibits the trees stripped of their leaves, and bare of their fruits, so has it now fared with our city. For the help from

above having forsaken her, she stands desolate stripped of almost all her inhabitants.

4. Nothing is sweeter than one's own country; but now, it has come to pass that nothing is more bitter! All flee from the place which brought them forth, as from a snare. They desert it as they would a dungeon; they leap out of it, as from a fire. And just as when a house is seized upon by the flames, not only those who dwell therein, but all who are near, take their flight from it with the utmost haste, eager to save but their bare bodies; even so now too, when the wrath of the Emperor is expected to come as a fire from above, everyone presses to go forth in time, and to save the bare body, before the fire in its progress reaches them. And now our calamity has become an enigma; a flight without enemies; an expulsion of inhabitants without a battle; a captivity without capture! We have not seen the fire of barbarians, nor beheld the face of enemies: and yet we experience the sufferings of captives. All men now hear of our calamities; for receiving our exiles, they learn from them the stroke which has fallen upon our city.

5. Yet I am not ashamed, nor blush at this. Let all men learn the sufferings of the city, that, sympathizing with their mother, they may lift up their united voice to God from the whole earth; and with one consent entreat the King of heaven for their universal nurse and parent. Lately our city was shaken; but now the very souls of the inhabitants totter! Then the foundations of the houses shook, but now the very foundations of every heart quiver; and we all see death daily before our eyes! We live in constant terror, and endure the penalty of Cain; a more pitiable one than that of those who were the former inmates of the prison; undergoing as we now do a new

and strange kind of siege, far more terrible than the ordinary kind. For they who suffer this from enemies, are only shut up within the walls; but even the forum has become impassable to us, and everyone is pent up within the walls of his own house! And as it is not safe for those who are beseiged to go beyond the walls, while the enemy without is encamped around; so neither, to many of those who inhabit this city, is it safe to go out of doors, or to appear openly; on account of those who are everywhere hunting for the innocent as well as the guilty; and seizing them even in the midst of the forum, and dragging them to the court of justice, without ceremony, and just as chance directs. For this reason, free-men sit in doors shackled up with their domestics; anxiously and minutely enquiring of those to whom they may safely put the question, "Who has been seized to-day; who carried off; or punished? How was it? And in what manner?" They live a life more wretched than any kind of death; being compelled daily to mourn the calamities of others; while they tremble for their own safety, and are in no better case than the dead; inasmuch as they are already dead with fear.

6. But if anyone who is devoid of this fear and anguish, chooses to enter the forum, he is presently driven back to his own dwelling, by the cheerless spectacle; finding hardly perchance one or two people, and those hanging their heads and creeping about with downcast looks, where but a few days before the multitude swept along more incessantly than the streams of rivers. Yet all these have now been driven away from us! And, as when many trees in a thick wood of oak are cut down in all directions, the spectacle becomes a melancholy one, even like that of a head with many patches of baldness; even so the city itself, its inhabitants being diminished and but

few appearing here and there, is now become dreary, and sheds a heavy mist of sorrow over those who witness it. And not the ground only, but the very nature of the air, and even the circle of the sun's beams, seem now to me to look mournful, and to shine more dimly; not that the elements change their nature, but that our eyes being confused by the cloud of sadness, are unable to receive the light of the rays clearly, or with the same relish. This is what the prophet of old bewailed, when he said, "The sun shall go down at noon, and the day shall be darkened." And this he said, not as though the Day Star should be eclipsed, or the day should disappear, but because those who are in sorrow, are not able to perceive the light even of noon day on account of the darkness of their anguish; which indeed has been the case now. And wherever any one looks abroad, whether upon the ground or upon the walls; whether upon the columns of the city, or upon his neighbors, he seems to see night and deep gloom; so full is all of melancholy! There is a silence big with horror, and loneliness everywhere; and that dear hum of the multitude is stifled; and even as though all were gone beneath the earth, so speechlessness hath now taken possession of the city; and all men seem like stones, and being oppressed by the calamity like a gag on their tongues; they maintain the profoundest silence, yea, such a silence as if enemies had come on them, and had consumed them all at once by fire and sword!

7. Now is it a fit season to say, "Call for the mourning women, that they may come, and for the cunning women, and let them take up a wailing. Let your eyes run down with water, and your eyelids gush out with tears." Ye hills take up wailing, and ye mountains lamentation! Let us call the whole creation into sympathy

with our evils. So great a city, and the head of those which lie under the eastern sky, is in danger of being torn away from the midst of the civilized world! She that had so many children, has now suddenly become childless, and there is no one who shall come to her aid! For he who has been insulted has not an equal in dignity upon earth; for he is a monarch; the summit and head of all here below! On this account then let us take refuge in the King that is above. Him let us call in to our aid. If we may not obtain the favor of heaven, there is no consolation left for what has befallen us!

8. Here I could wish to end this discourse; for the minds of those who are in anguish are indisposed to extend their discourses to a great length. And as when some dense cloud has formed, and flying under the solar rays, returns back to him all his splendor again, so indeed does the cloud of sadness, when it stands before our souls, refuse to admit an easy passage for the word, but chokes it and restrains it forcibly within. And this is the case not only with those who speak, but with those who hear; for as it does not suffer the word to burst forth freely from the soul of the speaker, so neither does it suffer it to sink into the mind of those who listen, with its natural power. Therefore also the Jews of old time, while slaving at the mud and bricks, had not the heart to listen to Moses, while he repeatedly told them great things respecting their future deliverance; despondency making their minds inaccessible to the address, and shutting up their sense of hearing. I could have wished then, as to myself, to have put an end here to my discourse; but thinking that it is not only the nature of a cloud to intercept the forward passage of the sun's rays, but that often just the opposite happens to the cloud; since the sun continually falling upon it with

much warmth, wears it away, and frequently breaks through the midst of it; and shining forth all at once, meets cheerfully the gaze of the beholders. This also I myself expect to do this day; and the word being continually associated with your minds, and dwelling in them, I hope to burst the cloud of sadness, and to shine through your understandings again, with the customary instruction!

9. But afford me your attention! Lend me your ears awhile! Shake off this despondency! Let us return to our former custom; and as we have been used always to meet here with gladness, so let us also do now, casting all upon God. And this will contribute towards our actual deliverance from calamity. For should the Lord see that His words are listened to carefully; and that our love of divine wisdom stands the trial of the difficulty of these times, He will quickly take us up again, and will make out of the present tempest a calm and happy change. For this too is a thing in which it behooves the Christian to differ from the unbelievers, the bearing all things nobly; and through hope of the future, soaring above the attack of human evils. The believer hath his stand on the Rock; for this reason he cannot be overthrown by the dashing of the billows. For should the waves of temptation rise, they cannot reach to his feet. He stands too lofty for any such assault. Let us not then sink down, beloved! We do not care so much for our own safety, as God who made us. There is not so much solicitude on our part, lest we suffer any dreadful misfortune, as with Him who bestowed upon us a soul, and then gave us so many good things beside. Let us mount on the wings of these hopes, and hear the things about to be spoken with our accustomed readiness.

10. I made a prolonged discourse lately unto you beloved, and yet I saw all following it up, and no one turning back in the middle of the course. I return thanks to you for that readiness, and have received the reward of my labors. But there was another reward, besides that attention, which I asked of you at that time; perchance you know and recollect it. And what was the reward? That you should punish and chastise the blasphemers that were in the city; that ye should restrain those who are violent and insolent against God! I do not think that I then spoke these things of myself; but that God, foreseeing what was coming, injected these words into my mind; for if we had punished those who dared to do such things, that which has now happened would never have happened. How much better would it have been, if necessity so required, to run into danger; yea, to suffer in castigating and correcting such persons (which would have brought us a martyr's crown), than now to fear, to tremble, and to expect death, from the insubordination of such persons! Behold, the crime was that of a few, but the blame comes on all! Behold, through these, we are all now placed in fear, and are ourselves suffering the punishment of what these men dared to do! But if we had taken them in time, and cast them out of the city, and chastised them, and corrected the sick member, we should not have been subjected to our present terror. I know that the manners of this city have been of a noble character from old times; but that certain strangers, and men of mixed race,—accursed and pernicious characters,— hopeless of their own safety, have perpetrated what has been perpetrated. For this very reason I was always lifting up my voice, and unceasingly bearing my testimony, saying, Let us punish the madness of those

blasphemers,—let us control their spirit, and provide for their salvation;—yea, though it be necessary to die in doing it, the deed would yet bring us great gain: let us not overlook the insult done to our common Lord; overlooking such things will bring forth some great evil to our city!

11. These things I foretold, and they have now actually taken place;—and we are paying the penalty of that listlessness! You overlooked the insult that was done unto God!—Behold, he hath permitted the Emperor to be insulted, and peril to the utmost to hang over all, in order that we might pay by this fear the penalty of that listlessness; was it then vainly, and to no purpose I foretold these things, and assiduously urged your Charity? But nevertheless, nothing was done. Let it, however, be done now; and being chastened by our present calamity, let us now restrain the disorderly madness of these men. Let us shut up their mouths, even as we close up pestiferous fountains; and let us turn them to a contrary course, and the evils which have taken hold of the city shall undoubtedly be stayed. The Church is not a theatre, that we should listen for amusement. With profit ought we to depart hence, and some fresh and great gain should we acquire ere we leave this place. For it is but vainly and irrationally we meet together, if we have been but captivated for a time, and return home empty, and void of all improvement from the things spoken.

12. What need have I of these plaudits, these cheers and tumultuous signs of approval? The praise I seek, is that ye show forth all I have said in your works. Then am I an enviable and happy man, not when ye approve, but when ye perform with all readiness, whatsoever ye hear from me? Let everyone then correct

his neighbor, for "edify ye one another," it is said, and if we do not this, the crimes of each one will bring some general and intolerable damage to the city. Behold, while we are unconscious of any part in this transaction, we are no less affrighted than those who were daringly engaged in it! We are dreading lest the wrath of the Emperor should descend upon all; and it is not sufficient for us to say in defense, "I was not present; I was not an accomplice, nor a participator in these acts." "For this reason," he may reply, "thou shalt be punished, and pay the extreme penalty, because thou wert not present; and didst not check, nor restrain the rioters, and didst not run any risk for the honor of the Emperor! Have you no part in these audacious deeds? I commend this, and take it well. But thou didst not check these things when being done. This is a cause of accusation!" Such words as these, we shall also hear from God, if we silently suffer the continuance of the injuries and insults committed against Him. For he also who had buried his talent in the earth, was called to account, not for crimes done by himself, for he had given back the whole of that which was entrusted to him, but because he had not increased it; because he had not instructed others; because he had not deposited it in the hands of the bankers; that is, he had not admonished, or counselled, or rebuked, or amended those unruly sinners who were his neighbors. On this account he was sent away without reprieve to those intolerable punishments! But I fully trust that though ye did not before, ye will now at least perform this work of correction, and not overlook insult committed against God. For the events which have taken place are sufficient, even if no one had given any warning, to convince men ever so disposed to be insensible, that they must exert themselves for their own safety.

13. But it is now time that we should proceed to lay out before you the customary table from St. Paul, by handling the subject of this day's reading, and placing it in view for you all. What then was the text read today? "Charge them that are rich in this world that they be not high-minded." When he says, "the rich in this world," he makes it manifest, that there are others who are rich, that is, in the world to come: such as was that Lazarus, poor as to the present life, but rich as to the future; not in gold and silver, and such like perishable and transitory store of wealth; but in those unutterable good things "which eye hath not seen, nor ear heard, nor hath it entered into the heart of man." For this is true wealth and opulence, when there is good unmixed, and not subject to any change. Not such was the case of that rich man who despised him, but he became the poorest of mankind. Afterwards at least when he sought to obtain but a drop of water, he did not get possession even of that, to such extreme poverty was he come. For this reason he calls them rich "in the present world," to teach thee that along with the present life, worldly wealth is annihilated. It goes no further, neither does it change its place with its migrating possessors, but it often leaves them before their end; which therefore he shows by saying, "Neither trust in uncertain riches;" for nothing is so faithless as wealth; of which I have often said, and will not cease to say, that it is a runaway, thankless servant, having no fidelity; and should you throw over him ten thousand chains, he will make off dragging his chains after him. Frequently, indeed, have those who possessed him shut him up with bars and doors, placing their slaves round about for guards. But he

has over-persuaded these very servants, and has fled away together with his guards; dragging his keepers after him like a chain, so little security was there in this custody. What then can be more faithless than this? What more wretched than men devoted to it? When men endeavor with all eagerness to collect so frail and fleeting a thing, they do not hear what the prophet says: "Woe unto them who trust in their power, and boast themselves in the multitude of their riches." Tell me why is this woe pronounced?—"He heaped up treasure," says he, "and knows not for whom he will gather it,"—forasmuch as the labor is certain, but the enjoyment uncertain. Very often you toil and endure trouble for enemies. The inheritance of your wealth after your decease, coming as it does, in many instances, to those who have injured you, and plotted against you in a thousand ways, has assigned you the sins for your part, but the enjoyment to others!

14. But here, it is worthy of enquiry, for what reason he does not say, "Charge those who are rich in the present world, not to be rich; charge them to become poor; charge them to get rid of what they have;" but, "charge them, not to be high-minded." For he knew that the root and foundation of riches is pride; and that if any man understood how to be unassuming, he would not make much ado about the matter. Tell me, indeed, for what reason thou leads about so many servants, parasites, and flatterers, and all the other forms of pomp? Not for necessity, but only for pride; to the end that by these thou may seem more dignified than other men! Besides, he knew that wealth is not forbidden if it be used for that which is necessary. For as I observed, wine is not a bad thing, but drunkenness is so. A covetous man is one thing, and a rich man is another thing. The covetous man is not

rich; he is in want of many things, and while he needs many things, he can never be rich. The covetous man is a keeper, not a master, of wealth; a slave, not a lord. For he would sooner give anyone a portion of his flesh, than his buried gold. And as though he were ordered and compelled of someone to touch nothing of these hidden treasures, so with all earnestness he watches and keeps them, abstaining from his own, as if it were another's. And certainly, they are not his own. For what he can neither determine to bestow upon others, nor to distribute to the necessitous, although he may sustain infinite punishments, how can he possibly account his own? How does he hold possession of those things, of which he has neither the free use, nor enjoyment? But besides this,— Paul is not accustomed to enjoin everything on every man, but accommodates himself to the weakness of his hearers, even, indeed, as Christ also did. For when that rich man came to him, and asked him concerning Life, he did not say at once, "Go, sell that thou hast," but omitting this, he spoke to him of other commandments. Nor afterwards, when he challenged Him and said, "What lack I yet?" did He simply say, "Sell what thou hast;" but, "If thou wilt be perfect, go and sell that thou hast." "I lay it down for your determination. I give you full power to choose. I do not lay upon you any necessity." For this reason also, Paul spoke nothing to the rich concerning poverty, but concerning humility; as well because of the weakness of his hearers, as because he perfectly knew, that could he bring them to exercise moderation, and to be free from pride, he should also quickly free them from eagerness about being rich.

15. And further, after giving this admonition, "not to be high-minded," he also taught the manner in which

they would be able to avoid being so. And how was it? That they should consider the nature of wealth, how uncertain and faithless it is! Therefore he goes on to say, "Neither trust in uncertain riches." The rich man is not one who is in possession of much, but one who gives much. Abraham was rich, but he was not covetous; for he turned not his thoughts to the house of this man, nor prayed into the wealth of that man; but going forth he looked around wherever there chanced to be a stranger, or a poor man, in order that he might succor poverty, and hospitably entertain the traveler. He covered not his roof with gold, but fixing his tent near the oak, he was contented with the shadow of its leaves. Yet so illustrious was his lodging, that angels were not ashamed to tarry with him; for they sought not splendor of abode, but virtue of soul. This man then let us imitate, beloved, and bestow what we have upon the needy. That lodging was rudely prepared, but it was more illustrious than the halls of kings. No king has ever entertained angels; but he, dwelling under that oak, and having but pitched a tent, was thought worthy of that honor: not receiving the honor on account of the meanness of his dwelling, but enjoying that benefit on account of the magnificence of his soul, and the wealth therein deposited.

16. Let us too, then, adorn not our houses, but our souls in preference to the house. For is it not disgraceful to clothe our walls with marble, vainly and to no end, and to neglect Christ going about naked? What does thy house profit thee, O man! For wilt thou take it with thee when thou departs? This thou canst not take with thee, when thou departs. But thy soul, when thou departs, thou shalt assuredly take with thee! Behold now this great danger has overtaken us! Let your houses stand by you! Let them

deliver you from the threatened peril! But they cannot! And ye yourselves are witnesses, who are leaving them solitary, and hurrying forth to the wilderness; fearing them as ye would do snares and nets! Let riches now lend assistance! But it is no time for them to do so! If then the power of riches is found wanting before the wrath of man, much rather will this be the case, before the divine and inexorable tribunal! If it is but a man that is provoked and offended, and even now gold is of no avail, much more will the power of money be utterly impotent then, when God is angry, who has no need of wealth! We build houses that we may have a habitation; not that we may make an ambitious display. What is beyond our wants, is superfluous and useless. Put on a sandal which is larger than your foot! You will not endure it; for it is a hindrance to the step. Thus also a house larger than necessity requires, is an impediment to your progress towards heaven. Do you wish to build large and splendid houses? I forbid it not; but let it be not upon the earth! Build thyself tabernacles in heaven, and such that thou may be able to receive others;—tabernacles which never fall to pieces. Why art thou mad about fleeting things; and things that must be left here? Nothing is more slippery than wealth. Today it is for thee; tomorrow it is against thee. It arms the eyes of the envious everywhere. It is a hostile comrade, a domestic enemy; and ye are witnesses of this, who possess it, and are in every way burying and concealing it from view; as even now too our very wealth makes the danger more insupportable to us! Thou sees indeed the poor ready for action, disengaged, and prepared for all things; but the wealthy in great perplexity, and wandering about, seeking where they may bury their gold, or seeking with whom they may deposit it! Why, O man, dost thou seek thy fellow slaves? Christ stands ready to receive, and to keep thy deposits for thee; and not to keep only, but also to augment them, and to pay them back with much interest. Out of His hand no man can forcibly take them away. And He not only keeps the deposit, but for this very thing He also frees thee from thy perils. For among men, they who receive treasures in trust think that they have done us a favor, in keeping that of which they took charge; but with Christ it is the contrary; for He does not say that He has conferred, but that He has received a favor, when He receives thy deposited treasures; and for the guardianship which He exercises over thy wealth, He does not demand a recompense of thee, but gives thee a recompense!

17. What defense then can we claim, or what excuse, when we pass by Him who is able to keep, and who is thankful for the trust giving in return great and unspeakable rewards, and in place of this guardianship commit our treasures to men who have not the power to keep them, and who think they grant us a favor, and pay us back at last only that which was given them. Thou art a stranger and a pilgrim with respect to the things here! Thou hast a country which is thine own in the heavens! There transfer all;—that before the actual enjoyment, thou may enjoy the recompense here. He who is nourished with good hopes, and is confident respecting things to come, hath here already tasted of the kingdom! For nothing ordinarily so repairs the soul, and makes a man better, as a good hope of things to come; so that if thou transfer thy wealth there, thou may then provide for thy soul with suitable leisure. For they who spend all their endeavors upon the decoration of their dwelling, rich as they are in outward things, are careless of that which is

within, letting their soul abide desolate and squalid, and full of cobwebs. But if they would be indifferent to exterior things, and earnestly expend all their attention upon the mind, adorning this at all points; then the soul of such men would be a resting place for Christ. And having Christ for its inhabitant, what could ever be more blessed? Would you be rich? Have God for thy friend, and thou shalt be richer than all men!—Would you be rich? Be not high-minded!—this rule is suitable not only to things future, but to things present. For there is no such object of envy, as a man of wealth; but when pride is super-added, a two-fold precipice is formed; the war becomes fiercer on all sides. But if you know how to exercise moderation, you undermine the tyranny of envy by your humility; and you possess whatever you do possess with safety. For such is the nature of virtue, that it not only profits us, as it respects futurity, but it also here bestows a present reward.

18. Let us not then be high-minded in reference to riches, or indeed to any other thing; for if even in spiritual things the man who is high-minded is fallen, and undone, much more so as to carnal things. Let us be mindful of our nature. Let us recollect our sins. Let us understand what we are; and this will provide a sufficient groundwork for complete humility. Tell me not, "I have laid up the revenues of this or that number of years; myriads of talents of gold; gains that are increasing every day." Say as much as you will, you say all in vain, and to no purpose. Very often in one hour, yea, in one short moment, just as the light dust, when the wind rushes down upon it from above, are all these things swept out of the house by a blast. Our life is full of such examples, and the Scriptures abound with lessons of this sort. He who is

rich to-day, is poor tomorrow. Wherefore, I have often smiled, when reading wills that said, let such a man have the ownership of these fields, or of this house, and another the use thereof. For we all have the use, but no man has the ownership. For although riches may remain with us all our lifetime, undergoing no change, we must transfer them in the end, whether we will or no, into the hands of others; having enjoyed only the use of them, and departing to another life naked and destitute of this ownership! Whence it is plain, that they only have the ownership of property, who have despised its use, and derided its enjoyment. For the man that has cast his substance away from him, and bestowed it on the poor, he uses it as he ought; and takes with him the ownership of these things when he departs, not being stripped of the possession even in death, but at that time receiving all back again; yea, and much more than these things, at that day of judgment, when he most needs their protection, and when we shall all have to render up an account of the deeds we have done. So that if any one wishes to have the possession of his riches, and the use and the ownership entire, let him disencumber himself from them all; since, truly, he who doth not this must at all events be separated from them at death; and frequently before his death will lose them, in the midst of dangers and innumerable ills.

19. And this is not the only disaster, that the change comes suddenly; but that the rich man comes unpracticed to the endurance of poverty. But not so the poor man; for he confides not in gold and silver, which are lifeless matter, but in "God, who giveth us all things richly to enjoy." So that the rich man stands in more uncertainty than the poor man, experiencing, as he does, frequent and diversified changes. What is the sense of

this? "Who giveth to us all things richly to enjoy." God giveth all those things with liberality, which are more necessary than riches; such, for example, as the air, the water, the fire, the sun; all things of this kind. The rich man is not able to say that he enjoys more of the sunbeams than the poor man; he is not able to say that he breathes more plenteous air: but all these are offered alike to all. And wherefore, one may say, is it the greater and more necessary blessings, and those which maintain our life, that God hath made common; but the smaller and less valuable (I speak of money) are not thus common. Why is this? In order that our life might be disciplined, and that we might have training ground for virtue. For if these necessaries were not common, perhaps they who are rich, practicing their usual covetousness, would strangle those who were poor. For if they do this for the sake of money, much rather would they do so for the things referred to. Again, if money was also an universal possession, and were offered in the same manner to all, the occasion for almsgiving, and the opportunity for benevolence, would be taken away.

20. That we may live then securely, the sources of our existence have been made common. On the other hand, to the end that we may have an opportunity of gaining crowns and good report, property has not been made common; in order that hating covetousness, and following after righteousness, and freely bestowing our goods upon the poor, we may by this method obtain a certain kind of relief for our sins. God hath made thee rich, why makes thou thyself poor? He hath made thee rich that thou may assist the needy; that thou may have release of thine own sins, by liberality to others. He hath given thee money, not that thou may shut it up for thy

destruction, but that thou may pour it forth for thy salvation. For this reason also He hath made the possession of riches uncertain and unstable, that by this means he might slack the intensity of thy madness concerning it. For if its possessors, even now whilst they can have no confidence in regard to it, but behold a multitude of snares produced from this quarter, are so inflamed with the desire of these things; if the elements of security and stability were added to wealth, whom would they have spared? From whom would they have refrained? From what widows? From what orphans? From what poor?

21. Wherefore let us not consider riches to be a great good; for the great good is, not to possess money, but to possess the fear of God and all manner of piety. Behold, now if there were any righteous man here, having great boldness toward God, notwithstanding he might be the poorest of mortals, he would be sufficient to liberate us from present evils! For he only needed to spread forth his hands towards heaven, and to call upon God, and this cloud would pass away! But now gold is treasured up in abundance; and yet it is more useless than mere clay for the purpose of deliverance from the impending calamities! Nor is it only in a peril of this kind; but should disease or death, or any such evil befall us, the impotency of wealth is fully proved, since it is at a loss, and has no consolation of its own to offer us amidst these events.

22. There is one thing in which wealth seems to have an advantage over poverty, viz. that it lives in a state of daily luxury, and is supplied with an abundance of pleasure in its banquets. This however may also be seen exemplified at the table of the poor; and these enjoy there a pleasure superior to that of the rich. And marvel not at

this, nor think what I say a paradox; for I will make the matter clear to you from the evidence of facts. Ye know of course, and ye all confess that in feasts it is not the nature of the viands, but the disposition of those who feast upon them, which usually causes the pleasure; for instance, when any one comes to the table hungry, the food will taste sweeter than any delicacy, or condiment, or a thousand exquisite preparations for the palate, although it may be the most common article of diet. But he who without tarrying for necessity, or first waiting till he is hungry, (as the custom is with the wealthy), when he comes to the table, notwithstanding he finds the most refined dainties spread before him, has no sensation of pleasure, his appetite not being previously excited. And that you may learn that this is the actual state of the case, besides that you are all witnesses to it, let us hear the Scripture telling us the same truth; "The full soul," it is said, "loathes the honey comb, but to the hungry soul every bitter thing is sweet." Yet what can be sweeter than honey, and the honey comb? Still he says it is not sweet to the man that is not hungry. And what can be more disagreeable than bitter things? And yet to those who are poverty stricken they are sweet. But that the poor come to the meal with need and hunger, and that the rich do not wait for this is manifest, I suppose, to everyone. Hence they do not reap the fruit of a genuine and unmixed pleasure. Nor is it only in the article of food, but any one may perceive that the same thing occurs with respect to drinks; and as in the one case hunger is the cause of pleasure, far more than the quality of the viands, so also in the other, thirst usually makes the draught sweetest, although what is drunk is only water. And this is that which the prophet intimated, when he said, "He satisfied them with honey out of the rock." But we do not read in any part of Scripture that Moses brought honey out of the rock, but throughout the history we read of rivers, and waters, and cool streams. What then is it that was meant? For the Scripture by no means speaks falsely. Inasmuch, then, as they were thirsty and wearied with drought, and found these streams of water so cooling, in order to show the pleasure of such a draught, he calls the water honey, not as though its nature were changed into honey, but because the condition of the drinkers made these streams sweeter than honey. You see how the condition of the thirsty is wont to make the draught sweet? Yea oftentimes have many of the poor, when wearied, and distressed, and parched with thirst, partaken of such streams even with such pleasure as I have said. But the rich, whilst drinking wine that is sweet, and has the fragrance of flowers, and every perfection that wine can have, experience no such enjoyment.

23. The same thing happens as everyone may perceive with regard to sleep. For not a soft couch, nor a bedstead overlaid with silver, nor the quietness that exists throughout the house, nor anything else of this kind, are so generally wont to make sleep sweet and pleasant, as labor and fatigue, and the need of sleep, and drowsiness when one lies down. And to this particular the experience of facts, nay, before actual experience, the assertion of the Scriptures bears witness. For Solomon, who had passed his life in luxury, when he wished to make this matter evident, said, "The sleep of a laboring man is sweet, whether he eat little or much?" Why does he add, "whether he eat little or much?" Both these things usually bring sleeplessness, viz. indigence, and excess of food; the one drying up the body, stiffening the eyelids and not

suffering them to be closed; the other straitening and oppressing the breath, and inducing many pains. But at the same time so powerful a persuasive is labor, that though both these things should befall him, the servant is able to sleep. For since throughout the whole day, they are running about everywhere, ministering to their masters, being knocked about and hard pressed, and having but little time to take breath, they receive a sufficient recompense for their toils and labors in the pleasure of sleeping. And thus it hath happened through the goodness of God toward man, that these pleasures are not to be purchased with gold and silver, but with labor, with hard toil, with necessity, and every kind of discipline. Not so the rich. On the contrary, whilst lying on their beds, they are frequently without sleep through the whole night; and though they devise many schemes, they do not obtain such pleasure. But the poor man when released from his daily labors, having his limbs completely tired, falls almost before he can lie down into a slumber that is sound, and sweet, and genuine, enjoying this reward, which is not a small one, of his fair day's toils. Since therefore the poor man sleeps, and drinks, and eats with more pleasure than the rich man, what further value is left to riches, now deprived of the one advantage they seemed to have over poverty? For this reason also, from the beginning, God tied the man to labor, not for the purpose of punishing or chastising, but for amendment and education. When Adam lived an unlaborious life, he fell from Paradise, but when the Apostle labored abundantly, and toiled hard, and said, "In labor and travail, working night and day," then he was taken up into Paradise, and ascended to the third heaven!

24. Let us not then despise labor; let us not despise work; for before the kingdom of Heaven, we receive the greatest recompense from thence, deriving pleasure from that circumstance; and not pleasure only, but what is greater than pleasure, the purest health. For in addition to their want of relish, many diseases also attack the rich; but the poor are freed from the hands of physicians; and if at times they do fall into a sickness, they recover themselves quickly, being far removed from all effeminacy, and having robust constitutions. Poverty, to those who bear it wisely, is a great possession, a treasure that cannot be taken away; the stoutest of staves; a way of gain that cannot be thwarted; a lodging that is safe from snares. The poor man, it may be objected, is oppressed. But then the rich man is still more subject to adverse designs. The poor man is looked down upon and insulted. But the rich man is the subject of envy. The poor man is not so easily assailed as the rich man, offering, as the latter does on every side, countless handles to the devil, and to his secret foes; and being the servant of all, on account of the great extent of his business. Standing in need of many things, he is compelled to flatter many persons, and to minister to them with much servility. But the poor man, if he knows how to be spiritually wise, is not assailable even by the devil himself. Job therefore, strong as he was before this, when he lost all, became still more powerful, and bore away an illustrious victory from the devil!

25. But besides this, the poor man cannot possibly be injured, if he knows how to be spiritually wise. Now what I said of pleasure, that it consisted not in a costly provision of meats, but in the disposition of those who eat, this also I say respecting an insult; that the insult is

either created or destroyed, not by the intention of those who insult, but by the disposition of those who bear it. For example. Someone hath insulted thee with much language, fit or unfit to repeat. If thou shalt laugh at the insults, if thou take not the words to heart, if thou shows thyself superior to the blow, thou art not insulted. And just as if we possessed an adamantine body, we should not be hurt, were we even attacked on all sides by a thousand darts, for darts beget wounds not from the hand of him who hurls them, but from the bodies of those who receive them, so too in this case, insults are constituted real and dishonorable ones, not from the folly of those who offer them, but from the weakness of the insulted. For if we know how to be truly wise, we are incapable of being insulted, or of suffering any serious evils. Someone it may be hath offered thee an insult, but thou hast not felt it? Thou hast not been pained. Then thou art not insulted, but hast given rather than received a blow! For when the insulting person perceives that his blow did not reach the soul of those who were reviled, he is himself the more severely fretted; and whilst those who are reproached remain silent, the insulting blow is turned backwards, and recoils of its own accord upon him who aimed it.

26. In all things then, beloved, let us be spiritually wise, and poverty will be able to do us no harm, but will benefit us exceedingly, and render us more illustrious and wealthy than the richest. For tell me who was poorer than Elias? Yet for this reason he surpassed all the wealthy, in that he was so poor, and this very poverty of his was his own choice from an opulence of mind. For since he accounted the wealth of all riches to be beneath his magnanimity, and not worthy of his spiritual wisdom, therefore he welcomed this kind of poverty; so that if he

had considered present things as of much worth, he would not have possessed only a mantle. But so did he contemn the vanity of the life that now is, and regard all gold as clay cast into the street, that he possessed himself of nothing more than that covering. Therefore the king had need of the poor man, and he who had so much gold hung upon the words of him who had nothing more than a sheepskin. Thus was the sheepskin more splendid than the purple, and the cave of the just man than the halls of kings. Therefore also when he went up to heaven, he left nothing to his disciple save the sheepskin. "By the help of this," said he, "I have wrestled with the devil, and taking this, be thou armed against him!" For indigence is a powerful weapon, an unassailable retreat, an unshaken fortress! Elisha received the sheepskin as the greatest inheritance; for it was truly such; a more precious one than all gold. And thenceforth that Elias was a twofold person; an Elias above and an Elias below! I know ye account that just person blessed, and ye would each desire to be that person. What then if I show you that all among us, who are initiated, have received something far greater than he did? For Elias left a sheepskin to his disciple, but the Son of God ascending left to us His own flesh! Elias indeed, cast off his mantle, before he went up; but Christ left it behind for our sakes; and yet retained it when He ascended. Let us not then be cast down. Let us not lament, nor fear the difficulty of the times, for He who did not refuse to pour out His blood for all, and has suffered us to partake of His flesh and of His blood again, what will He refuse to do for our safety? Confident then in these hopes, let us beseech Him continually; let us be earnest in prayers and supplications; and let us with all strictness give our attention to every other virtue; that so we may escape the danger that now threatens, and obtain the good things to come; which God grant we may all be worthy of, through the grace and lovingkindness of our Lord Jesus Christ, by Whom, and with Whom be glory to the Father together with the Holy Ghost, forever and ever. Amen.

Homily III.

On the departure of Flavian, Bishop of Antioch, who was gone on an embassy to the Emperor Theodosius, on behalf of the city. Of the dignity of the Priesthood. What is true fasting. Slander worse than devouring the human body. And finally of those who had been put to death on account of the sedition; and against those who complained that many innocent persons were apprehended.

1. When I look on that throne, deserted and bereft of our teacher, I rejoice and weep at the same time. I weep, because I see not our father with us! But I rejoice that he hath set out on a journey for our preservation; that he is gone to snatch so great a multitude from the wrath of the Emperor! Here is both an ornament to you, and a crown to him! An ornament to you, that such a father hath been allotted to you; a crown to him, because he is so affectionate towards his children, and hath confirmed by actual deeds what Christ said. For having learnt that "the good shepherd lays down his life for the sheep," he took his departure; venturing his own life for us all, notwithstanding there were many things to hinder his absence, and enforce his stay. And first, his time of life, extended as it is to the utmost limits of old age; next, his bodily infirmity, and the season of the year, as well as the

necessity for his presence at the holy festival; and besides these reasons, his only sister even now at her last breath! He has disregarded, however, the ties of kindred, of old age, of infirmity, and the severity of the season, and the toils of the journey; and preferring you and your safety above all things, he has broken through all these restraints. And, even as a youth, the aged man is now hastening along, borne upon the wings of zeal! For if Christ (says he) gave Himself for us, what excuse or pardon should we deserve, having undertaken the charge of so numerous a people, if we were not ready to do and to suffer anything for the security of those committed into our hands. For if (continues he) the patriarch Jacob, when in charge of flocks, and feeding brute sheep, and having to give account to man, passed sleepless nights, and bore heat and cold, and all the inclemency of the elements, to the end that not one of those animals might perish, much less doth it become us, who preside over those, who are not irrational, but spiritual sheep; who are about to give an account of this charge, not to man, but to God, to be slack in any respect, or shrink from anything which might benefit the flock. Besides, in proportion as the latter flock is superior to the former; men to brutes, and God to men; so it behooves us to manifest a greater and more intense anxiety and diligence. He knows well that his concern is now, not for one city only, but for the whole of the East. For our city is the head and mother of all that lie towards the East. For this reason he would encounter every danger, and nothing would avail to detain him here.

2. On this account I trust that there may be a good hope; for God will not disdain to look upon such earnestness and zeal, nor will He suffer his servant to return without success. I know that when he has barely

seen our pious Emperor, and been seen by him, he will be able at once by his very countenance to allay his wrath. For not only the words of the saints, but their very countenances are full of grace. And he is a person too endowed with abundant wisdom; and being well skilled in the divine laws, he will say to him as Moses said to God, "Yet now, if thou wilt forgive their sin;—and if not, slay me together with them." For such are the bowels of the saints, that they think death with their children sweeter than life without them. He will also make the special season his advocate and shelter himself behind the sacred festival of the Passover; and will remind the Emperor of the season when Christ remitted the sins of the whole world. He will exhort him to imitate his Lord. He will also remind him of that parable of the ten thousand talents, and the hundred pence. I know the boldness of our father, that he will not hesitate to alarm him from the parable, and to say, "Take heed lest thou also hear it said in that day, 'O thou wicked servant, I forgave thee all that debt, because thou desires me; you ought also to forgive thy fellow-servants!' Thou dost to thyself a greater benefit than them, since by pardoning these few offences thou gains an amnesty for greater." To this address he will add that prayer, which those who initiated him into the sacred mystery taught him to offer up, and say, "Forgive us our debts, as we forgive our debtors."

3. He will moreover inform him, that the offence was not common to the whole city, but the deed of certain strangers and adventurers, men that act upon no deliberate plan, but with every sort of audacity and lawlessness; and that it would not be just for the disorderly conduct of a few to extirpate so great a city, and to punish those who had done no wrong; and that even though all had been

transgressors, they had paid a sufficient punishment, being consumed by fear so many days, and expecting every day to be put to death, and being exiles and fugitives; thus living more wretchedly than condemned criminals, carrying their life in their hands, and having no confidence of escape! "Let this punishment (he will say) suffice. Carry not thy resentment further! Make the Judge above merciful to thyself, by humanity towards thy fellow-servants! Think of the greatness of the city, and that the question now is not concerning one, or two, or three, or ten souls, but of a vast multitude too numerous to be reckoned up! It is a question which affects the capital of the whole world. This is the city in which Christians were first called by that name. Honor Christ. Reverence the city which first proclaimed that name, so lovely and sweet to all! This city hath been the tabernacle of Apostles; the dwelling place of the just! And now this is the first and only instance of insurrection against its rulers; and all past time will bear favorable witness to the manners of the city. For had the people been continually given to sedition, it might have been necessary to make an example of such iniquity; but if this hath happened only once in all time, it is plain that the offence has not arisen from the habit of the city, but that it was the transgression of those who had in an evil hour by mere random chance arrived there."

4. These things and more than these the priest will say with still greater boldness; and the Emperor will listen to them; and one is humane, and the other is faithful; so that on both sides we entertain favorable hopes. But much more do we rely upon the mercy of God, than upon the fidelity of our Teacher and the humanity of the Emperor. For whilst the Emperor is supplicated, and the priest is

supplicating, He Himself will interpose, softening the heart of the Emperor, and exciting the tongue of the priest; facilitating his utterance;—preparing the mind of the other to receive what is said and with much indulgence, to accede to the petitions. For our city is dearer to Christ than all others both because of the virtue of our ancestors, and of your own. And as Peter was the first among the apostles to preach Christ, so as I said before, this city was the first of cities that adorned itself by assuming the Christian appellation, as a sort of admirable diadem. But if where only ten just men were found, God promised to save all who dwelt therein, why should we not expect a favorable issue, and become assured of all our lives, when there are not only ten, twenty, or twice so many only, but far more; who are serving God with all strictness.

5. I have heard many saying, "The threats of a king are like the wrath of a lion;" being full of dejection and lamentation. What then should we say to such? That He who said, "The wolves and the lambs shall feed together; and the leopard shall lie down with the kid, and the lion shall eat straw like the ox," will be able to convert the lion into a mild lamb. Let us therefore supplicate Him; let us send an embassy to Him; and He will doubtless allay the Emperor's wrath, and deliver us from the impending distress. Our Father hath gone thither on this embassy. Let us go on embassy from hence to the Majesty of heaven! Let us assist him by prayers! The community of the Church can do much, if with a sorrowful soul, and with a contrite spirit, we offer up our prayers! It is unnecessary to cross the ocean, or to undertake a long journey. Let every man and woman among us, whether meeting together at church, or remaining at home, call

upon God with much earnestness, and He will doubtless accede to these petitions.

Whence does this appear evident? Because He is exceedingly desirous, that we should always take refuge in Him, and in everything make our requests unto Him; and do nothing and speak nothing without Him. For men, when we trouble them repeatedly concerning our affairs, become slothful and evasive, and conduct themselves unpleasantly towards us; but with God it is quite the reverse. Not when we apply to him continually respecting our affairs, but when we fail to do so, then is he especially displeased. Hear at least what He reproves the Jews for, when He says, "Ye have taken counsel, but not of Me, and made treaties, but not by My Spirit." For this is the custom of those who love; they desire that all the concerns of their beloved should be accomplished by means of themselves; and that they should neither do anything, nor say anything, without them. On this account did God not only on that occasion, but again elsewhere, uttering a reproof, speak the same language. "They have reigned, but not by Me; they have ruled, and they made it not known to Me." Let us not then be slow to take refuge in Him continually; and whatever be the evil, it will in any case find its appropriate solution.

6. Doth a man affright you? Hasten to the Lord above, and thou wilt suffer no evil. Thus the ancients had release from their calamities; and not men only, but also women. There was a certain Hebrew woman, Esther was her name. This Esther rescued the whole people of the Jews, when they were about to be delivered over to destruction, by this very method. For when the Persian king gave orders that all the Jews should be utterly destroyed, and there was no one who was able to stand in

the way of his wrath,—this woman having divested herself of the splendid robe, and clothed herself with sackcloth and being besprinkled with ashes, supplicated the merciful God to go in with her to the king; and offering up her prayer to Him, these were the words she uttered, "O Lord, make my words acceptable, and put eloquent speech in my mouth." Let this be the prayer which we offer to God for our Teacher. For if a woman, supplicating on behalf of the Jews, prevailed to allay the wrath of a barbarian, much rather will our Teacher, entreating on behalf of so great a city, and in conjunction with so great a Church, be able to persuade this most mild and merciful Emperor. For if he hath received authority to loose sins committed against God, much more will he be able to take away and blot out those which have been committed against a man. He is also himself a ruler and a ruler of more dignity than the other. For the sacred laws take and place under his hands even the royal head. And when there is need of any good thing from above, the Emperor is accustomed to fly to the priest: but not the priest to the Emperor. He too hath his breast-plate, that of righteousness. He too hath his girdle, that of truth, and sandals of much greater dignity, those of the Gospel of peace. He too hath a sword, not of iron, but of the Spirit; he too hath a crown resting on his head. This panoply is the more splendid. The weapons are grander, the license of speech greater, and mightier the strength. So that from the weight of his authority, and from his own greatness of soul; and more than all the rest, from the hope which he has in God, he will address the Emperor with much freedom and much discretion.

7. Let us not then despair of our safety, but let us pray; let us make invocation; let us supplicate; let us go

on embassy to the King that is above with many tears! We have this fast too as an ally, and as an assistant in this good intercession. Therefore, as when the winter is over and the summer is appearing, the sailor draws his vessel to the deep; and the soldier burnishes his arms, and makes ready his steed for the battle; and the husbandman sharpens his sickle; and the traveler boldly undertakes a long journey, and the wrestler strips and bares himself for the contest. So too, when the fast makes its appearance, like a kind of spiritual summer, let us as soldiers burnish our weapons; and as husbandmen let us sharpen our sickle; and as sailors let us order our thoughts against the waves of extravagant desires; and as travelers let us set out on the journey towards heaven; and as wrestlers let us strip for the contest. For the believer is at once a husbandman, and a sailor, and a soldier, a wrestler, and a traveler. Hence St. Paul says, "We wrestle not against flesh and blood, but against principalities, against powers. Put on therefore the whole armor of God." Hast thou observed the wrestler? Hast thou observed the soldier? If thou art a wrestler, it is necessary for thee to engage in the conflict naked. If a soldier, it behooves thee to stand in the battle line armed at all points. How then are both these things possible, to be naked, and yet not naked; to be clothed, and yet not clothed! How? I will tell thee. Divest thyself of worldly business, and thou hast become a wrestler. Put on the spiritual armor, and thou hast become a soldier. Strip thyself of worldly cares, for the season is one of wrestling. Clothe thyself with the spiritual armor, for we have a heavy warfare to wage with demons. Therefore also it is needful we should be naked, so as to offer nothing that the devil may take hold of, while he is wrestling with us; and to be fully armed at all points, so as on no side to receive a deadly blow. Cultivate thy soul. Cut away the thorns. Sow the word of godliness. Propagate and nurse with much care the fair plants of divine wisdom, and thou hast become a husbandman. And Paul will say to thee, "The husbandman that labored must be first partaker of the fruits." He too himself practiced this art. Therefore writing to the Corinthians, he said, "I have planted, Apollos watered, but God gave the increase." Sharpen thy sickle, which thou hast blunted through gluttony—sharpen it by fasting. Lay hold of the pathway which leads towards heaven; rugged and narrow as it is, lay hold of it, and journey on. And how may thou be able to do these things? By subduing thy body, and bringing it into subjection. For when the way grows narrow, the corpulence that comes of gluttony is a great hindrance. Keep down the waves of inordinate desires. Repel the tempest of evil thoughts. Preserve the bark; display much skill, and thou hast become a pilot. But we shall have the fast for a groundwork and instructor in all these things.

8. I speak not, indeed, of such a fast as most persons keep, but of real fasting; not merely an abstinence from meats; but from sins too. For the nature of a fast is such, that it does not suffice to deliver those who practice it, unless it be done according to a suitable law. "For the wrestler," it is said, "is not crowned unless he strive lawfully." To the end then, that when we have gone through the labor of fasting, we forfeit not the crown of fasting, we should understand how, and after what manner, it is necessary to conduct this business; since that Pharisee also fasted, but afterwards went down empty, and destitute of the fruit of fasting. The Publican fasted not; and yet he was accepted in preference to him who

had fasted; in order that thou may learn that fasting is unprofitable, except all other duties follow with it. The Ninevites fasted, and won the favor of God. The Jews, fasted too, and profited nothing, nay, they departed with blame. Since then the danger in fasting is so great to those who do not know how they ought to fast, we should learn the laws of this exercise, in order that we may not "run uncertainly," nor "beat the air," nor while we are fighting contend with a shadow. Fasting is a medicine; but a medicine, though it be never so profitable, becomes frequently useless owing to the unskillfulness of him who employs it. For it is necessary to know, moreover, the time when it should be applied, and the requisite quantity of it; and the temperament of body that admits it; and the nature of the country, and the season of the year; and the corresponding diet; as well as various other particulars; any of which, if one overlooks, he will mar all the rest that have been named. Now if, when the body needs healing, such exactness is required on our part, much more ought we, when our care is about the soul, and we seek to heal the distempers of the mind, to look, and to search into every particular with the utmost accuracy.

9. Let us see then how the Ninevites fasted, and how they were delivered from that wrath—"Let neither man nor beast, herd nor flock, taste anything," says (the prophet). What say you? Tell me—must even the irrational things fast, and the horses and the mules be covered with sackcloth? "Even so," he replies. For as when, at the decease of some rich man, the relatives clothe not only the men servants and maid servants, but the horses also with sackcloth, and give orders that they should follow the procession to the sepulcher, led by their grooms; thus signifying the greatness of the calamity, and

inviting all to pity; thus also, indeed, when that city was about to be destroyed, even the irrational nature was enveloped in sackcloth, and subjected to the yoke of fasting. "It is not possible," says he, "that irrational creatures should learn the wrath of God by means of reason; let them be taught by means of fasting, that this stroke is of divine infliction. For if the city should be overturned, not only would it be one common sepulcher for us, the dwellers therein, but for these likewise. Inasmuch then as these would participate in the punishment, let them also do so in the fast." But there was yet another thing which they aimed at in this act, which the prophets also are wont to do. For these, when they see some dreadful chastisement proceeding from heaven, and those who are to be punished without anything to say for themselves;—laden with shame,—unworthy of the least pardon or excuse:—not knowing what to do, nor from whence they may procure an advocacy for the condemned, they have recourse to the things irrational; and describing their death in tragical fashion, they make intercession by them, putting forward as a plea their pitiable and mournful destruction. When therefore, aforetime, famine had seized upon the Jews, and a great drought oppressed their country, and all things were being consumed, one of the prophets spoke thus, "The young heifers leaped in their stalls; the herds of oxen wept, because there was no pasture; all the cattle of the field looked upward to Thee, because the streams of waters were dried up." Another prophet bewailing the evils of drought again speaks to this effect: "The hinds calved in the fields and forsook it, because there was no grass. The wild asses did stand in the forests; they snuffed up the wind like a dragon; their eyes did fail, because there was no grass." Moreover, ye have heard Joel saying to-day, "Let the bridegroom go forth of his chamber, and the bride out of her closet;—the infants that suck the breast." For what reason, I ask, does he call so immature an age to supplication? Is it not plainly for the very same reason? For since all who have arrived at the age of manhood, have inflamed and provoked God's wrath, let the age, says he, which is devoid of transgressions supplicate Him who is provoked.

10. But, as I said before, we may see what it was that dissolved such inexorable wrath. Was it, forsooth, fasting only and sackcloth? We say not so; but the change of their whole life. Whence does this appear? From the very language of the prophet. For he who hath discoursed of the wrath of God, and of their fasting, himself too, when speaking of the reconciliation, and teaching us the cause of the reconciliation, speaks to this effect; "And God saw their works." What kind of works? That they had fasted? That they had put on sackcloth? Nothing of the sort: but passing all these points in silence, he adds, "That they turned everyone from their evil ways, and the Lord repented of the evil that He had said He would do unto them." See that fasting did not rescue from this danger, but it was the change of life, which rendered God propitious and kind to these barbarians?

11. I have said these things, not that we may disparage fasting, but that we may honor fasting; for the honor of fasting consists not in abstinence from food, but in withdrawing from sinful practices; since he who limits his fasting only to an abstinence from meats, is one who especially disparages it. Do you fast? Give me proof of it by thy works! Is it said by what kind of works? If thou sees a poor man, take pity on him! If thou sees in enemy,

be reconciled to him! If thou sees a friend gaining honor, envy him not! If thou sees a handsome woman, pass her by! For let not the mouth only fast, but also the eye, and the ear, and the feet, and the hands, and all the members of our bodies. Let the hands fast, by being pure from rapine and avarice. Let the feet fast, by ceasing from running to the unlawful spectacles. Let the eyes fast, being taught never to fix themselves rudely upon handsome countenances, or to busy themselves with strange beauties. For looking is the food of the eyes, but if this be such as is unlawful or forbidden, it mars the fast; and upsets the whole safety of the soul; but if it be lawful and safe, it adorns fasting. For it would be among things the most absurd to abstain from lawful food because of the fast, but with the eyes to touch even what is forbidden. Do you not eat flesh? Feed not upon lasciviousness by means of the eyes. Let the ear fast also. The fasting of the ear consists in refusing to receive evil speaking and calumnies. "Thou shalt not receive a false report," it says.

12. Let the mouth too fast from disgraceful speeches and railing. For what doth it profit if we abstain from birds and fishes; and yet bite and devour our brethren? The evil speaker eats the flesh of his brother, and bites the body of his neighbor. Because of this Paul utters the fearful saying, "If ye bite and devour one another, take heed that ye be not consumed one of another." Thou hast not fixed thy teeth in the flesh, but thou hast fixed the slander in the soul, and inflicted the wound of evil suspicion; thou hast harmed, in a thousand ways, thyself and him, and many others, for in slandering a neighbor thou hast made him who listens to the slander worse; for should he be a wicked man, he becomes more careless when he finds a partner in his wickedness; and

should he be a just man, he is lifted to arrogance, and puffed up; being led on by the sin of others to imagine great things concerning himself. Besides, thou hast struck at the common welfare of the Church; for all those who hear not only accuse the supposed sinner, but the reproach is fastened on the Christian community; neither dost thou hear the unbelievers saying, "Such a person is a fornicator, or a libertine;" but instead of the individual who hath sinned, they accuse all Christians. In addition to this, thou hast caused the glory of God to be blasphemed; for as His Name is glorified when we have good report, so when we sin, it is blasphemed and insulted!

13. A fourth reason is, that thou hast disgraced him who is ill reported; and hast thus rendered him more shameless than he was, by placing him in a state of enmity and hostility. Fifthly, thou hast made thyself liable to chastisement and vengeance; by involving thyself in matters which in no way concerned thee. For let not anyone tell me in reply, "Then I am an evil speaker when I speak falsely, but if I speak what is true, I cease to be so." Although it be with truth thou speaks evil, this also is a crime. For that Pharisee spoke evil of the Publican with truth; but nevertheless this availed him not. For was not the latter, I ask, a publican and a sinner? It is manifest to everyone that he was a publican. But at the same time inasmuch as the Pharisee spoke ill of him, he departed from the temple with the loss of every advantage. Do you wish to correct a brother? Weep; pray unto God; taking him apart, admonish, counsel, entreat him! So also Paul did, "Lest," says he, "when I come again, my God will humble me among you, and I shall bewail many which have sinned already, and have not repented of the uncleanness and fornication and lasciviousness which

they have committed." Show thy charity towards the sinner. Persuade him that it is from care and anxiety for his welfare, and not from a wish to expose him, that you put him in mind of his sin. Take hold of his feet; embrace him; be not ashamed, if thou truly desires to cure him. Physicians too do things of this sort, oftentimes, when their patients are hard to please; by embraces and entreaties they at length persuade them to take a salutary medicine. Thus also do thou. Show the wound to the priest; that is the part of one who cares for him, and provides for him, and is anxious on his behalf.

14. But not only do I now admonish the evil speakers; but those besides, who hear others ill spoken of, I exhort to stop up their ears, and to imitate the prophet who says, "Whoso privily slandered his neighbor, him will I punish." Say to thy neighbor, "Hast thou anyone to praise or highly to commend? I open my ears, to receive the fragrant oil; but if thou hast any evil to say, I block up the entrance to thy words,—for I am not to admit dung and dirt. What profit doth it afford me to learn that such a one is a bad man? The greatest injury indeed results from this, and the worst loss!" Say to him, "Let us be anxious about our own faults; how we may render up an account of our own transgressions; and exhibit this sort of curiosity and meddlesome activity respecting our own lives. What excuse or pardon shall we find; whilst we never even take into consideration our own affairs, but thus inquisitively pry into those of others!" And as it is mean and extremely disgraceful to peer into a house, and to observe what is within as one passes, so also to make inquisition into another man's life is the last degree of illiberality. But what is yet more ridiculous is, that those who lead this sort of life, and are neglectful of their own

affairs, when they have mentioned any of these secret matters, beseech and adjure him who has heard it, not to mention it more to any other person; thus making it plain that they have done an action which deserves censure. For if thou beseeches him to tell this to no other person, much more did it not become thee to tell these things first to him. The matter was safe while in thy possession; now, after betraying it, thou art grown anxious for its safety. If thou art desirous that it be not carried abroad to another, do not thyself tell it. But when thou hast betrayed the custody of the matter to another, thou does what is superfluous and useless, in charging him, and putting him on oath for the safety of what has been spoken.

15. "But it is sweet to slander." Nay, it is sweet not to speak evil. For he that hath spoken evil is henceforth contentious; he is suspicious and he fears, repents, and gnaws his own tongue. Being timorous and trembling, lest at any time, what he said should be carried to others, and bring great peril, and useless and needless enmity, on the sayer. But he who keeps the matter to himself, will spend his days in safety, with much pleasantness. "Thou hast heard a word," we read, "let it die with thee; and be bold; it will not burst thee." What is the meaning of this? "Let it die with thee?" Extinguish it; bury it; neither permit it to go forth, nor even to move at all; but, as the best course, be careful not to tolerate others in the practice of evil speaking. And should you perchance, at any time receive an impression from it, bury it, destroy what has been uttered, deliver it over to oblivion; in order that you may become like those who have not heard it; and spend the present life with much peace and security. Should the slanderers learn that we abhor them more than those do whom they accuse, they

themselves will henceforth abandon this evil habit, and correct the sin; and will afterwards applaud, and proclaim us as those who were their saviors and benefactors. For, as to speak well, and to applaud, is the beginning of friendship, so to speak ill and to calumniate, has been the beginning and foundation of enmity, and hatred, and a thousand quarrels. From nothing else have our own affairs been more neglected, than from the habit of prying into and meddling with the concerns of others; for it is not possible for one who is given to evil speaking, and busying himself with other men's lives, ever to look after his own life. His whole study being expended upon meddling with other men's matters, all those which belong to himself must of necessity be left at hazard and neglected. For it is well if one who spends all his leisure on the anxious consideration of his own sins, and the judgment of them, can make any progress. But when thou art always busy about other men's matters, when wilt thou pay any heed to thy own evils?

16. Let us flee then, beloved, let us flee slander! Knowing that it is the very gulph of Satan, and the place where he lurks with his snares. For in order that we may be careless of our own state, and may thus render our account heavier, the devil leads us into this custom. But more than this it is not only a very serious matter, that we shall hereafter have to give account of what we have spoken, but that we shall make our own offences the heavier by these means; depriving ourselves of all excuse. For he who scans with bitterness the conduct of others, can never obtain pardon for the sins committed by himself. For God will determine the sentence, not only from the nature of our transgressions, but from the judgment which thou hast passed upon others. Therefore

He gave the admonition, "Judge not, that ye be not judged." For the sin, of whatever kind, will not there appear anymore such as it was when committed, but will receive a great and unpardonable addition from the judgment passed by thee upon thy fellow servants. For as he who is humane, and merciful, and forgiving, cuts away the greater mass of his sins, so he who is bitter, and cruel, and implacable, greatly increases the magnitude of his own offences. Let us then expel from our mouth all slander, knowing that if we do not abstain from it, though we might feed upon ashes, this austerity would avail us nothing. "For not that which entered into, but that which cometh out of the mouth defiles the man." If any one were to stir up a cesspool, when you were passing, say, would you not reproach and rate the man who did it? This then also do with respect to the slanderer. For the stirred cesspool does not so grossly offend the sense of those who smell that ill savor, as the stirring up other men's sins, and the exposure of an impure life, offends and disturbs the soul of those who hear of it. Therefore let us abstain from evil speaking, from foul language, from blasphemy; and let us not speak ill of our neighbor, nor of God!

17. For many of our evil speakers have run into such madness, as to lift up their own tongue from their fellow servants against their Master. But how great an evil this is, you may learn from the affairs in which we are now involved. A man is insulted, and, lo! We are all fearing and trembling, both those who were guilty of the insult, and those who are conscious of nothing of the kind! But God is insulted every day! Why do I say every day?—every hour rather, by the rich, by the poor, by those who are at ease, by the afflicted, by those who

calumniate, and those who are calumniated, and yet no one ever hears a word of this!

Therefore He has permitted our fellow servant to be insulted, in order that from the danger which has happened through this insult, thou may learn the benignity of the Lord! And notwithstanding that this is our first and only offence, we do not on that account expect to gain an excuse, or pardon. But we provoke God every day, and we show no signs of returning to Him, and yet He endures it with all long-suffering! See you then how great the benignity of the Lord is? Yet, in this present outrage, those who had done amiss were taken and thrust into prison, and paid the penalty; nevertheless we are still in fear, for he who has been insulted has not as yet heard what has taken place, nor pronounced sentence, and we are all trembling. But God every day hears of the insults offered Him, and no one heeds it, although God is thus merciful and loving toward man. With Him it suffices only to acknowledge the sin, and so to cancel the accusation. But with man it is altogether the reverse. When those who have sinned confess, then they are punished the more; which indeed has happened in the present instance. And some have perished by the sword, some by fire; some given to wild beasts, and not men only, but children. And neither this immaturity of age, nor the tumult of the people, nor the circumstance that they were infuriated by demons when they perpetrated these deeds; nor that the exaction was thought to be intolerable; nor poverty, nor having offended in company with all; nor promising that they would never hereafter dare to repeat such deeds; nor anything else, could at all rescue them; but they were led away to the pit, without reprieve; armed soldiers conducting and guarding them on either side, lest anyone should carry off the criminals; whilst mothers also followed afar off, seeing their children beheaded, but not daring to bewail their calamity; for terror conquered grief, and fear overcame nature! And just as when men beholding from the land those who are shipwrecked, are deeply distressed, but are not able to approach and to rescue the drowning, so too here, the mothers restrained through fear of the soldiers, as it were by so many waves, not only dared not go near to their children, and rescue them from condemnation, but were afraid even to shed tears?

18. Assuredly ye gather from thence the mercy of God, how unspeakable, how boundless, how transcending all description! Here indeed the person who has been insulted is of the same nature; and only once in all his lifetime has experienced this; and then it was not done to his face; nor while he was present to see or hear it; and nevertheless, none of those who perpetrated these deeds obtained pardon. But with regard to God nothing of the kind can be said; for the interval between man and God, is so great, as no language can at all express; and throughout every day He is insulted, although present, and seeing and hearing it: and yet He sends not forth the lightning, nor commands the sea to overflow the land, and submerge all men; nor does He bid the earth to cleave asunder and swallow up all the contumelious; but He forbears, and suffers long, and still offers to pardon those who have insulted Him, if they only repent and promise to do these things no more! Truly now is the season to proclaim, "Who can utter the mighty acts of the Lord? Who can show forth all His praise?" How many men have not only cast down, but also trodden underfoot the images of God! For when thou throttles a debtor, when thou stripes him,

when thou drags him away, thou tramples under foot God's image. Hear for a certainty Paul saying, that "a man ought not to cover his head, forasmuch as he is the image and glory of God." And again, hear God Himself saying, "Let us make man in Our Image, after Our likeness." But if thou says that man is not of the same substance as God,—what matters that? For neither was the brazen statue of the same substance as the Emperor; yet nevertheless, they who defied it paid the penalty. Thus also with regard to mankind, if men are not of the same substance as God, (as indeed they are not), still they have been called His image; and it were fitting they should receive honor on account of the appellation. But thou for the sake of a little gold dost trample them under foot, dost throttle them, and drag them away; and hast not to this day in any wise paid the penalty!

19. May there be then speedily some favorable and propitious change! This certainly I foretell and testify, that although this cloud should pass away, and we yet remain in the same condition of listlessness, we shall again have to suffer much heavier evils than those we are now dreading; for I do not so much fear the wrath of the Emperor, as your own listlessness. Surely it is not sufficient by way of apology that we supplicate two or three days, but it is necessary that we should make a change in our whole life, and that whilst abstaining from wickedness we should persevere continually in virtue. For as those who are sickly, unless they keep up a constant regimen, would find no advantage by their observing a two or three days' discipline; so those who are in sin, if they do not exercise sobriety at all times, will find no benefit in two or three days' amendment. For as it is said, that he who is washed, and is again afterwards polluted

with the mire, hath gained nothing; so he who has repented for three days, and has again returned to his former state, has accomplished nothing. Let us not therefore, now act as we have always done hitherto. For many times, when we have been surprised by earthquakes, as well as famine and drought, after becoming more sober and gentle for three or four days, we did but return again to the former course. For this cause our present troubles have happened. But if we have not done so before; yet, now at least let us all persevere in the same piety; let us preserve the same meekness, that we may not again need another stroke. Was not God able to have prevented what has taken place? He did, however, permit it, that He might make those who despised Him more sober minded, through dread of a fellow-servant!

20. But let not anyone say that many of the guilty escaped, and that many of the innocent incurred punishment. For I hear of numerous persons who frequently say this; not only in the case of the present sedition, but also in many other circumstances of this nature. What then should I reply to those who make such observations? Why, that if he who was captured was innocent of the present sedition, he had wrought some other transgression before this still more grievous, for which, not having afterwards repented, he has paid the penalty at the present time. For thus is the custom of God to deal with us. When we sin, He does not straightway visit the transgression, but lets it pass, giving us space for repentance, in order that we may be amended and converted. But if, because we have not paid the penalty, we suppose that the offence too is blotted out, and make light of it; then somewhere, where we think not of it, we are sure afterwards to be punished. And this takes place in

order that, when we sin and are not punished, we may not be free from fear, unless we amend, knowing that we shall certainly fall into punishment where we do not expect it. So that if you sin, beloved, and art not punished, do not grow presumptuous, but for this very cause be the more alarmed, knowing that it is an easy matter with God to recompense again when he pleases. For this reason then he hath not punished thee, that thou might receive space for repentance. Let us not therefore say, that such a person whilst innocent incurred punishment; and another whilst guilty escaped, for he who incurred it, being guiltless, as I observed, paid the punishment of other transgressions; and he who now escapes it, if he repents not, will be captured in another snare. If our minds are thus disposed, we shall never forget our own sins, but, always fearful and trembling lest we should have to pay the penalty, we shall readily recollect them. For nothing is so apt to bring sin to remembrance as punishment and chastisement. And this is shown by Joseph's brethren. For when they had sold the just man, and thirteen years had passed away, suspecting they had fallen into punishment, and fearing for their lives, they remembered their sin, and said one to another, "We are verily guilty concerning our brother Joseph." See you, how fear brought their guilt to recollection? And yet when they were sinning they perceived it not, but when they were fearful of being punished, then they remembered it? Knowing, therefore, all these things, let us make a change and amendment of our lives; and let us think of religion and virtue, before we think of deliverance from the impending distress.

21. And in the meanwhile I desire to fix three precepts in your mind, to the end that you may accomplish me these during the fast,—viz. to speak ill of

no one; to hold no one for an enemy; and to expel from the mouth altogether the evil custom of oaths. And as when we hear that some money tax is imposed, each one going within, and calling his wife and children and servants, considers and consults with them how he may pay this tribute, so also let us do with respect to these spiritual precepts. Let everyone when he has returned home call together his wife and children, and let him say, that a spiritual tribute was imposed this day: a tribute by which there will be some deliverance and removal of these evils; a tribute which does not make those who pay it poor, but richer; that is to say, to have no enemy, to speak evil of no man, and to swear not at all. Let us consider; let us think; let us resolve how we may fulfill these precepts. Let us exert every endeavor. Let us admonish each other. Let us correct each other, that we may not go to the other world as debtors, and then, needing to borrow of others, suffer the fate of the foolish virgins, and fall from immortal salvation. If we thus set our lives in order, I warrant you and promise, that from this there will be deliverance from the present calamity, and a removal of these dreadful ills; and what is greater than all, there will be the enjoyment of the good things to come. For it were fitting that I should commit to you the whole body of virtue; but I think it the best method of correction, to take the laws by parts, and reduce them to practice, and then to proceed to others. For as in a given field, the husbandman, digging it all up piecemeal, gradually comes to the end of his task; so we too if we make this rule for ourselves, in any wise to reduce to a correct practice these three precepts during the present Lent, and to commit them to the safe custody of good habit, we shall proceed with greater ease to the rest; and by this means arriving at the summit of spiritual wisdom, we shall both reap the fruit of a favorable hope in the present life; and in the life to come we shall stand before Christ with great confidence, and enjoy those unspeakable blessings; which, God grant, we may all be found worthy of, through the grace and loving kindness of Jesus Christ our Lord, with Whom be glory to the Father and the Holy Spirit forever and ever. Amen.

Homily IV.

An exhortation to the people respecting fortitude and patience, from the examples of Job and the Three Children in Babylon. The Homily concludes with an address on the subject of abstaining from oaths.

1. Blessed be God! Who hath comforted your sorrowing souls, and stayed your agitated spirits! For that ye have received no small consolation is evident by the desire and readiness to listen which ye are now showing. For it is impossible that a soul in anguish, and oppressed with the cloud of despondency, should have power to hear with readiness anything that is spoken. But I see you are attending to us with much good will, and with an intense earnestness; and that you have shaken off gloomy thoughts, and put aside the sense of present distress, in your affectionate desire of listening. For this cause, I thank God heartily together with you, that the calamity has not overmatched your philosophy; nor fear relaxed your vigor; nor tribulation quenched your alacrity; nor danger dried up your zeal: nor the fear of men overcome the desire for God; nor the difficulty of the times overthrown your earnestness; nay, so far from

overthrowing, it has strengthened it; so far from slackening, it has given it more intensity; so far from quenching, has kindled it the more. The forum is indeed empty, but the church is filled; the former supplies material for melancholy, the latter is an occasion of joy and spiritual gladness! When therefore, beloved, you betake yourself to the forum, and the sight of the solitude calls forth a groan, fly back to thy Mother, and straightway she will console thee with the multitude of her offspring and will show thee the chorus of the Brethren complete, and will drive away all thy despondency! For in the city we are as earnestly longing to see human beings, as those who inhabit the deserts; but when we take refuge in the church, we are straitened for room by the multitude. And as when the sea is in uproar, and rendered furious by the violent tempest, fear compels all to fly for refuge from without into the harbor; so also now, the waves of the forum, and the tempest of the city, drives together every one from all sides into the church, and by the bond of love knits the members close to one another.

 2. Let us then give thanks to God even for these things, that we have reaped so much fruit from the tribulation; that we have received so great an advantage from the trial. If there were no trial, there would be no crown; if there were no wrestling, there would be no prize; if there were no lists marked out, there would be no honors; if there were no tribulation, there would be no rest; if there were no winter, there would be no summer. And this may be observed, not only amongst men, but even with the very seeds; for if, in that case, we expect the ear of corn to spring and flourish, there must be much rain, much gathering of the clouds, and much frost; and

the time of sowing is also a rainy season. Since therefore the winter, a winter not of the elements, but of souls, has now set in, let us too sow in this winter that we may reap in the summer; let us sow tears, that we may reap gladness. This is not my word, it is a prophetic promise, "They who sow in tears, shall reap in joy." The rain which cometh down, doth not so make the seeds to sprout and grow, as the shower of falling tears makes the seed of godliness to spring up and flourish. This it is that cleanses the soul; waters the mind, and causes the growing germ of doctrine to push rapidly forwards. For this reason also, it is needful to plough up a deep furrow. This the Prophet signified when he spoke thus, "Break up your fallow ground, and sow not among thorns." Therefore, as when he who has set the plough on the field, turns up the earth from below, preparing beforehand a safe lodgment for the seeds, in order that they may not lie dispersed over the surface, but may be hidden in the very womb of the earth, and deposit their roots in safety: so also it is our business to act; and making use of the plough of tribulation to break up the depth of the heart. For another Prophet admonishes of this, when he says, "Rend your hearts and not your garments." Let us then rend our hearts, that if any evil plant, any treacherous thought be present in us, we may tear it up by the roots, and provide a pure soil for the seeds of godliness. For if we do not now break up the fallow ground; if we do not now sow; if we do not now water it with tears, whilst it is a time of tribulation and fasting, when shall we ever be brought to compunction? Will it be when we are at ease, and in luxury? But this is impossible. For ease and luxury generally lead to indolence, just as tribulation leads back again to diligence; and restores to itself the mind that had wandered abroad, and been dreaming after a multitude of objects.

3. Let us not then grieve on account of this despondency, but even give thanks to God, for great is the gain that comes of tribulation. The husbandman, when he has sown the seed he had gathered with so much labor, prays that a shower may come; and the ignorant man, looking on, will be surprised at all that takes place; and perhaps say to himself, "what can this man be doing? He is scattering what he has collected; and not only scattering, but he is also mixing it up in the earth with much industry, so that it will be no easy matter for him to collect these together again; and besides mixing them with the earth, he is moreover desiring a heavy rain, so that all he has cast therein will rot, and become mire." Such a person is also terrified when he observes the thunders bursting through the clouds, and the lightning striking downwards. But not so the farmer. He is glad and rejoices whilst beholding the heavy rain. For he does not regard what is present, but awaits the future. He does not attend to the thundering, but is reckoning the number of his sheaves. He thinks not of the decaying seed, but of the flourishing ears of corn; not of the tedious rain, but of the delightful dust of the threshing floor. Thus indeed, also, should we regard, not our present tribulation, nor the pain of it, but the benefit that may arise from it—the fruit that it will bring forth. Let us wait for the sheaves of the threshing floor; for if we be sober, we shall be able to collect much fruit from the present time, and to fill the granaries of our minds. If we be sober, we shall not only be far from taking any harm from this trouble, but we shall also reap innumerable benefits. But should we be slothful, even tranquility will destroy us! Either of these

things is injurious to him who takes no heed; but they both profit him who lives with strictness. And even as gold if it be covered with water, still shows its own proper beauty, and although it should fall into the furnace, would again come forth brighter than before; but on the other hand, should clay or grass be mixed with water, the one dissolves and the other corrupts; and should they fall into the fire, the one is parched and the other is burnt up; so also in truth it is with the just man and the sinner! For should the former enjoy repose, he remains illustrious, even as gold is when immersed in water; and though he falls into trial, he becomes the more illustrious, like gold when subjected to the test of fire; but the sinner, if he obtains rest, is enervated and corrupted like the grass and the clay, when they come in contact with water; and should he undergo trial, he is burnt up and destroyed, in the same way as the grass and the clay are by the action of fire!

4. Let us not then be out of heart for the present evils; for if thou hast any sins remaining, they will disappear, and easily be burnt up by the tribulation; but if thou possesses virtue, thou wilt become thereby more illustrious and distinguished; for if thou art continually vigilant and sober, thou wilt be superior to all injury. For it is not the nature of the trials, but the listlessness of those who are tried, that is apt to cause their overthrow. So that if thou desires to rejoice, and to enjoy ease and pleasure, seek neither for pleasure nor ease, but seek for a soul full of patience, and one that is able to manifest fortitude; since if thou hast not this, not only will trial put thee to shame, but repose will destroy and overthrow thee yet more signally. For to prove that it is not the attack of evils, but the listlessness of the mind which subverts our

salvation, hear what Christ says: "Whosoever hears these sayings of mine, and doeth them, I will liken him unto a wise man, which built his house upon a rock; and the rain descended, and the floods came, and the winds blew, and beat upon that house; and it fell not, for it was founded upon a rock." And again: "Everyone who hears these sayings of mine, and doeth them not, shall be likened unto a foolish man, which built his house upon the sand; and the rain descended, and the floods came, and the winds blew, and beat upon that house; and it fell, and great was the fall of it." Do you perceive that it was not the attack of these trials that produced the overthrow, but the folly of the builders? For there was rain there, and there was rain here; there were floods there, and there were floods here; here the beating of winds, and there again the same. The one man built a house, and the other built a house. The building was the same; the trials were the same; but the end was not the same; because there was not the same foundation. For the folly of the builder, not the nature of the trials, caused the fall of the building; otherwise the house that was founded upon the rock should have fallen, whereas nothing of that kind befell it. But do not suppose that these things were spoken merely of a house; for the discourse relates to a soul, giving proof by its works that it hears the divine word, or rejects it. Thus Job built up his soul. The rain descended;—for the fire fell from heaven and devoured all his flocks; the floods came;—the frequent,—the constant,—the successive messengers of his calamities, telling him of the destruction of his herds—of his camels—of his children. The winds blew,—the bitter words of his wife:—"Curse God," she said, "and die." Yet the house fell not: the soul was not supplanted: the just man did not blaspheme; but even gave thanks thus, saying, "The Lord gave and the Lord hath taken away. As it pleased the Lord, so is it come to pass." See you that not the nature of the trials, but the negligence of the indolent, is wont to cause the overthrow? Since tribulation makes the strong man stronger. Who says this? It is the man who lived in tribulation, the blessed Paul; he speaks thus: "Tribulation worked patience, and patience probation, and probation hope." And even as the violence of the wind, when it rushes upon strong trees, and sways them in all directions, does not root them up, but renders them still firmer and stronger by these attacks; so the soul that is holy, and lives in a religious state, is not supplanted by the inroads of trial and tribulation, but stimulated thereby to more patience; even as the blessed Job, whom they made more illustrious and honorable.

5. At the present time then, a man is angry with us, a man of like passions, and of like soul, and we are afraid: but in the case of Job it was an evil and malignant demon who was angry; nay, he was not simply angry, but set in motion all sorts of machinations, and brought forward every stratagem; and yet even with all he could not conquer the fortitude of the just man. But here is a man, who is at one time angry, at another time is reconciled; and we are nevertheless dead with fear. On that occasion it was a devil that waged war, who is never reconciled to human nature, but has engaged in a war without treaty, and a battle without truce against our race; yet nevertheless, the just man laughed his darts to scorn. What apology then, or what pardon can be ours, if we cannot sustain a human trial; we who are taught such spiritual wisdom under grace; when this man before grace, and before the Old Testament, endured this most grievous war so nobly! These things, beloved, we should

therefore always discourse of with one another; and by words of this kind encourage ourselves. For ye are witnesses, and your conscience is a witness how much gain we have already received from this trial! The dissolute man hath now become sober; the bold man meek; the slothful man active. They who never at any time saw a church, but constantly spent their time at the theatre, now remain in the church the whole day long. Tell me then, dost thou grieve on this account, that God hath made thee earnest through fear; that He hath led thee by tribulation to a sense of thine own safety? But is thy conscience pained? Yea, is thy mind pierced every day as with a dart, expecting death, and the greatest wrath? Nevertheless, from thence too we shall gain a great advance toward virtue, if our piety is made more earnest by means of the distress. For God is able to free you from all these evils this day. But not until He sees that you are purified; not until He sees that a conversion has taken place, and a repentance firm and unshaken, will He entirely remove the tribulation. The goldsmith, until he perceives the gold well refined, will not draw it out from the furnace; and even so God will not take away this cloud before He hath thoroughly amended us. For He Himself who hath permitted this trial, knows the time for removing it. So it is also with one who plays the harp; he neither overstrains the string, lest he break it, nor relaxes it too much, lest he mar the consonance of its harmony. Thus does God act. He neither places our souls in a state of constant repose, nor of lengthened tribulation; making use of both these at His discretion; for he neither suffers us to enjoy continual repose, lest we should grow listless, nor on the other hand does he permit us to be in constant tribulation, lest we sink under it, and become desperate.

6. Let us then leave to Him the time for the removal of our evils; let *us* only pray; let *us* live in piety: for this is our work, to turn to virtue; but to set us free from these evils is God's work! For indeed He is more desirous to quench this fire than thou who art tried by it: but He is waiting for thy salvation. As tribulation then came of rest, so also after tribulation, rest must be expected. For neither is it always winter, nor always summer; neither are there always waves, nor always a calm; neither always night, nor always day. Thus tribulation is not perpetual, but there will be also repose; only in our tribulation, let us give thanks to God always. For the three youths were cast into the furnace, and did not even for this forget their piety; neither did the flames affright them, but more earnestly than men sitting in a chamber, and suffering nothing to alarm them, did they, whilst encircled by the fire, send up to heaven those sacred prayers—therefore the fire became a wall unto them, and the flame a robe; and the furnace was a fountain; and whereas it received them bound, it restored them free. It received bodies that were mortal, but abstained from them as if they had been immortal! It knew their nature, yet it reverenced their piety! The tyrant bound their feet, and their feet bound the operation of the fire! O marvelous thing! The flame loosed those who were bound, and was itself afterwards bound by those who had been in bonds; for the piety of the youths changed the nature of things; or rather it did not change the nature, but, what was far more wonderful, it stayed the operation of them, even whilst their nature remained. For it did not quench the fire, but though burning, made it powerless. And it was truly marvelous and unaccountable, that this not only happened with respect to the bodies of

these saints, but also with respect to their garments, and their shoes. And as it was in the case of the Apostles, the garments of Paul expelled diseases and demons, and the shadow of Peter put death to flight; so indeed also in this case, the shoes of these youths extinguished the power of the fire.

7. I know not how I should speak, for the wonder surpasses all description! The force of the fire was both quenched and not quenched: for whilst it came in contact with the bodies of these saints, it was quenched; but when it was needful to burst their bonds, it was not quenched; wherefore it broke their bonds, but touched not their ankles. Do you see how very near it was? Yet the fire was not deceived, and dared not penetrate within the bonds. The tyrant bound, and the flame set loose; that thou might learn at once the fierceness of the barbarian, and the submissiveness of the element. For what reason did he bind, when he was about to cast into the fire? In order that the miracle might be the greater; that the sign might be the more unaccountable; that thou may not suppose that the things seen were an optical delusion. For if that fire had been no fire, it would not have consumed the bands; and what is much more, it would not have seized upon the soldiers who were placed without the furnace; but as the case was, it showed its power upon those without; but towards those within, its submissiveness. But observe, I pray, in everything, how the devil by the very same means with which he fights with the servants of God, pulls down his own power; not intentionally, but because the wisdom and abundant contrivance of God turns all his weapons and devices upon his own head; which assuredly happened on that occasion. For the devil at that time inspiring the tyrant, neither suffered the heads of the

saints to be cut off with the sword, nor that they should be delivered to wild beasts, nor punished in any such manner; but that they should be thrown into the fire; to the end that not even any relics of these saints should remain, their bodies being altogether consumed, and their ashes being mingled with the ashes of the fagots. But God accordingly employed this very circumstance for the taking away of impiety. And how? I will tell you. Fire is accounted by the Persians to be a god; and the barbarians, who inhabit that country even now honor it with much worship. God, therefore, being desirous to pull up by the roots the material of impiety, permitted the punishment to take this form, in order that He might give the victory to His servants before the eyes of all these fire-worshippers; persuading them by the plain fact, that the gods of the Gentiles are in dread not of God only, but even of the servants of God.

8. Consider, moreover, how the crown of this victory was woven by the adversaries, and the enemies themselves were made witnesses of this trophy. For "Nebuchadnezzar," it says, "sent to gather together the princes, the governors, and the captains, the judges, the sheriffs, and all the rulers of the provinces, to come to the dedication of the image, and they were all gathered together." The enemy prepares the theatre, and he himself collects together the spectators, and prepares the lists; a theatre too, not of chance persons, or of some private individuals, but of all those who were honorable and in authority, to the end that their testimony may be worthy of credit with the multitude. They had come summoned for one thing; but they all departed having beheld another thing. They came in order to worship the image; and they departed, having derided the image, and struck with

wonder at the power of God, through the signs which had taken place with respect to these young men. And observe, where the field for this display was spread out. No city, nor select enclosure furnished room for this theatre of the whole world, but smooth and naked plains. For in the plain of Dura, outside the city, he set up the image, and the herald came and cried, "To you it is commanded, O people, nations, and languages, that at what time ye hear the sound of the cornet, flute, harp, sackbut, psaltery, dulcimer, and all kinds of music, ye fall down and worship the golden image;" (for a fall indeed it was to worship the idol) "and whoso falls not down, and worshiped, shall the same hour be cast into the midst of a burning fiery furnace." See you how difficult these struggles are made; how irresistible the snare; and how deep the gulf, and a precipice on either hand? But be not afraid. In whatever degree the enemy increases his machinations, so much the more does he display the courage of the young men. For this reason is there this symphony of so many musicians; for this reason the burning furnace; in order that both pleasure, and fear, may besiege the souls of those present. Is there any one of harsh and unyielding character among them? "Let the melody of every kind of music," says he, "enchant and soften him." But is he superior to this artifice, "let the sight of the flame affright and astound him." Thus was fear as well as pleasure present; the one entering to assault the soul by the ears, the other by the eyes. But the noble character of these youths was not by any such means to be conquered; but even as, when they fell into the fire, they mastered the flames, even so they derided all desire and all fear. For it was for them the devil had prepared all these things beforehand. For he had no doubts of his own subjects, but was exceedingly confident that no one would resist the royal mandate. But when all fell down, and were subdued, then the youths alone are led into the midst; in order that from this too the conquest may become the more illustrious, they alone conquering and being proclaimed victors among so vast a multitude. For this would not have been so surprising if they had acted courageously at the first, when as yet no one had been overthrown. But the greatest, and most astonishing fact was, that the multitude of those who fell down, neither affrighted, nor enfeebled them. They did not say to themselves any such things as many are ofttimes wont to say; "If we were the first, and the only persons to worship the image, this would have been a sin: but if we do this with so many myriads, who will not make allowance? Who will not think us worthy of defense?" nothing of that sort did they say or think, when they beheld the prostrate forms of so many tyrants. Consider thou also with me the wickedness of those who were their accusers, and how maliciously and bitterly they brought the accusation! "There are," say they, "certain Jews whom thou hast set up over the works of the province of Babylon." They did not merely make mention of the nation, but they also bring to mind their honorable condition, that they may inflame the wrath of the king; almost as if they had said, "These slaves, these captives, who are without a city, thou hast made rulers over us. But they shew contempt for such honor, and treat insolently him who has given them this honor!" Therefore they say this; "The Jews whom thou hast set over the works of the province of Babylon, obey not thy decree, nor serve thy gods." The accusation becomes their greatest praise; and the crimes imputed, their encomium; a testimony indeed that is indubitable, since their enemies bring it forward. What then does the king? He commands that they should be brought into the midst, so that he may affright them in every way. But nothing dismayed them, neither the wrath of the king, nor their being left alone in the midst of so many, nor the sight of the fire, nor the sound of the trumpet, nor the whole multitude looking fire at them; for deriding all these things, as if they were about to be cast into a cool fountain of water, they entered the furnace uttering that blessed sentence, "We will not serve thy gods, nor worship the golden image which thou hast set up."

9. I have not referred to this history without reason, but that ye may learn that whether it be the wrath of a king, or the violence of soldiers, or the envy of enemies, or captivity, or destitution, or fire, or furnace, or ten thousand terrors, nothing will avail to put to shame or terrify a righteous man. For if where the king was godless the youths were not dismayed at the tyrant's wrath, how much more ought we to be confident, having an emperor who is humane and merciful, and to express thankfulness to God for this tribulation, knowing from what has now been said, that tribulations render men more illustrious both in the presence of God and of man, if they know how to bear them with fortitude! For indeed if these had not been made slaves, we should not have known their freedom! If they had not been captives, we should not have learned their nobility of soul! If they had not been exiles from their country below, we should not have known the excellency of their citizenship above! If the earthly king had not been angry with them, we should not have known the favor with which they were regarded by the heavenly King!

10. Thou too then, if thou hast Him for thy Friend, be not despairing, although thou falls into the furnace: and in like manner if He be angry, think not thou art safe though thou be in Paradise. For Adam indeed was in Paradise, yet, when he had provoked God, Paradise profited him nothing. These youths were in the furnace; yet, since they were approved, the furnace injured them not at all. Adam was in Paradise, but when he was supine, he was supplanted! Job sat down on the dunghill, yet, since he was vigilant he prevailed! Yet how much better was Paradise than a dunghill! Still the excellency of the place benefitted in no degree the inhabitant; forasmuch as he had betrayed himself; as likewise indeed the vileness of the place did to one no injury, who was fortified on every side with virtue. As to ourselves then, let us fortify our souls; for if the loss of wealth should threaten us, or even death, and yet no one can rob us of our religion, we are the happiest of men, Christ commended this when he said, "Be ye wise as serpents." For just as he exposes the whole body in order that he may save the head, so also do thou. Although it should be necessary to expose wealth, or the body, or the present life, or all things, for the purpose of preserving thy religion; be not cast down! For if thou depart hence in possession of that, God will restore to thee all things with more abundant splendor, and will raise again thy body with greater glory; and instead of riches, there will be the good things that surpass all power of description. Did not Job sit naked on a dunghill, sustaining a life more grievous than ten thousand deaths? Yet since he did not cast away his piety, all his former things came back to him in greater abundance, soundness and beauty of body; his full band of children; his possessions; and what was greater than all, the splendid

crown of his patience. For as it happens with trees, should anyone pluck away the fruit and the leaves together; should he even cut off all the branches letting the root only remain; the tree will rise again entire, with greater beauty, so indeed is it also with us. If the root of piety remain, although wealth be taken away, although the body destroyed, all things again revert to us with greater glory than before. Casting away therefore all anxiety and superfluous care, let us return to ourselves; and let us adorn the body and the soul with the ornament of virtue; converting our bodily members into instruments of righteousness and not instruments of sin.

11. And first of all, let us discipline our tongue to be the minister of the grace of the Spirit, expelling from the mouth all virulence and malignity, and the practice of using disgraceful words. For it is in our power to make each one of our members an instrument of wickedness, or of righteousness. Hear then how men make the tongue an instrument, some of sin, others of righteousness! "Their tongue is a sharp sword." But another speaks thus of his own tongue: "My tongue is the pen of a ready writer." The former wrought destruction; the latter wrote the divine law. Thus was one a sword, the other a pen, not according to its own nature, but according to the choice of those who employed it. For the nature of this tongue and of that was the same, but the operation was not the same. And again, as to the mouth likewise, we may see this same thing. For these had a mouth full of filth and of wickedness, therefore against such it is said by way of accusation, "Their mouth is full of cursing and bitterness;" not such was his, but "My mouth shall speak of wisdom, and the meditation of my heart shall be of understanding." Again, there were others who had their

hands full of iniquity, and accusing these he said, "Iniquities are in their hands, and their right hand is filled with gifts." But he himself had hands practiced in nothing but in being stretched out towards heaven. Therefore he said of these too, "The lifting up of my hands (let it be) an evening sacrifice." The same may also be perceived with reference to the heart; for their heart indeed was foolish, but this man's was true; hence he speaks of them thus, "Their heart is vain;" but of his own, "My heart is inditing of a good matter." And as to the ear, one may see that the case is the same; for some have a sense of hearing like that of beasts, which is not to be charmed or moved to pity; and reproaching such the Psalmist says, "They are like the deaf adder, that stopped her ears." But his ear was the receptacle of the divine words, and this he again makes manifest, when he says, "I will incline mine ear to a parable, I will open my dark speech upon the harp."

12. Knowing these things then, let us fortify ourselves with virtue on all sides, and thus we shall avert the wrath of God, and let us make the members of the body instruments of righteousness; and let us discipline eyes, and mouth, and hands, and feet, and heart, and tongue, and the whole body, to be employed only in the service of virtue. And let us remember those three precepts, of which I discoursed to your Charity, exhorting you to consider no one as an enemy, nor to speak evil of any one of those who have aggrieved you; and to expel from your mouth the evil custom of oaths. And with respect to the two former precepts, we will discourse to you on another occasion; but we shall speak to you during the whole of the present week respecting oaths; thus beginning with the easier precept. For it is no labor at all to overcome the habit of swearing, if we would but apply

a little endeavor, by reminding each other; by advising; by observing; and by requiring those who thus forget themselves, to render an account, and to pay the penalty. For what advantage shall we gain by abstinence from meats, if we do not also expel the evil habits of the soul? Lo, we have spent the whole of this day fasting; and in the evening we shall spread a table, not such as we did on yester-eve, but one of an altered and more solemn kind. Can any one of us then say that he has changed his life too this day; that he has altered his ill custom, as well as his food? Truly, I suppose not! Of what advantage then is our fasting? Wherefore I exhort, and I will not cease to exhort, that undertaking each precept separately, you should spend two or three days in the attainment of it; and just as there are some who rival one another in fasting, and shew a marvelous emulation in it; (some indeed who spend two whole days without food; and others who, rejecting from their tables not only the use of wine, and of oil, but of every dish, and taking only bread and water, persevere in this practice during the whole of Lent); so, indeed, let us also contend mutually with one another in abolishing the frequency of oaths. For this is more useful than any fasting; this is more profitable than any austerity. And this same care which we display in abstaining from food, let us exhibit with respect to abstinence from oaths; since we shall be chargeable with the reproach of extreme folly, while we regard not things that are forbidden, and expend all our care upon things indifferent; for to eat is not forbidden, but to swear is forbidden; we, however, abstaining from those things that are permitted, daringly venture upon those things that are forbidden! On this account I beseech your Charity to make some change, and to let the beginning of it be visible from this day. For if we spend the whole of the present fast with such zeal, having in this week attained the practice of not swearing at all; and in the following having extinguished wrath; and in that which succeeds it, having pulled up evil-speaking by the roots; and after that, having amended what yet remains; thus going forward in our course, we shall come by little and little to the very summit of virtue; and we shall escape the present danger; and shall make God propitious; and the multitude will come back again to our city; and we shall teach the fugitives that we are to place our hopes of safety neither in security of place, nor in flight and retirement; but in piety of soul, and in virtue of manners. And thus shall we obtain the good things of this and of the future life; which, God grant! we may all be found worthy of, by the grace and loving-kindness of our Lord Jesus Christ, through whom and with whom be glory to the Father, together with the Holy Ghost, now and for ever and ever. Amen.

Homily V.

The exhortation of the last Homily is continued in this. The people are exhorted to bear with fortitude the impending wrath of the Emperor. The cases of Job and the Ninevites are referred to as examples. It is shewn that men ought not to fear death, but sin. What it is to die miserably is explained; and the Homily concludes with an earnest dissuasive against the use of oaths.

1. The discourse concerning the three young men, and the Babylonian furnace, did, as it would seem, yesterday give no small comfort to your Charity; and still more the example in the case of Job, and that dunghill more to be venerated than any kingly throne. For from seeing a royal throne no advantage results to the spectators, but only a temporary pleasure, which has no profit; but from the sight of Job's dunghill, one may derive every kind of benefit, yea, much divine wisdom and consolation, in order to patience. Therefore to this day many undertake a long pilgrimage, even across the sea, hastening from the extremities of the earth, as far as Arabia, that they may see that dunghill; and having beheld it, may kiss the land, which contained the wrestling-ground of such a victor, and received the blood that was more precious than all gold! For the purple shines not so brilliantly, as did that body when dyed not in another's blood, but in its own! Even those very wounds were more precious than all manner of jewels! For the nature of pearls is of no help to our life; nor do they satisfy any necessary want on the part of those who have them. But those wounds are a consolation for all sadness; and that

thou may learn this to be the truth, suppose any one were to lose a beloved and only son. Shew him ten thousand pearls, and you will not console his grief, or lighten his anguish; but recall to his mind the wounds of Job, and thou would easily be able to minister comfort by speaking thus: "Why sorrows thou, O man? Thou hast lost one son; but that blessed man, after he had been bereaved of the whole family of his children, both received a plague in his own flesh, and sat down naked upon the dunghill, streaming with gore from every part, and his flesh gradually wasting away; even he who was just, and true, so devout a man, who stained from every evil deed, and had even God for a witness to his virtue." By speaking thus thou would extinguish all the sufferer's sadness, and remove all his distress. Thus the wounds of the just man become more useful than pearls!

2. Figure to yourselves then this wrestler; and imagine that you see that dunghill, and himself sitting in the midst of it! That golden statue! Set with gems! I know not how to express it: for I am unable to find any material so precious as to compare it with that body stained with blood! So far above every substance, however costly, was the nature of that flesh, beyond all comparison more precious, and those wounds more splendid than the sun's beams; for these illumine the eyes of the body; but those enlighten the eyes of the mind! Those struck the devil with utter blindness! Therefore it was, that after that blow, he started back and appeared no more. And do thou, O beloved, learn thence too what advantage there is in tribulation! For when the just man was rich, and enjoyed ease, he had the means of accusing him. However falsely, yet still he had it in his power to say, "Doth Job serve thee for naught?" But after he had stripped him and made him

poor, he dared not even open his mouth any more. When he was wealthy, he prepared to wrestle with him, and threatened to overthrow him; but when he had made him poor, and taken away all he had, and thrown him into the deepest distress, then he started back. When indeed his body was sound, he lifted up his hands against him, but when he had battered his flesh, then he fled,—defeated! See you how to the vigilant, poverty is much better and more beneficial than riches; and infirmity and sickness, than health; and trial, than tranquility; inasmuch as it makes the combatants more illustrious and vigorous?

3. Who hath seen or heard of such an astonishing contest? The fighters in worldly contests, when they have battered the heads of their adversaries, are then victorious, and are crowned! But this adversary, when he had battered the body of the just man, perforating it with ulcers of every kind, and had reduced him to great weakness, was then conquered, and drew back. Even when he had pierced his ribs in every direction, he was no gainer thereby; for he spoiled him not of his hidden treasure, but he made him more conspicuous to us; and through that piercing he gave to all the privilege to look into his interior, and to discern completely the whole of his wealth! When he expected to prevail, then he withdrew with much ignominy, and never again uttered a syllable! What is the matter, O devil? For what cause withdraws thou? Was not everything done that thou choses? Hast thou not taken away his flocks, his herds, his droves of horses and of mules? Hast thou not also destroyed his troop of children? And battered his flesh to pieces. For what reason withdraws thou? "Because," says he, "everything I chose is come to pass, and yet that which I most desired should come to pass, and for which I

did all those things, is not come to pass; he hath not blasphemed! For it was in order to this, continues he, that I was doing all those things; and as this is not come to pass, I am no gainer by having deprived him of his wealth; or by the destruction of his children; or by the plague inflicted upon his body; but the reverse of what I purposed hath come to pass; I have made my enemy more illustrious; I have added luster to his reputation." Perceives thou, O beloved, how great was the reward of tribulation? His body was fair and sound before, but it became more venerable, when pierced through and through by these wounds! And thus wool, fair as it is before the dyeing, when it becomes purple, takes an indescribable beauty, and an additional grace. But if he had not stripped him, we should not have known the good condition of the victor; if he had not pierced the body with ulcers, the rays within would not have shone forth. If he had not made him sit down upon a dunghill, we should not have known his wealth. For a king sitting on a throne is not so illustrious, as this man was notable and conspicuous, whilst sitting upon his dunghill! For after the royal throne, comes death; but after that dunghill, the kingdom of heaven!

4. Collecting then all these reasons, let us raise ourselves from the dejection which oppresses us. For I have laid these histories before you, not that ye may applaud what is spoken, but that ye may imitate the virtue and the patience of such noble men; that ye may learn from the very facts, that there is nothing of human ills to be dreaded, save sin only; neither poverty, nor disease, nor insult, nor malicious treatment, nor ignominy, nor death, which is accounted the worst of all evils. To those who love spiritual wisdom, such things are only the

names of calamities; names which have no substantial reality. But the true calamity consists in offending God, and in doing aught which is displeasing to Him. For tell me, what is there in death which is terrible? Is it because it transports thee more quickly to the peaceful haven, and to that life which is free from tumult? Although man should not put thee to death, will not the very law of nature, at length stealing upon thee, separate the body from the soul; and if this event which we fear does not happen now, it will happen shortly.

5. I speak thus, not anticipating any dread or melancholy event: God forbid! But because I am ashamed for those who are afraid of death. Tell me, whilst expecting such good things as "eye hath not seen, nor ear heard, nor have entered the heart of man," dost thou demur about this enjoyment, and art negligent and slothful; and not only slothful, but fearful and trembling? And is it not shameful that thou art distressed on account of death, whereas Paul groaned on account of the present life, and writing to the Romans said, "The creation groans together, and ourselves also which have the first fruits of the Spirit do groan." And he spoke thus, not as condemning the things present, but longing for the things to come. "I have tasted," says he, "of the grace, and I do not willingly put up with the delay. I have the first fruits of the Spirit, and I press on towards the whole. I have ascended to the third heaven; I have seen that glory which is unutterable; I have beheld the shining palaces; I have learnt what joys I am deprived of, while I linger here, and therefore do I groan." For suppose anyone had conducted thee into princely halls, and shewn thee the gold everywhere glittering on the walls, and all the rest of the glorious show; if from thence he had led thee back

afterward to a poor man's hut, and promised that in a short time he would bring thee back to those palaces, and would there give thee a perpetual mansion; tell me, would you not indeed languish with desire, and feel impatient, even at these few days? Thus think then of heaven, and of earth, and groan with Paul, not because of death, but because of the present life!

6. But grant me, says one, to be like Paul, and I shall never be afraid of death. Why, what is it that forbids thee, O man, to become like Paul? Was he not a poor man? Was he not a tent maker? Was he not a man of humble position? For if he had been rich and high born, the poor, when called upon to imitate his zeal, would have had their poverty to plead; but now thou canst say nothing of this sort. For this man was one who exercised a manual art, and supported himself too by his daily labors. And thou, indeed, from the first hast inherited true religion from thy fathers; and from thy earliest age hast been nourished in the study of the sacred writings; but he was "a blasphemer, and a persecutor, and injurious," and ravaged the Church! Nevertheless, he so changed all at once, as to surpass all in the vehemence of his zeal, and he cries out, saying, "Be ye imitators of me, even as I also am of Christ." He imitated the Lord; and wilt not thou who hast been educated in piety from the first, imitate a fellow-servant; one who by conversion was brought to the faith at a later period of life? Knows thou not, that they who are in sins are dead whilst they live; and that they who live in righteousness, although they be dead, yet they live? And this is not my word. It is the declaration of Christ speaking to Martha, "He that believeth in me though he were dead yet shall he live." Is our doctrine, indeed, a fable? If thou art a Christian, believe in Christ;

if thou believes in Christ, show me thy faith by thy works. But how may you show this? By thy contempt of death: for in this we differ from the unbelievers. They may well fear death; since they have no hope of a resurrection. But thou, who art travelling toward better things, and hast the opportunity of meditating on the hope of the future; what excuse hast thou, if whilst assured of a resurrection, thou are yet at the same time as fearful of death, as those who believe not the resurrection?

7. But I have no fear of death, says one, nor of the act of dying, but of a miserable death, of being beheaded. Did John then, I ask, die miserably? For he was beheaded. Or did Stephen die miserably? for he was stoned; and all the martyrs have thus died wretchedly, according to this objection: since some have ended their lives by fire; and others by the sword; and some cast into the ocean; others down a precipice; and others into the jaws of wild beasts, have so come by their death. To die basely, O man, is not to come to one's end by a violent death, but to die in sin! Hear, at least, the prophet moralizing on this very matter, and saying, "The death of sinners is evil." He does not say that a violent death is evil; but what then? "The death of sinners is evil." And justly so; for after the departure from this life, there is an intolerable punishment; undying vengeance, the envenomed worm; the fire unquenchable, the outer darkness, the chains indissoluble; the gnashing of teeth, the tribulation, and the anguish, and the eternal justice.

8. Since therefore such evils await sinners, what advantage can it be to them, though they should end their days at home, and in their bed? Even so, on the other hand, it can do no harm to the righteous to lay down the present life through sword, or steel, or fire, when they are

to depart to the good things that are immortal. Truly "the death of sinners is evil." Such a death was that of the rich man, who despised Lazarus. He, when he had terminated his life by a natural end, at home and on his bed, and with his relatives about him, experienced after his departure to the other world a fiery torment; nor was he able to obtain there even a little comfort, out of all the pleasure he had enjoyed in the present life! But not so was it with Lazarus; for when lying upon the pavement, while the dogs came and licked his sores, he had suffered a violent death (for what could be more painful than hunger?), but on his departing hence he enjoyed eternal blessings, luxuriating in the bosom of Abraham! In what respect, then, did it injure him that he died a violent death? Or what did it profit the rich man, that he died not with violence?

9. But, says someone, "We have no fear of dying by violence, but of dying unjustly; and of being punished in a similar way with the guilty,—we who have had nothing to do with the crimes of which we are suspected." What says thou, tell me? Art thou afraid of dying unjustly, and would you wish to die justly. But who is there so wretched and miserable, that when he had the alternative of dying unjustly, would rather depart by an act of justice? For if it be necessary to fear death, it is necessary to fear it when it comes upon us justly; since he indeed who dies unjustly, is by this very means made a partaker with all the saints. For many of those who were approved and distinguished by God, have been subjected to an unjust end; and first of all Abel. For it was not that he had sinned against his brother, or done Cain any harm; but inasmuch as he had honored God, therefore was he slaughtered. But God permitted it. Was it, think you,

because He loved him, or because He hated him? Most clearly, because He loved him, and wished to make his crown the brighter, by that most unjust murder. See you then, that it becomes us not to be afraid of dying by violence; nor yet of dying unjustly; but of dying in a state of sin? Abel died unjustly. Cain lived, groaning and trembling! Which then, I would ask, was the more blessed of the two; he who went to rest in righteousness, or he who lived in sin; he who died unjustly, or he who was justly punished? Would you have me declare unto your Charity, whence it is that we are afraid of death? The love of the kingdom hath not penetrated us, nor the desire of things to come inflamed us: otherwise we should despise all present things, even as the blessed Paul did. Add to this, on the other hand, that we do not stand in awe of hell; therefore death is terrible. We are not sensible of the insufferable nature of the punishment there; therefore, instead of sin, we fear death; since if the fear of the one held possession of our souls, the fear of the other would not be able to enter.

10. And this I will endeavor to make manifest, not from anything of a remote nature, but from what is at our own doors; and from the events which have happened among us in these days. For when the Emperor's letter came, ordering that tribute to be imposed which was thought to be so intolerable, all were in a tumult; all quarreled with it; thought it a sore grievance, resented it; and when they met one another said, "Our life is not worth living, the city is undone;—no one will be able to stand under this heavy burden;" and they were distressed as if placed in the extremest danger. After this, when the rebellion was actually perpetrated, and certain vile, yea, thoroughly vile persons, trampling underfoot the laws,

threw down the statues, and involved all in the utmost peril; and now that we are in fear for our very lives, through the indignation of the Emperor, this loss of money no longer stings us. But instead of such complaints, I hear from all a language of a different kind. "Let the Emperor take our substance, we will gladly be deprived of our fields and possessions, if anyone will but ensure us safety for the bare body." As therefore, before the fear of death pressed upon us, the loss of our wealth tormented us; and after these lawless outrages had been perpetrated, the fear of death succeeding, expelled the grief for that loss; so if the fear of hell had held possession of our souls, the fear of death would not have possessed them. But even as it is with the body, when two kinds of pain seize upon us, the more powerful usually overshadows the weaker one, so also would it now happen; if the dread of future punishment remained in the soul, that would overshadow all human fear. So that if anyone endeavors always to have the remembrance of hell, he will deride every kind of death; and this will not only deliver him from the present distress, but will even rescue him from the flame to come. For he who is always afraid of hell, will never fall into the fire of hell; being made sober by this continual fear!

11. Permit me, that I now say to you at a fitting time, "Brethren, be not children in understanding; howbeit in malice be ye children." For this is a childish terror of ours, if we fear death, but are not fearful of sin. Little children too are afraid of masks, but fear not the fire. On the contrary, if they are carried by accident near a lighted candle, they stretch out the hand without any concern towards the candle and the flame; yet a mask which is so utterly contemptible terrifies them; whereas

they have no dread of fire, which is really a thing to be afraid of. Just so we too have a fear of death, which is a mask that might well be despised; but have no fear of sin, which is truly dreadful; and, even as fire, devours the conscience! And this is wont to happen not on account of the nature of the things, but by reason of our own folly; so that if we were once to consider what death is, we should at no time be afraid of it. What then, I pray you, is death? Just what it is to put off a garment. For the body is about the soul as a garment; and after laying this aside for a short time by means of death, we shall resume it again with the more splendor. What is death at most? It is a journey for a season; a sleep longer than usual! So that if thou fears death, thou should also fear sleep! If for those who are dying thou art pained, grieve for those too who are eating and drinking, for as this is natural, so is that! Let not natural things sadden thee; rather let things which arise from an evil choice make thee sorrowful. Sorrow not for the dying man; but sorrow for him who is living in sin!

12. Would you have me mention another reason on account of which we fear death? We do not live with strictness, nor keep a clear conscience; for if this were the case nothing would alarm us, neither death, nor famine, nor the loss of wealth, nor anything else of this kind. For he who lives virtuously, cannot be injured by any of these things, or be deprived of his inward pleasure. For being supported by favorable hopes, nothing will be able to throw him into dejection. What is there that anyone can possibly effect, by which he can cause the noble-minded man to become sorrowful? Take away his riches? He has yet wealth that is in the heavens! Cast him out of his country? He will take his journey to that city which is

above! Load him with fetters? He has still his conscience free, and is insensible to the external chain! Put his body to death? Yet he shall rise again! And as he who fights with a shadow, and beaten the air, will be unable to hit anyone; so he who is at war with the just man, is but striking at a shadow, and wasting his own strength, without being able to inflict any injury upon him. Grant me then to be sure of the kingdom of heaven; and, if thou wishes, slay me this day. I shall be thankful to thee for the slaughter; forasmuch as thou sends me quickly to the possession of those good things! "This, however," says someone, "is what we especially lament, that hindered as we are by the multitude of our sins, we shall not attain to that kingdom." Such being the case then, leave off lamenting death, and lament thy sins, in order that thou may be freed from them! Grief, indeed, hath had its existence, not that we should sorrow for the loss of wealth, nor for death, nor for anything else of that kind, but that we may employ it for the taking away of our sins. And I will make the truth of this evident by an example. Healing medicines have been made for those diseases only which they are able to remove; not for those which are in no respect assisted by them. For instance (for I wish to make the matter still plainer), the medicine which is able to benefit a malady of the eyes only, and no other disease, one might justly say was made only for the sake of the eyes; not for the stomach, nor for the hands, nor any other member. Let us then transfer this argument to the subject of grief; and we shall find, that in none of those things which happen to us, is it of any advantage, except to correct sin; whence it is apparent that it hath had its existence only for the destruction of this. Let us now take a survey of each of those evils which befall us, and let us apply despondency as a remedy, and see what sort of advantage results from it.

13. Someone is mulcted in property: he becomes sad, but this does not make good his loss. Someone hath lost a son: he grieves, but he cannot raise the dead, nor benefit the departed. Someone hath been scourged, beaten, and insulted; he becomes sorrowful. This does not recall the insult. Someone falls into sickness, and a most grievous disease; he is dejected. This does not remove his disease, but only makes it the more grievous. Do you see that in none of these cases does sadness answer any useful purpose? Suppose that anyone hath sinned, and is sad. He blots out the sin; he gets free from the transgression. How is this shewn? By the declaration of the Lord; for, speaking of a certain one who had sinned, He said, "Because of his iniquity I made him sad for a while; and I saw that he was grieved, and he went on heavily; and I healed his ways." Therefore also Paul says, "Godly sorrow worked repentance unto salvation not to be repented of." Since then what I have said clearly shews, that neither the loss of riches, nor insult, nor abuse, nor stripes, nor sickness, nor death, nor any other thing of that kind can possibly be relieved by the interference of grief, but sin only can it blot out and do away, it is evident that this is the only reason why it hath its existence. Let us therefore no more grieve for the loss of wealth, but let us grieve only when we commit sin. For great in this case is the gain that comes of sorrow. Art thou amerced? Be not dejected, for thus thou wilt not be at all benefited. Hast thou sinned? Then be sorry: for it is profitable; and consider the skill and wisdom of God. Sin hath brought forth for us these two things, sorrow and death. For "in the day thou eats," He says, "thou shalt surely die;" and to

the woman, "In sorrow thou shalt bring forth children." And by both of these things he took away sin, and provided that the mother should be destroyed by her offspring. For that death as well as grief takes away sin, is evident, in the first place, from the case of the martyrs; and it is plain too from what Paul says to those who had sinned, speaking on this wise, "For this cause many are weak and sickly among you, and many sleep." Inasmuch, he observes, as ye have sinned, ye die, so that ye are freed from sin by death. Therefore he goes on to say, "For if we would judge ourselves, we should not be judged. But when we are judged, we are chastened of the Lord, that we should not be condemned with the world." And even as the worm is brought forth from the wood, and devours the wood; and a moth consumes the wool, from whence it originates; so grief and death were born of sin, and devour sin.

14. Let us not then fear death, but let us only fear sin, and grieve on account of this. And these things I speak, not anticipating anything fearful, God forbid! But wishing you when alarmed to be always thus affected, and to fulfil the law of Christ in very deed. For "he," says Christ, "that takes not his cross, and follows after Me, is not worthy of Me." This He said, not that we should bear the wood upon our shoulders, but that we should always have death before our eyes. Even so as Paul, that is, died daily, and laughed at death, and despised the present life. For indeed thou art a soldier, and stands continually at arms; but a soldier who is afraid of death, will never perform a noble action. Thus then neither will a Christian man, if fearful of dangers, perform anything great or admirable; nay, besides this, he will be apt to be easily vanquished. But not so is it with the man who is bold and

lofty minded. He remains impregnable and unconquerable. As then the Three Children, when they feared not the fire, escaped from the fire, so also we, if we fear not death, shall entirely escape from death. They feared not the fire (for it is no crime to be burnt), but they feared sin, for it is a crime to commit impiety. Let us also imitate these and all such, and let us not be afraid of dangers, and then we shall pass safely through them.

15. As for me, "I am not a prophet nor the son of a prophet,"1258 yet I understand clearly thus much of the future, and I proclaim, both loudly and distinctly, that if we become changed, and bestow some care upon our souls, and desist from iniquity, nothing will be unpleasant or painful. And this I plainly know from the love of God toward man, as well as from those things which He hath done for men, and cities, and nations, and whole populations. For He threatened the city of Nineveh, and said, "There are yet three days, and Nineveh shall be overthrown." What then, I ask, Was Nineveh overthrown? Was the city destroyed? Nay, quite the contrary; it both arose, and became still more distinguished; and long as is the time which has elapsed, it has not effaced its glory, but we all still celebrate and admire it even to this day. For from that time it hath been a sort of excellent haven for all who have sinned, not suffering them to sink into desperation, but calling all to repentance; and by what it did, and by what it obtained of God's favor, persuading men never to despair of their salvation, but exhibiting the best life they can, and setting before them a good hope, to be confident of the issue as destined in any wise to be favorable. For who would not be stirred up on hearing of such an example, even if he were the laziest of mortals?

16. For God even preferred that His own prediction should fall to the ground, so that the city should not fall. Or rather, the prophecy did not even so fall to the ground. For if indeed while the men continued in the same wickedness, the sentence had not taken effect, someone perhaps might have brought a charge against what was uttered. But if when they had changed, and desisted from their iniquity, God also desisted from His wrath, who shall be able any longer to find fault with the prophecy, or to convict the things spoken of falsehood. The same law indeed which God had laid down from the beginning, publishing it to all men by the prophet, was on that occasion strictly observed. What then is this law? "I shall speak a sentence," says He, "concerning a nation or a kingdom, to pluck up, and to pull down, and to destroy it; and it shall be, that if they repent of their evil, I will also repent of the wrath which I said I would do unto them." Guarding then this law, he saved those who were converted and released from His wrath those who desisted from their wickedness. He knew the virtue of the barbarians; therefore He hastened the prophet thither. Thus was the city agitated at the time, when it heard the prophet's voice, but instead of being injured it was benefited by fear. For that fear was the cause of its safety. The threatening effected the deliverance from the peril. The sentence of overthrow put a stop to the overthrow. O strange and astonishing event! The sentence threatening death, brought forth life! The sentence after it was published became cancelled; the very opposite to that which takes place among temporal judges! For in their case the proclamation of the sentence causes it to become valid, is fully to ratify it; but on the contrary, with God, the publication of the sentence, caused it to be cancelled.

For if it had not been published, the offenders would not have heard; and if they had not heard, they would not have repented, and if they had not repented, they would not have warded off the punishment, nor would they have obtained that astonishing deliverance. For how is it less than astonishing, when the judge declares sentence, and the condemned discharge the sentence by their repentance! They, indeed, did not flee from the city as we are now doing, but remaining in it they caused it to stand. It was a snare, and they made it a fortification! It was a gulph, and a precipice, and they turned it into a tower of safety! They had heard that the buildings would fall, and yet they fled not from the buildings, but they fled from their sins. They did not depart each from his house as we do now, but each departed from his evil way; for, said they, "why should we think the walls have brought forth the wrath? We are the causes of the wound; we then should provide the medicine." Therefore they trusted for safety, not to a change of habitations, but of habits.

17. Thus did the barbarians! and are we not ashamed, and ought we not to hide our faces, whilst instead of changing our habits, as they did, we change only our habitations; privily removing our goods, and doing the deeds of men that are drunken? Our Master is angry with us; and we, neglecting to appease His wrath, carry about our household stuff from place to place, and run hither and thither, seeking where we may deposit our substance; while we ought rather to seek where we may deposit our soul in safety; or rather, it behooved us not to seek, but to entrust its safety to virtue and uprightness of life. For when we were angry and displeased with a servant, if he, instead of defending himself against our displeasure, went down to his apartment, and collecting

together his clothes, and binding up together all his movables, meditated a flight, we could not tamely put up with this contempt. Let us then desist from this unseasonable endeavor, and let us each say to God, "Whither shall I go from Thy Spirit, and whither shall I flee from Thy presence?" Let us imitate the spiritual wisdom of the barbarians. They repented even on uncertain grounds! For the sentence had no such clause, "If you turn and repent, I will set up the city;" but simply, "Yet three days, and Nineveh shall be overthrown." What then said they? "Who knows whether God will repent of the evil He said He would do unto us?" Who knows? They know not the end of the event, and yet they do not neglect repentance! They are unacquainted with God's method of shewing mercy, and yet they change upon the strength of uncertainties! For neither was it in their power to look at other Ninevites who had repented and been saved; nor had they read prophets; nor had they heard patriarchs; nor had they enjoyed counsel, or partaken of admonition; nor had they persuaded themselves that they should certainly propitiate God by repentance. For the threatening did not imply this: but they were doubtful, and hesitating concerning it; and yet they repented with all diligence. What reason then shall we have to urge, when those, who had no ground for confidence as to the issue, are seen to have exhibited so great a change; but thou who hast ground of confidence in the mercy of God, and who hast frequently received many pledges of His care, and hast heard prophets, and apostles, and hast been instructed by actual events; hast yet no emulation to reach the same measure of virtue as these did! Great assuredly was their virtue! But greater by far was the mercy of God! And this may be seen from the very greatness of the threat. For this reason God did not add to the declaration, "But if ye repent. I will spare:" in order that by setting forth a sentence without limitation, He might increase the fear and having increased the fear, He might constrain them more speedily to repentance.

18. The prophet is indeed ashamed, foreseeing what the issue would be, and conjecturing that what he had prophesied, would remain unaccomplished; God however is not ashamed, but is desirous of one thing only, viz. the salvation of men, and corrects His own servant. For when he had entered the ship, He straightway there raised a boisterous sea; in order that thou might know that where sin is, there is a tempest; where there is disobedience, there is the swelling of the waves. The city was shaken because of the sins of the Ninevites; and the ship was shaken because of the disobedience of the prophet. The sailors therefore threw Jonah in the deep, and the ship was preserved. Let us then drown our sins, and our city will assuredly be safe! Flight will certainly be no advantage to us; for it did not profit him; on the contrary, it did him injury. He fled from the land indeed, but he fled not from the wrath of God; he fled from the land, but he brought the tempest after him on the sea; and so far was he from obtaining any benefit by his flight, that he plunged those also who received him into the extremest peril. And whilst he sat sailing in the ship, although the sailors, the pilots, and all the necessary apparatus of the ship were there present, he was placed in the utmost danger. After, however, having been thrown out into the deep, and having put away his sin by means of the punishment, he had been conveyed into that unstable vessel, I mean, the whale's belly, he enjoyed great security. This was for the purpose of teaching thee,

that as no ship can be of any use to him who is living in sin, so him who has put away his sin, the sea cannot drown, nor monsters destroy. Of a truth, the waves received, but they did not suffocate him. The whale received him, but did not destroy him; but both the animal and the element gave back to God unhurt that, with which they were entrusted; and by all these things the prophet was taught to be humane and merciful; and not to be more cruel than wild beasts, or thoughtless sailors, or unruly waves. For even the sailors did not immediately at first give him up, but after much compulsion; and the sea and the monster guarded him with great kindness; all these things being under God's direction.

19. Therefore he came back again; he preached; he threatened; he persuaded; he preserved; he affrighted; he amended; he established; by one, and that the first preaching! Many days he needed not, nor continued counsel; but speaking these simple words only, he brought all to repentance! On this account God did not lead him directly from the ship into the city; but the sailors committed him to the sea; the sea to the whale; the whale to God; God to the Ninevites; and by this long circuit he brought back the fugitive, that he might instruct all, that it is impossible to fly from the hands of God; that whithersoever any one may roam, dragging his sin after him, he will have to undergo a thousand evils; and though no mortal were present, yet on every side the whole creation will rise up against him with the utmost vehemence! Let us not then provide for our safety by flight, but by a change of the moral character. Is it for remaining in the city that God is angry with thee, that thou should fly? It is because thou hast sinned, that He is indignant. Lay aside therefore the sin, and where the

cause of thy wound lies, thence remove the fountain of the evil. For the physicians too give us directions to cure contraries by contraries. Is fever, for instance, produced by a full diet? They subject the disease to the regimen of abstinence. Does anyone fall sick from sadness? They say that mirth is the suitable medicine for it. Thus also it befits us to act with respect to diseases of the soul. Hath listlessness excited the wrath? Let us shake this off by zeal, and let us manifest in our conduct a great change. We have the fast, a very great auxiliary and ally in our warfare; and besides the fast, we have the impending distress, and the fear of danger. Now then, in season, let us be at work on the soul; for we shall easily be able to persuade it to whatever we choose; since he who is alarmed and trembling, and set free from all luxury, and who lives in terror, is able to practice moral wisdom without difficulty, and to receive the seeds of virtue with much alacrity.

20. Let us therefore persuade it to make this first change for the better, by the avoidance of oaths; for although I spoke to you yesterday, and the day before, on this same subject; yet neither to-day, nor to-morrow, nor the day after, will I desist giving my counsel on this subject. And why do I say to-morrow and the day following? Until I see that you are amended, I will not abstain from doing so. If those, indeed, who transgress this law, are not ashamed, far less should we who bid them not transgress it, feel this frequency of the admonition to be a matter worthy of shame. For to be continually reminding men of the same topics is not the fault of the speaker, but of the hearers, needing as they do perpetual instruction, upon simple and easily-observed precepts. What indeed is easier than not to swear? It is

only a good work of habit. It is neither labor of the body, nor expenditure of wealth. Art thou desirous to learn how it is possible to get the better of this infirmity, how it is possible to be set free from this evil habit? I will tell thee of a particular method by which if pursued thou wilt certainly master it. If thou sees either thyself or any other person, whether it be one of thy servants, or of thy children, or thy wife, ensnared in this vice; when thou hast continually reminded them of it, and they are not amended, order them to retire to rest supperless; and impose this sentence upon thyself, as well as upon them, a sentence which will bring with it no injury, but a gain. For such is the nature of spiritual acts; they bring profit and a speedy reformation. The tongue when constantly punished, when straitened by thirst. And pained by hunger, receives a sufficient admonition, even whilst no one is its monitor; and though we were the most stupid of mortals, yet when we are thus reminded by the greatness of the punishment during a whole day, we shall need no other counsel and exhortation.

21. Ye have applauded what I have spoken. But still shew me your applause too by deeds. Else what is the advantage of our meeting here? Suppose a child were to go to school every day, yet if he learnt nothing the more for it, would the excuse satisfy us that he every day went there? Should we not esteem it the greatest fault, that going there daily, he did it to no purpose. Let us consider this with ourselves, and let us say to ourselves, For so long a time have we met together at church, having the benefit of a most solemn Communion, which has in it much profit; and should we return back again just as we came, with none of our defects corrected, of what advantage is our coming here? For most actions are done,

not for themselves, but for the effects which follow through their means; as, for example, the sower does not sow for the mere sake of sowing, but in order that he may reap too; since if this were not to follow, the sowing would be a loss, the seeds rotting without any kind of advantage. The merchant doth not take a voyage merely for sailing's sake, but that he may increase his substance by going abroad; since, if this be not attained beside, extreme mischief will result, and the voyage of merchants were but for loss. Let us indeed consider this in relation to ourselves. We also meet together in the church, not for the mere purpose of spending time here, but in order that we may return having gained a great and spiritual benefit. Should we then depart empty, and without having received any advantage, this our diligence becomes our condemnation! In order that this may not occur, and extreme mischief result, on departing from this place, let friends practice with one another; fathers with children; and masters with servants; and train yourselves to perform the task assigned you; so that when ye come back again, and hear us giving you counsel on the same subjects, ye may not be put to shame by an accusing conscience, but may rejoice and be glad, whilst ye perceive that ye have accomplished the greatest part of the admonition.

22. Let us not moralize on these things here only. For this temporary admonition does not suffice to extirpate the whole evil; but at home also, let the husband hear of these things from the wife, and the wife from the husband. And let there be a kind of rivalry among all in endeavoring to gain precedence in the fulfilment of this law; and let him who is in advance, and hath amended his conduct, reproach him who is still loitering behind; to the end that he may stir him up the more by these gibes. He

who is deficient, and hath not yet amended his conduct, let him look at him who hath outstripped him, and strive with emulation to come up with him quickly. If we take advice on these points, and are anxiously concerned about them, our other affairs will speedily be well adjusted. Be thou solicitous about God's business, and he will take care of thine! And do not say to me, "What if anyone should impose upon us the necessity of taking oaths? What if he should not believe us?" For assuredly, where a law is transgressed, it is improper to make mention of necessity; forasmuch as there is but one necessity which cannot be dispensed with, viz. that of not offending God! This, however, I say further; cut off in the meantime superfluous oaths, those that are taken uselessly, and without any necessity; those to your own family, those to your friends, those to your servants; and should you take away these, you will have no further need of me for the others. For the very mouth that has been well disciplined to dread and to avoid the frequent oath, should anyone constrain it a thousand times, would never consent to relapse again into the same habit. On the contrary, as now, with much labor and vast importunity, by alarming, threatening, exhorting, and counselling, we have scarcely been able to bring it over to a different habit, so in that case, although any one were to impose ever so great necessity, he could not possibly persuade to a transgression of this law. And as a person would never choose to take a particular poison, however urgent the necessity might be, so neither would he to utter an oath!

23. Should this amendment then take place, it will be an encouragement and inducement to the attainment of the remaining parts of virtue. For he who has not accomplished anything at all becomes listless, and quickly

falls; but he who is conscious with himself that he has fulfilled at least one precept, coming by this to have a good hope, will go on with greater alacrity towards the rest; so that, after he has reached one, he will presently come to another; and will not halt until he has attained the crown of all. For if with regard to wealth, the more anyone obtains of it, the more he desires, much rather may this be seen with reference to spiritual attainments. Therefore I hasten, and am urgent that this work may take its commencement, and that the foundation of virtue may be laid in your souls. We pray and beseech, that ye will remember these words, not only at the present time, but also at home, and in the market, and wheresoever ye pass your time. Oh! That it were possible for me familiarly to converse with you! Then this long harangue of mine would have been unnecessary. But now since this may not be, instead of me, remember my words: and while you are sitting at table, suppose me to enter, and to be standing beside you, and dinning into you the things I now say to you in this place. And wheresoever there may be any discourse concerning me among you, above all things remember this precept, and render me this recompense for my love toward you. If I see that you have fulfilled it, I have received my full return, and have obtained a sufficient recompense for my labors. In order then that ye may both render us the more active, and that yourselves too may be in the enjoyment of a good hope; and may provide for the accomplishment of the remaining precepts with greater facility; treasure up this precept in your souls with much care, and ye will then understand the benefit of this admonition. And since a vestment broidered with gold is a beautiful and conspicuous object, but seems much more so to us when it is worn upon our own person;

thus also the precepts of God are beautiful when being praised, but appear far more lovely when they are rightly practiced. For now indeed ye commend what is spoken during a brief moment of time, but if ye reduce it to practice, you will alike commend both yourselves and us all day long, and all your lives long. And this is not the grand point, that we shall praise one another; but that God will accept us; and not only accept us, but will also reward us with those gifts that are great and unspeakable! Of which may we all be deemed worthy, through the grace and lovingkindness of our Lord Jesus Christ, through whom, and with whom, to the Father together with the Holy Ghost, be glory, now and always, for ever and ever. Amen.

Homily VI.

This Homily is intended to shew that the fear of Magistrates is beneficial. It also contains an account of what occurred, during their journey, to those who were conveying the tidings of the sedition to the Emperor. The case of Jonah is further cited in illustration. The exhortation on the fear of death is here continued; and it is shewn, that he who suffers unjustly, and yet gives thanks to God, by whose permission it happens, is as one suffering for God's sake. Examples are again adduced from the history of the Three Children, and the Babylonian furnace. The Homily concludes with an address on the necessity of abstaining from oaths.

1. We have spent many days addressing words of comfort to your Charity. We would not, however, on that account lay the subject aside; but as long as the sore of

despondency remains, we will apply to it the medicine of consolation. For if in the case of bodily wounds, physicians do not give over their fomentations, until they perceive that the pain has subsided; much less ought this to be done in regard to the soul. Despondency is a sore of the soul; and we must therefore foment it continually with soothing words. For not so naturally is warm water efficacious to soften a hard tumor of the flesh, as words of comfort are powerful to allay the swelling passions of the soul. Here, there is no need of the sponge as with physician, but instead of this we employ the tongue. No need of fire here, that we may warm the water; but instead of fire, we make use of the grace of the Spirit. Suffer us then to do so today. For if we were not to comfort you, where else could ye obtain consolation? The judges affright; the priests therefore must console! The rulers threaten; therefore must the Church give comfort! Thus it happens with respect to little children. The teachers frighten them, and send them away weeping to their mothers; but the mothers receiving them back to their own bosoms, keep them there, embrace them, and kiss them, while they wipe away their tears, and relieve their sorrowing spirits; persuading them by what they say, that it is profitable for them to fear their teachers. Since therefore the rulers also make you afraid, and render you anxious, the Church, which is the common mother of us all, opening her bosom, and cradling us in her arms, administers daily consolation; telling us that the fear of rulers is profitable, and profitable too the consolation that comes from hence. For the fear of the former does not permit us to be relaxed by listlessness, but the consolation of the latter does not allow us to sink under the weight of sadness; and by both these means God provides for our safety. He Himself hath armed magistrates with power; that they may strike terror into the licentious; and hath ordained His priests that they may administer consolation to those that are in sorrow.

2. And both these things are taught us by the Scripture, and by actual experience of recent events. For if, whilst there are magistrates and soldiers living under arms, the madness of a few individuals, a motley crew of adventurers, hath kindled such a fire among us, in so short a moment of time, and raised such a tempest, and made us all to stand in fear of shipwreck, suppose the fear of magistrates to be wholly taken away? To what lengths would they not have gone in their madness? Would they not have overthrown the city from its foundations, turning all things upside down, and have taken our very lives? If you were to abolish the public tribunals, you would abolish all order from our life. And even as if you deprive the ship of its pilot, you sink the vessel; or as, if you remove the general from the army, you place the soldiers bound in the hands of the enemy; so if you deprive the city of its rulers, we must lead a life less rational than that of the brutes, biting and devouring one another; the rich man, the poorer; the stronger man, the weaker; and the bolder man, him who is more gentle. But now by the grace of God none of these things happen. For they who live in a state of piety, require no correction on the part of the magistrates; for "the law is not made for a righteous man," says one. But the more numerous being viciously inclined, if they had no fear of these hanging over them, would fill the cities with innumerable evils; which Paul knowing, observed, "There is no power, but of God, the powers that be are ordained of God." For what the tie-beams are in houses, that rulers are in cities; and in the

same manner as if you were to take away the former, the walls, being disunited, would fall in upon one another of their own accord; so were you to deprive the world of magistrates, and of the fear that comes of them, houses at once, and cities, and nations, would fall on one another in unrestrained confusion, there being no one to repress, or repel, or persuade them to be peaceful, by the fear of punishment!

3. Let us not then be grieved, beloved, by the fear of our rulers, but let us give thanks to God that He hath removed our listlessness, and rendered us more diligent. For tell me, what harm hath arisen from this concern and anxiety? Is it that we are become more grave, and gentle; more diligent, and attentive? That we see no one intoxicated, and singing lascivious airs? Or is it that there are continual supplications, and prayers, and tears? That unseasonable laughter, and impure words, and all dissoluteness is banished; and that the city is now in all respects, like the pattern of a modest and virtuous woman? Do you grieve, I ask, for any of these reasons? For these things, assuredly, it were right to rejoice, and to be thankful to God, that by the terror of a few days He hath put an end to such stupidity!

"Very true," says someone, "if our danger did not go beyond fear, we should have reaped a sufficient benefit; but we are now in dread lest the mischief should proceed much farther, and we should be all placed in the extremest peril."

Nevertheless, I say, fear not. Paul comforted you, saying, "God is faithful, who will not suffer you to be tempted above that ye are able, but will with the temptation also make the way of escape, that ye may be able to bear it." He indeed Himself hath said, "I will never leave thee, nor forsake thee." For had He resolved to punish us in deed, and in actual endurance, He would not have given us over to terror during so many days. For when He would not punish, He affrights; since if He were intending to punish, fear would be superfluous, and threatening superfluous. But now, we have sustained a life more grievous than countless deaths; fearing and trembling during so many days, and being suspicious of our very shadows; and paying the punishment of Cain; and in the midst of our sleep, starting up, through constant agony of mind. So that if we have kindled God's wrath, we have appeased Him in the endurance of such a punishment. For if we have not paid the satisfaction due to our sins, yet it hath been enough to satisfy the mercy of God.

4. But not this, but many other grounds for confidence ought we to have. For God hath already given us not a few pledges for favorable hopes. And first of all, those who carried the evil tidings departing hence with the speed of wings, supposing they should long ere this have reached the camp, are yet delayed in the midst of their journey. So many hindrances and impediments have arisen; and they have left their horses, and are now proceeding in vehicles; whence their arrival must of necessity be retarded. For since God here stirred up our priest, and common father, and persuaded him to go forth, and undertake this embassy, he detained the messengers for a while, when they were but half way on their road, lest arriving before him they might kindle the fire, and make our teacher's efforts to mend matters useless, when the royal ears had become inflamed. For that this hindrance on the road, was not without God's interposition is evident from this. Men who had been

familiar with such journeys all their lives, and whose constant business it was to ride on horseback, now broke down through the fatigue of this very riding; so that what hath now happened is the reverse of what took place in the case of Jonah. For God hastened him when unwilling, to go on his mission. But these, who were desirous to go, He hindered. O strange and wonderful event! He wished not to preach of an overthrow; and God forced him to go against his will. These men with much haste set forward to be the bearers of a message of overthrow, and against their will again He has hindered them! For what reason think you? Why, because in this case the haste was an injury; but in the other case, haste brought gain. On this account, He hastened him forward by means of the whale; and detained these by means of their horses. See you the wisdom of God? Through the very means by which each party hoped to accomplish their object, through these each received a hindrance. Jonah expected to escape by the ship, and the ship became his chain. These couriers, by means of their horses, expected the more quickly to see the Emperor; and the horses became the obstacles; or rather, neither the horses in one case, nor the ship in the other, but the Providence of God everywhere directing all things according to its own wisdom!

5. Consider also His care over us, and how He both affrighted and consoled us. For after permitting them to set out on the very day when all these outrages were committed, as if they would report all that had taken place to the Emperor; He alarmed us all at their sudden departure. But when they were gone, and two or three days had elapsed, and we thought the journey of our Priest would now be useless, as he would arrive when it was too late, He delivered us from this fear, and

comforted us by detaining them, as I observed, midway; and by providing persons coming to us from thence by the same road, to announce to us all the difficulties they had met with on their journey, that we might thus take a little breath, as indeed we did, and were relieved of a great part of our anxiety. Having heard of this, we adored God who had done it, who hath even now more tenderly than any father disposed all things for us, delaying by some invisible power those evil messengers, and all but saying to them, "Why do ye hasten? Why do ye press on, when ye are going to overwhelm so great a city? For are ye the bearers of a good message to the Emperor? Wait there till I have made ready my servant, as an excellent physician, to come up with you and anticipate you in your course." But if there was so much of providential care in the first breaking out of this wound of iniquity, much more shall we obtain a greater freedom from anxiety, after conversion, after repentance, after so much fear, after tears and prayers. For Jonah was very properly constrained, in order that he might be forcibly brought to repentance; but ye have already given striking evidences of repentance, and conversion. Therefore, it is necessary that you should receive consolation, instead of a threatening messenger. For this reason also hath He sent our common father hence, notwithstanding the many things to hinder it. But if He had not been tender of our safety, He would not have persuaded him to this, but would have hindered him, however disposed he might be to undertake the journey.

6. There is a third reason by which I may possibly persuade you to have confidence; I mean, the present sacred season, which almost all, even unbelievers, respect; but to which this our divinely-favored Emperor

has shewn such reverence and honor, as to surpass all the Emperors who have reigned with a regard for religion before him. As a proof of this, by sending a letter on these days in honor of the feast, he liberated nearly all those who were lodged in prison; and this letter our Priest when he arrives will read to him; and remind him of his own laws, and will say to him, "Do thou exhort thyself, and remember thine own deeds! Thou hast an example for thy philanthropy at home! Thou didst choose to forbear from executing a justifiable slaughter, and wilt thou endure to perpetrate one that is unjust. Reverencing the feast, thou didst discharge those who had been convicted and condemned; and wilt thou, I ask, condemn the innocent, and those who have not committed any violence, and this when the sacred season is present? That be far from thee, O Emperor! Thou, speaking by this Epistle to all the cities, didst say, 'Would it were possible for me to raise even the dead.' This philanthropy and these words we now stand in need of. To conquer enemies, doth not render kings so illustrious, as to conquer wrath and anger; for in the former case, the success is due to arms and soldiers; but here the trophy is simply thine own, and thou hast no one to divide with thee the glory of thy moral wisdom. Thou hast overcome barbarian war, overcome also Imperial wrath! Let all unbelievers learn that the fear of Christ is able to bridle every kind of authority. Glorify thy Lord by forgiving the trespasses of thy fellow-servants; that He also may glorify thee the more; that at the Day of Judgment, He may bend on thee an Eye merciful and serene, being mindful of this thy lovingkindness!" This, and much more, he will say, and will assuredly rescue us from the Emperor's wrath. And not only will this fast be of the greatest assistance to us in influencing the Emperor in our favor, but also towards enduring what befalls us with fortitude; for we reap no small consolation from this season. For our very meeting together daily as we do, and having the benefit of hearing the divine Scriptures; and beholding each other; and weeping with each other; and praying, and receiving Benedictions, and so departing home, takes off the chief part of our distress.

7. Let us, therefore, not despond, nor give ourselves up by reason of our distress; but let us wait, expecting a favorable issue; and let us give heed to the things that are now about to be spoken. For it is my purpose to discourse to you again today respecting contempt for death. I said to you, yesterday, that we are afraid of death, not because he is really formidable; but because the love of the kingdom hath not kindled us, nor the fear of hell laid hold of us; and because besides this we have not a good conscience. Are you desirous that I should speak of a fourth reason for this unseasonable distress, one which is not less, and truer than the rest? We do not live with the austerity that becomes Christians. On the contrary, we love to follow this voluptuous and dissolute and indolent life; therefore also it is but natural that we cleave to present things; since if we spent this life in fasting, vigils, and poverty of diet, cutting off all our extravagant desires; setting a restraint upon our pleasures; undergoing the toils of virtue; keeping the body under like Paul, and bringing it into subjection; not "making provision for the lusts of the flesh;" and pursuing the straight and narrow way, we should soon be earnestly desirous of future things, and eager to be delivered from our present labors. And to prove that what I say is not untrue, ascend to the tops of the mountains, and observe

the monks who are there; some in sackcloth; some in bonds; some in fasting; some shut up in darkness. Thou wilt then perceive, that all these are earnestly desiring death, and calling it rest. For even as the pugilist is eager to leave the stadium, in order that he may be freed from wounds; and the wrestler longs for the theatre to break up, that he may be released from his toils; so also he who by the aid of virtue leads a life of austerity, and mortification, earnestly longs for death in order that he may be freed from his present labors, and may be able to have full assurance in regard to the crowns laid up in store, by arriving in the still harbor, and migrating to the place where there is no further apprehension of shipwreck. Therefore, also, hath God provided for us a life that is naturally laborious and troublesome; to the end that being here urged by tribulation, we may conceive an eager longing for future blessings; for if now, whilst there are so many sorrows, and dangers, and fears, and anxieties, surrounding us on all sides, we thus cling to the present life; when should we ever be desirous of the life to come, if our present existence were altogether void of grief and misery?

8. Thus also God acted towards the Jews. For wishing to infuse into them a desire of returning (to Canaan), and to persuade them to hate Egypt, He permitted them to be distressed by working in clay, and brick-making, that being oppressed by that weight of toil and affliction, they might cry unto God respecting their return. For if, indeed when they departed after these things had happened, they did again remember Egypt, with their hard slavery, and were urgent to turn back to that former tyranny; what if they had received no such treatment from these barbarians? When would they have

ever wished to leave that strange land? To the end, therefore, that we may not be too closely attached to the earth, and grow wretched whilst gaping after present things, and become unmindful of futurity, God hath made our lives here full of labor. Let us not then cherish the love of the present life beyond what is necessary. For what doth it profit us? Or what is the advantage of being closely riveted to the desire of this present state? Art thou willing to learn in what respect this life is advantageous? It is so, inasmuch as it is the ground-work and starting point of the life to come; the wrestling-school and the arena for crowns of victory hereafter! So that if it does not provide these for us, it is worse than a thousand deaths. For if we do not wish to live so as to please God, it is better to die. For what is the gain? What have we the more? Do we not every day see the same sun, and the same moon, the same winter, the same summer, the same course of things? "The thing that hath been, shall be; and that which is done, is that which shall be done." Let us not then at once pronounce those happy, who are alive, and bewail the dead, but let us weep for those who are in their sins, whether they be dead or alive. And on the other hand, let us call those happy in whatsoever condition they be, who are in a state of righteousness. Thou, forsooth, fears and laments "one" death; but Paul, who was dying daily, was so far from shedding a tear on that account, that he rejoiced and exulted!

9. "O that I did endure the peril for God," says someone, "then I should have no anxiety!" But do not even now sink into despondency; for not only indeed is he well approved, who suffers in the cause of God: but he who is suffering anything unjustly: and bearing it nobly, and giving thanks to God who permits it, is not inferior to

him who sustains these trials for God's sake. The blessed Job is a proof of this, who received so many intolerable wounds through the devil's plotting against him uselessly, vainly, and without cause. Yet, nevertheless, because he bore them courageously, and gave thanks to God who permitted them, he was invested with a perfect crown. Be not sad then on account of death; for it is natural to die: but grieve for sin; because it is a fault of the will. But if thou grieves for the dead, mourn also for those who are born into the world; for as the one thing is of nature, so is the other too of nature. Should anyone, therefore, threaten thee with death, say to him, "I am instructed by Christ not to 'fear them which kill the body, but are not able to kill the soul.'" Or should he threaten thee with the confiscation of thy goods, say to him, "Naked came I out of my mother's womb, and naked shall I return thither. We brought nothing into this world, and it is certain we can carry nothing out." "And though thou take me not, death will come and take me; and though thou slay me not, yet the law of nature will presently interfere and bring the end." Therefore we should fear none of these things which are brought on us by the order of nature, but those which are engendered by our own evil will; for these bring forth our penalty. But let us continually consider this, that as regards the events which come upon us unexpectedly we shall not mend them by grieving, and so we shall cease to grieve.

  10. And moreover we should think of this again, that if we suffer any evil unjustly, during the present life, we discharge a multitude of sins. Therefore it is a great advantage to have out the chastisement of our sins here, and not there; for the rich man received no evil here, and therefore he was scorched in the flames there; and that

this was the reason why he did not enjoy any consolation, hear in proof what Abraham says, "Son, thou hast received thy good things; therefore thou art tormented." But that to the good things bestowed on Lazarus, not only his virtue, but his having here suffered a thousand ills, contributed, learn also from the patriarch's words. For having said to the rich man, "Thou hast received thy good things," he goes on to say, "and Lazarus evil things, and for this reason he is comforted." For as they who live virtuously, and are afflicted, receive a double reward from God, so he who lives in wickedness, and fares sumptuously, shall have a double punishment. Again, I declare this not for the purpose of accusing those who have taken flight, for it is said, "Add not more trouble to a heart that is vexed;" nor do I say it because I wish to rebuke; (for the sick man stands in need of consolation); but for the purpose of endeavoring to promote an amendment. Let us not entrust our safety to flight, but flee from sins, and depart from our evil way. If we escape from these things, although we be in the midst of ten thousand soldiers; not one of them will be able to smite us; but not flying from these, though we ascend to the very summit of the mountains, we shall there find innumerable enemies! Let us again call to mind those three children, who were in the midst of the furnace, yet suffered no evil, and those who cast them into it, how they that sat around were all consumed. What is more wonderful than this? The fire freed those it held possession of, and violently seized those whom it did not hold, to teach thee, that not the habitation, but the habit of life, brings safety or punishment. Those within the furnace escaped, but those without were consumed. To each alike were the same bodies, but not the same dispositions. For this reason neither were the effects on them the same; for hay, although it lie without the flame, is quickly kindled; but gold, although it remain within, becomes the more resplendent!

11. Where now are those who said, "Let the Emperor take all, and grant us our bodies free?" Let such go and learn what is a free body. It is not immunity from punishment that makes the body free, but perseverance in a life of righteousness. The bodies of these youths, for instance, were free, though they were given over to the furnace, because they had before put off the slavery of sin. For this alone is liberty; and not an immunity from punishment, or from suffering anything fearful. But having heard of the furnace, call thou to mind the "rivers of fire," which there shall be in that fearful day. For as on the above occasion, the fire seized upon some, but reverenced others, so also shall it be with those rivers. If anyone should then have hay, wood, stubble, he increases the fire; but if he has gold and silver, he becomes the brighter. Let us therefore get together this kind of material, and let us bear the present state of things nobly; knowing that this tribulation will both bring us deliverance from that punishment if we understand how to practice true wisdom, and will also make us better here; and not only us, but often those too, who throw us into trouble, if we be vigilant; so abundant is the force of this spiritual wisdom; which was the case then even with the tyrant. For when he knew that they had suffered no harm, hear how he changed his language. "Ye servants of the most high God, come forth, and come hither." Didst not thou say, a little before "Who is that God that shall deliver you out of my hands?" What hath happened? Whence this change? You saw those without destroyed, and do you

call on those within? Whence hath it come to pass that thou art grown wise in such matters. Thou sees how great a change took place in the monarch! Whilst he had not yet exercised his power over them, he blasphemed, but as soon as he had cast them into fire, he began to shew moral wisdom. For this reason also God permitted all to take place, whatsoever the tyrant wished, in order that He might make it manifest, that none will be able to injure those who are kept by Him. And what He did towards Job, He performed here. For on that occasion also, He permitted the devil to manifest all his power; and not till he had exhausted all his darts, and no further mode of plotting against him remained, was the combatant led out of the field, that the victory might be brilliant and indubitable. So here too He did the very same thing. He willed to overthrow their city, and God stayed him not: he willed to carry them away captive, and He hindered him not: he willed to bind them, and He permitted; to cast them into the furnace, and He allowed it: to heat the flame beyond its measure, and this too He suffered; and when there was nothing further left for the tyrant to do, and he had exhausted all his strength, then God manifested His own power, and the patience of the youths. See how God permitted these tribulations even to the end, that He might shew the assailants the spiritual wisdom of those whom they assailed, as well as His own providence. Both of which circumstances also that man then discerned, and cried out, "Ye servants of the most high God, come forth, and come hither."

12. But consider thou with me the magnanimity of the youths; for they neither sprang out before the call, lest some should suppose they feared the fire; nor when they were called did they remain within, lest anyone should

think that they were ambitious and contentious. "As soon," say they, "as thou hast learnt whose servants we are, as soon as thou hast acknowledged our Lord, we come forth to be heralds to all who are present of the power of God." Or rather, not only they themselves, but even the enemy with his own voice, yea, both orally, and by his epistle, proclaimed to all men both the constancy of the combatants, and the strength of Him who presided over the contest. And even as the heralds, when they proclaim the names of the victorious combatants in the midst of the theatre, mention also the cities to which they belong; "such a one, of such a city!" So he too, instead of their city, proclaimed their Lord, by saying, "Shadrach, Meshach, and Abednego, ye servants of the most high God, come forth, and come hither." What is come to pass, that thou calls them the servants of God? Were they not thy servants? "Yea," says he, "but they have overthrown my sovereignty; they have trampled underfoot my pride. They have shown by deeds, that He is their true Lord. If they were the servants of men, the fire would not have feared them; the flame would not have made way for them; for the creation knows nothing of reverencing or honoring the servants of men." Therefore again he says, "Blessed be the God of Shadrach, Meshach, and Abednego."

13. Contemplate with me also, how first he proclaims the Arbiter of the contest. "Blessed be God, who hath sent His angel and delivered His servants." This of the power of God. He speaks also of the virtue of the combatants. "Because they trusted in Him, and have changed the king's word, and have yielded their bodies, that they might not worship any god except their own God." Could anything equal the virtue of this? Before

this, when they said, "We will not serve thy gods," he was inflamed more fiercely than the very furnace; but now, when by their deeds they had taught him this, he was so far from being indignant, that he praised and admired them, for not having obeyed him! So good a thing is virtue, that it has even its enemies themselves to applaud and admire it! These had fought and conquered, but the vanquished party gave thanks, that the sight of the fire had not terrified them, but that the hope in their Lord had comforted them. And He names the God of the whole world after the three youths, not at all circumscribing His sovereignty, but inasmuch as these three youths were equivalent to the whole world. For this reason he both applauds those who had despised him, and passing by so many governors, kings, and princes, those who had obeyed him, he stands in admiration of the three captives and slaves, who derided his tyranny! For they did these things, not for the sake of contention, but for the love of wisdom; not of defiance, but of devotion; not as being puffed up with pride, but fired with zeal. For great indeed is the blessing of a hope in God; which then also the barbarian learned, and making it manifest that it was from that source they had escaped the impending peril, he exclaimed aloud: "Because they trusted in Him!"

14. But I say all this now, and select all the histories that contain trials and tribulations, and the wrath of kings, and their evil designs, in order that we may fear nothing, save only offending God. For then also was there a furnace burning; yet they derided it, but feared sin. For they knew that if they were consumed in the fire, they should suffer nothing that was to be dreaded; but that if they were guilty of impiety, they should undergo the extremes of misery. It is the greatest punishment to

commit sin, though we may remain unpunished; as on the other hand, it is the greatest honor and repose to live virtuously, though we may be punished. For sins separate us from God; as He Himself speaks; "Have not your sins separated between you and Me?" But punishments lead us back to God. As one says, "Give peace; for Thou hast recompensed us for all things." Suppose any one hath a wound; which is the most deserving of fear, gangrene, or the surgeon's knife? The steel, or the devouring progress of the ulcer? Sin is a gangrene, punishment is the surgeon's knife. As then, he who hath a gangrene, although he is not lanced, hath to sustain the malady, and is then in the worse condition, when he is not lanced; so also the sinner, though he be not punished, is the most wretched of men; and is then especially wretched, when he hath no punishment, and is suffering no distress. And as those who have a disease of the spleen, or a dropsy, when they enjoy a plentiful table, and cool drinks, and a variety of delicacies, and condiments, are then especially in a most pitiable state, increasing as they do their disease by luxury; but should they rigorously subject themselves to hunger and thirst, according to medical laws, they might have some hope of recovery; so also those who live in iniquity, if they are punished, may have favorable hopes; but if, together with their wickedness, they enjoy security and luxury, they become more wretched than those who cram their bellies, though they are in a state of dropsy; and so much the more, as the soul is better than the body. If then thou sees any who are in the same sins, and some of them struggling continually with hunger, and a thousand ills; while others are drinking their fill, and living sumptuously, and gormandizing; think those the better off, who endure sufferings. For not only is the flame of voluptuousness cut off by these misfortunes, but they also depart to the future Judgment, and that dread tribunal, with no small relief; and go hence, having discharged here the penalty of the greater part of their sins by the ills they have suffered.

15. But enough of consolation. It is time for us now, at last, to proceed to the exhortation on the subject of avoiding oaths, and to remove that seeming palliation on behalf of those who swear, which is but futile, and useless. For when we bring an accusation against them, they allege the case of others who do the very same thing; and they say, "such and such persons swear." Let us then say to these, Nevertheless; such a man does not swear: and God will give His judgment concerning thee, from those who do good works; for sinners do not profit sinners by fellowship in transgressions; but they who perform what is right condemn sinners. For they who gave not Christ food, or drink, were many; but they rendered no aid to each other. Similar also was the case of the five virgins, who found no pardon from companionship, but being condemned by a comparison with those who had acted wisely, both these and the former were alike punished.

16. Dismissing then this argument of frigid self-deception, let us not look at the case of those who fall, but at those who fashion their conduct rightly; and let us endeavor to carry along with us a memento of the present fast when it is over. And as it often happens when we have purchased a vestment, or a slave, or a precious vase, we recall again the time when we did so, and say to each other, "That slave I purchased at such a festival; that garment I bought at such a time;" so, in like manner, if we now reduce to practice this law, we shall say, I reformed the practice of swearing during that Lent; for till then I

was a swearer; but from barely hearing an admonition, I have abstained from the sin.

But "the custom," it may be objected, "is a hard thing to be reformed." I know it is; and therefore am urgent to throw you into another custom, which is good and profitable. For when you say, it is difficult for me to abstain from what is habitual; for that very reason, I say, you should make haste to abstain, knowing for certain, that if you once make another custom for yourself of not swearing, you will want no labor afterwards. Which is the more difficult thing; not to swear, or to remain the whole day without food; and to shrivel up on water-drinking, and meagre diet? It is evident that the latter surpasses the former; yet, notwithstanding, custom has made this matter so possible and easy of execution, that when the fast comes round, although anyone should exhort a thousand times, or as frequently constrain and compel one to partake of wine, or taste of any other of those things which are forbidden during fasts, yet a man would prefer to suffer anything, rather than touch the prohibited article of food; and that not for want of relish for the table, nevertheless, we bear it all with fortitude, from the habit of our conscience. And the case will be the same in regard to oaths; and just as if now, any one were to impose ever so great necessity, you would remain immovable, holding fast the habit; so also in that case, if anyone should urge you ten thousand times, you would not depart from your custom.

18. When you go home, therefore, discourse of all these things with those who are in your house; and as many persons often do, when they come back from a meadow, having plucked there a rose, or a violet, or some flower of that kind, they return twisting it about with their

fingers; and as some, again, when they quit the gardens to go home, take with them branches of trees, with their fruit upon them; and as others, moreover, from sumptuous feasts, carry away leavings of the entertainment for their dependents; so indeed do thou, departing from hence, take an exhortation home to thy wife, thy children, and all thine household. For this admonition is more profitable than the meadow, the garden, or the banqueting table. These roses never wither; these fruits never drop off; these dainties never corrupt. The former yield a temporary delight; but the latter a lasting advantage, not only after this reformation has taken place, but in the very act of reforming. For think what a good practice this would be, having dismissed all other matters public or private, to discourse only of the divine laws continually, at the table, in the forum, and in your other meetings. Would we give our attention to these things, we should say nothing of a dangerous or injurious nature, nor should we sin unwittingly. Giving our leisure to discourse respecting these things, we should be able to withdraw our soul even from this despondency that hangs over us, instead of looking with so much anxiety as we do, whilst we say one to another, "Hath the Emperor heard what hath happened? Is he incensed? What sentence hath he pronounced? Hath any one petitioned him? What? Will he himself endure to destroy utterly a city so great and populous?" Casting these and all such cares upon God, let us be anxious only as to what He hath commanded! Thus shall we rid ourselves of all these sorrows; and although ten only among us should succeed, the ten would quickly become twenty; the twenty fifty; the fifty a hundred; the hundred a thousand; the thousand all the city. And just as when ten lamps are lighted, one may easily fill the whole house with light, so also with respect to right actions; should only ten act rightly, we shall light up a general flame throughout the city, to shine forth, and to procure us safety. For not so naturally does the fire, when it falls upon a forest, kindle the neighboring trees successively, as will the emulation for virtue, when it seizes upon a few minds, be mighty in its progress to diffuse itself through the whole community.

19. Give me cause, then, to exult over you both in the present life, and at that future Day, when those to whom talents have been entrusted, shall be summoned! Your good reputation is a sufficient reward for my labors; and if I see you living in piety, I have all I wish. Do, then, what yesterday I recommended, and to-day will repeat, and will not cease to say it. Fix a penalty for those who swear; a penalty which is a gain, and not a loss; and prepare yourselves henceforth so as you may give us a proof of success. For I shall endeavor to hold a long conversation with each of you, when this assembly is dismissed; in order that in the continuance of discourse I may discover the persons who have been acting rightly, and those who have not. And if I find anyone still swearing, I shall make him manifest to all who are amended, that by reproving, rebuking, and correcting, we may quickly deliver him from this evil habit. For better it is that he should amend through being reproached here, than that he should be put to shame, and punished, in the presence of the whole assembled universe, on that Day, when our sins shall be revealed to the eyes of all men! But God forbid that any in this fair assembly should appear there suffering such things! But by the prayers of the holy fathers, correcting all our offences, and having shown forth the abundant fruit of virtue, may we depart hence

with much confidence, through the grace and lovingkindness of our Lord Jesus Christ, through whom, and with whom, be glory to the Father together with the Holy Spirit, for ever and ever. Amen.

Homily VII.

Recapitulation of former exhortations. Sin brought death and grief into the world, and they tend to its cure. Grief serviceable only for the destruction of sin. Remarks upon the passage, Gen. 1. 1. "In the beginning God created the heaven and the earth." It is argued that God's forethought for man in the work of creation affords grounds of comfort; and that mercy is shewn even in chastisement, as in the saying, "Adam, where art thou?" Concluding admonition on the avoidance of oaths.

1. Yesterday, I discoursed unto your Charity in many words, and upon many subjects; and if out of this variety, it be not possible for you to retain all, I wish more particularly to recall to memory the observation, that God hath implanted the affection grief in our natures for no other reason but because of sin, and He hath made this evident from actual experience. For whilst we are grieved and distressed through the loss of wealth; or by reason of sickness, and death, and the other evils that befall us, we not only reap no consolation from our sorrow, but we also increase the force of these calamities. But if we are in pain and sorrow for our sins, we diminish the weight of sin; we make that little which is great; and very often we blot it all out entirely. Ye should continually remember this, I repeat, in order that ye may mourn for sin only, and for nothing besides; and the additional fact, that sin,

though it brought death and sadness into our life, is again destroyed by both these; which I have recently made evident. Therefore, let us fear nothing so much as sin and transgression. Let us not fear punishment, and then we shall escape punishment. Even as the Three Children were not afraid of the furnace, and so escaped from the furnace. Such indeed it becomes the servants of God to be. For if those who were brought up under the Old dispensation, when death was not yet slain, nor his "brazen gates broken down," nor his "iron bars smitten in sunder;" so nobly encountered their end, how destitute of all defense or excuse shall we be, if, after having had the benefit of such great grace, we attain not even to the same measure of virtue as they did, now when death is only a name, devoid of reality. For death is nothing more than a sleep, a journey, a migration, a rest, a tranquil haven; an escape from trouble, and a freedom from the cares of this present life!

2. But here let us dismiss the subject of consolation; it is the fifth day we are engaged in speaking words of comfort to your Charity, and we might now seem to be troublesome. For what hath been already said is sufficient for those who give heed; but to those who are pusillanimous it will be no gain, even though we were to add to what we have said. It is now time to direct our teaching to the exposition of the Scriptures. For as, if we had said nothing in reference to the present calamity, one might have condemned us for cruelty, and a want of humanity; so, were we always discoursing of this, we might justly be condemned for pusillanimity. Commending then your hearts to God, who is able to speak into your minds, and to expel all grief from within, let us now take up our accustomed manner of instruction;

and that especially since every exposition of Scripture is matter of comfort and relief. So that, although we may seem to be desisting from the topic of consolation, we shall again light upon the same subject by means of Scriptural exposition. For that all Scripture furnishes consolation to those who give attention to it, I will make manifest to you from its own evidence. For I shall not go about among the Scripture narratives to search out certain arguments consolatory; but in order that I may make the proof of the matter which I have undertaken plainer, we will take in hand the book which has today been read to us; and bringing forward, if you will, the introduction and commencement of it, which may especially seem to present no trace of consolation, but to be altogether foreign to topics of comfort, I will make that which I affirm evident.

3. What then is this introduction? "In the beginning God made the heaven and the earth, and the earth was invisible, and unformed, and darkness was upon the face of the abyss." Do these words seem to some of you incapable of affording consolation under distress? Is it not an historical narrative, and an instruction about the creation? Would you then that I show the consolation that is hidden in this saying? Arouse yourselves then, and attend with earnestness to the things which are about to be spoken. For when thou hears that God made the heaven, the earth, the sea, the air, the waters, the multitude of stars, the two great lights, the plants, the quadrupeds, the swimming and the flying animals, and all things without exception which thou sees, for thee, and for thy safety and honor; dost thou not straightway take comfort and receive this as the strongest proof of the love of God, when thou thinks that He produced such a world as this, so fair, so

vast and wonderful, for such a puny being as thyself! When therefore thou hears that, "In the beginning God made the heaven and the earth," run not hastily over the declaration; but traverse in thy mind the breadth of the earth; and reflect how He hath spread out so sumptuous and exquisite a table for us, and provided us with such abundant gladness. And this is, indeed, the most marvelous thing, that He gave us not such a world as this in payment for services done; or as a recompense for good works; but at the very time He formed us, He honored our race with this kingdom. For He said, "Let us make man after our image, and after our likeness." What is the sense of this, "after our image, and after our likeness?" The image of government is that which is meant; and as there is no one in heaven superior to God, so let there be none upon earth superior to man. This then is one, and the first respect, in which He did him honor; by making him after His own image; and secondly, by providing us with this principality, not as a payment for services, but making it entirely the gift of His own love toward man; and thirdly, in that He conferred it upon us as a thing of nature. For of governments there are some natural, and others which are elective—natural as of the lion over the quadrupeds, or as that of the eagle over the birds; elective, as that of an Emperor over us; for he doth not reign over his fellow-servants by any natural authority. Therefore it is that he oftentimes loses his sovereignty. For such are things which are not naturally inherent; they readily admit of change and transposition. But not so with the lion; he rules by nature over the quadrupeds, as the eagle doth over birds. The character of sovereignty is, therefore, constantly allotted to his race; and no lion hath ever been seen deprived of it. Such a kind of sovereignty God bestowed upon us from the beginning, and set us over all things. And not only in this respect did He confer honor upon our nature, but also, by the very eminence of the spot in which we were placed, fixing upon Paradise as our choice dwelling, and bestowing the gift of reason, and an immortal soul.

4. But I would not speak of these things: for I say that such was the abundance of God's care, that we may know His goodness, and His love towards man, not only from the way in which He hath honored, but also from the way in which He hath punished us. And this, I especially exhort you to consider with attention, that God is alike good, not only whilst He is treating us with honor and beneficence, but also whilst He is punishing and chastising. And whether we should have to carry on our contest and combat against the heathen, or against the heretics, respecting the lovingkindness and goodness of God, we shall make His goodness evident, not only from the cases in which He bestows honor, but also from the cases in which He inflicts punishment. For if He is good only whilst honoring us, and not good whilst punishing us, He were but half good. But this is not the case. God forbid! Among men this may probably happen, when they inflict punishments in anger and passion; but God being free from passion, whether He exercise kindness, or whether He punish, He is alike good. Nor less does the threat of hell serve to show His goodness, than the promise of the kingdom. But how? I answer. If He had not threatened hell, if He had not prepared punishment, there are not many who would have attained the kingdom. For the promise of good things doth not so strongly induce the multitude to virtue; as doth the threat of evil things compel by fear, and arouse them to the care of the

soul. So that, although hell be the opposite of the kingdom of heaven, yet each hath respect to the same end—the salvation of men; the one alluring to itself, the other driving them towards its opposite, and by the operation of fear correcting those who are carelessly disposed.

5. I do not enlarge upon this subject without reason; but because there are many who often, when famines, and droughts, and wars take place, or when the wrath of an Emperor overtakes them, or when any other unexpected events of this kind happen, deceive the simpler class by saying, that these things are unworthy of the Providence of God.

I am therefore compelled to dwell on this part of my discourse, that we may not be beguiled by words, but that we may plainly perceive, that whether He brings upon us a famine, or a war, or any calamity, whatsoever, He doth it out of His exceeding great care and kindness. For even those fathers, who especially love their offspring, will forbid them the table, and inflict stripes, and punish them by disgrace, and in endless other ways of this kind correct their children when they are disorderly; yet are they nevertheless fathers, not only while doing them honor, but when acting thus; yea, they are preeminently fathers when they act thus. But if men, who are frequently carried away beyond what is meet by the force of angry feelings, are yet held to punish those whom they love, not from cruelty and inhumanity, but from a kind care and regard; much rather is it proper to be thus minded concerning God; who in the exceeding abundance of His goodness, far transcends every degree of paternal fondness. And that you may not suppose that what I say is a mere conjecture, let us, I pray you, direct our discourse to the Scripture itself. When man, then, had been deceived and beguiled by the wicked demon, let us observe how God treated him, after his committing so great a sin. Did He then altogether destroy him? Yet the reason of the thing in justice demanded this, that one who had displayed nothing that was good, but, after enjoying so much favor, had waxed wanton even from the very first, should be made away with, and utterly destroyed; yet God acted not so; neither did He regard with disgust and aversion him who had been so ungrateful towards his Benefactor, but He comes to him as a physician cometh to a sick man.

6. Do not, O beloved, pass over unthinkingly, what has just been said! but consider what an act it was, not to send an angel, or archangel, or any other of his fellow-servants, but that the Lord Himself should have descended to him who had fallen from the right way, and should have raised him when thus cast down; and should have approached him, One to one, as a friend comes to a friend when he is unfortunate, and is plunged in great distress! For that He acted thus out of His great kindness, the very words too which He spoke to him evidently show His ineffable affection. And why do I say, *all* the words? The first utterance signifies at once His tenderness. For He said not, what it was probable a person treated so contemptuously would say, "O wicked, yea most wicked man! When thou has enjoyed so great favor from Me, and has been honored with such a sovereignty, being exalted above all the creatures upon the earth for no merit of thine own; and having received in actual deeds the pledges of My care, and a true manifestation of My Providence, didst thou esteem a wicked and pestiferous demon, the enemy of thy salvation, to be worthy of more credit than thy Lord and Benefactor? What proof did he give of regard for

thee, like that which I have done? Did I not make for thee the heaven, the earth, the sea, the sun, the moon, and all the stars? For truly none of the angels needed this work of creation; but for thee, and for thy recreation, I made so great and excellent a world; and didst thou esteem mere words alone, a false engagement, and a promise full of deceit, as more worthy to be believed than the kindness and providence that was manifested by deeds; that thou gives thyself over to him, and didst trample My laws under foot!" These words, and more of this kind, one who had been treated contemptuously would probably say. But God acted not so; but quite in the contrary manner. For by His first word He at once raised him up from his dejection, and gave the fearful and trembling man confidence, by being the first Himself to call him, or rather, not by merely calling him first, but by addressing him by his own familiar appellation, and saying, "Adam, where art thou?" Thus He shewed His tenderness, and the great regard He had for him. For ye must all know, that this is a mark of intimate friendship. And thus those who call upon the dead are wont to do, continually repeating their names. And so, on the other hand, those who entertain hatred and enmity against any, cannot bear to mention the very names of those who have aggrieved them. Saul, for instance, though he had sustained no injury from David, but had wronged him exceedingly, since he abhorred and hated him, could not endure to mention his proper name; but when all were seated together, not seeing David to be present, what said he? He said not, "Where is David? But, 'Where is the son of Jesse?'" calling him by his father's name. And again, the Jews did the same with respect to Christ, for since they abhorred and hated Him, they did not say, "Where is Christ?" but, "Where is that man?"

7. But God, willing to show even by this that sin had not quenched His tenderness, nor disobedience taken away His favor toward him, and that He still exercised His Providence and care for the fallen one, said, "Adam, where art thou?" not being ignorant of the place where he was, but because the mouth of those who have sinned is closed up; sin turning the tongue backward, and conscience taking hold of it; so that such persons remain speechless, held fast in silence as by a kind of chain. And God wishing therefore to invite him to freedom of utterance, and to give him confidence, and to lead him to make an apology for his offences, in order that he might obtain some forgiveness, was Himself the first to call; cutting off much of Adam's distress by the familiar appellation, and dispelling his fear, and opening by this address the mouth that was shut. Hence also it was that he said, "Adam, where art thou?" "I left thee," says he, "in one situation, and I find thee in another. I left thee in confidence and glory; and I now find thee in disgrace and silence!" And observe the care of God in this instance. He called not Eve;—He called not the serpent,—but him who had sinned in the lightest degree of all, he brings first to the tribunal, in order that beginning from him who was able to find some degree of excuse, He might pass a more merciful sentence, even against her who had sinned the most. And judges, indeed, do not deign to make inquiry in their own person of their fellow-servants, and those who are partakers of a common nature with them, but putting forward some one of their attendants to intervene, they instruct him to convey their own questions to the criminal; and through him they say and hear whatever

they wish, when they examine the offenders. But God had no need of a go-between in dealing with man; but Himself in His own person at once judges and consoles him. And not only this is wonderful, but also that he corrects the crimes that had been committed. For judges in general, when they find thieves and grave-robbers, do not consider how they may make them better, but how they may make them pay the penalty of the offences committed. But God, quite on the contrary, when He finds a sinner, considers not how He may make him pay the penalty, but how He may amend him, and make him better, and invincible for the future. So that God is at the same time a Judge, a Physician, and a Teacher; for as a Judge He examines, and as a Physician He amends, and as a Teacher He instructs those who have sinned, directing them unto all spiritual wisdom.

8. But if one short and simple speech thus demonstrates the care of God, what if we should read through this whole judgment, and unfold its entire records? See how all Scripture is consolation and comfort? But of these records we will speak at a befitting season; before that, however, it is necessary to state at what time this Book was given; for these things were not written in the beginning, nor at once when Adam was made, but many generations afterwards; and it were worthwhile to enquire for what reason this delay took place, and why at length they were given to the Jews only, and not to all men; and why written in the Hebrew tongue; and why in the wilderness of Sinai? For the Apostle doth not mention the place merely in a cursory manner; but shews that in that circumstance too there was a great subject of contemplation for us, when he says to

us: "For these are two covenants, the one from Mount Sinai, which gendered to bondage."

9. Other things too besides these it were to our purpose to enquire into. But I see that the time doth not permit us to launch our discourse upon so wide a sea; wherefore prudently reserving these to a fit season, we would again address you on the subject of abstinence from oaths; and we would entreat your Charity to use much diligence respecting this matter. For what is it but an absurdity, that not even a servant dares to call his master by name, nor to mention him unceremoniously, and casually, but that he should everywhere bandy about the name of the Lord of Angels familiarly with much irreverence! And if it be necessary to take the book of the Gospel, thou receives it with hands that have been first washed; and fearfully and tremblingly, with much reverence and devotion; and dost thou unceremoniously bandy about upon thy tongue the Lord of the Gospel? Do you desire to learn how the Powers above pronounce that Name; with what awe, with what terror, with what wonder? "I saw the Lord," says the prophet, "sitting upon a throne, high, and lifted up; around Him stood the Seraphim; and one cried unto another, and said, Holy, Holy, Holy, Lord God of Sabbath; the whole earth is full of His glory!" Perceives thou, with what dread, with what awe, they pronounce that Name, whilst glorifying and praising Him? But thou, in thy prayers and supplications, calls upon Him with much listlessness; when it would become thee to be full of awe, and to be watchful and sober! But in oaths, where it is wholly unsuitable that this wonderful Name should be introduced, there thou makes a long string of divers forms of imprecation! What pardon then, or what excuse shall we have, howsoever we may

plead this "custom"? It is said, that a certain heathen orator, by a kind of foolish habit, was continually moving his right shoulder as he went along. He conquered this habit, however, by fastening sharp knives on each side over his shoulders, so that the fear of being cut controlled the member in its unseasonable movement by fear of the wound! Do thou too, then, act thus with regard to thy tongue, and instead of the knife, suspend over it the fear of God's chastisement, and thou wilt assuredly get the better! For it seems impossible, utterly impossible, that those should ever be overcome, who are solicitous and earnest about this, and really make it their business.

10. Ye applaud what is now said, but when ye have amended, ye will applaud in a greater degree not only us, but also yourselves; and ye will hear with more pleasure what is spoken; and ye will call upon God with a pure conscience, who is so sparing of thee, O man! That He says, "Neither shalt thou swear by thy head." But thou so despises Him as to swear even by His glory. "But what shall I do," says one, "with those who impose necessity on me?" What kind of necessity can there be, O man? Let all men understand that thou wilt choose to suffer anything rather than transgress the law of God; and they will abstain from compelling thee. For as a proof that it is not an oath which rendered a man worthy of credit, but the testimony of his life, the uprightness of his conversation, and his good reputation, many have often split their throats with swearing, and yet have been able to convince no one; whereas others by a mere expression of assent, have been esteemed more deserving of belief than they who swore never so much. Knowing, therefore, all these things, and placing before our eyes the punishment that is in store for those who swear, as well as for those

who swear falsely, let us abstain from this evil custom, that advancing from hence to the correction of what remains, we may enjoy the blessedness of the life to come, which God grant that we may all be found worthy to obtain, by the grace and love toward man of our Lord Jesus Christ, through Whom and with Whom to the Father with the Holy Ghost be glory, and power, and honor, now and ever, and world without end. Amen.

Homily VIII.

An exhortation to virtue—and particularly upon the passage, "God was walking in Paradise in the cool of the day:"—and again on the subject of abstaining from oaths.

Ye have lately heard, how all Scripture brings consolation and comfort, although it be an historical narrative. For instance, "In the beginning, God created the heaven and the earth," was an historical declaration; but it was shewn in our discourse, that this sentence was one pregnant with comfort; as, for example, that God made us a twofold table, by spreading out the sea and the land at the same time; by kindling above the twofold lights, the sun and moon; by determining the twofold seasons of their course, the day and night, the one for labor, and the other for rest. For the night ministers to us no less benefit than the day. But as I said with reference to trees, those which are barren, rival in their utility those which bear fruit; since we are thus not necessitated to touch those trees which are pleasant for food, for the purposes of building. The wild and untamed animals are also subservient to our need, in no less a degree than the tame animals; by driving us together, through the fear of them, into cities; making us more cautious, and binding us to one another; and by exercising the strength of some, and freeing others from their sicknesses; for the physicians concoct many medicines out of these; and by reminding us of our ancient sin. For when I hear it said, "The fear of you, and the dread of you, shall be upon all the wild beasts of the earth:" and then observe, that this honor was afterwards curtailed, I am reminded of sin, which hath dissipated the fear of us, and undermined our authority. Thus I become a better and a wiser man, whilst I learn the harm that sin hath occasioned us. As then, what I said was, that the things alluded to, and others of a similar kind, which God, who is the Maker, knows of, contribute not a little to our present life; so now also I say, that the night no less than the day brings along with it its advantage, being a rest from labors, and a medicine for disease. Often, indeed, physicians, though exerting themselves in many ways, and preparing an endless variety of remedies, are not able to deliver the man who is laboring under infirmity. But sleep coming upon him of its own accord hath entirely removed the disease, and freed them from an infinite deal of trouble. Night, again, is not only a medicine for bodily labors, but also for mental diseases, in giving rest to anguished souls. Ofttimes it happened that someone hath lost a son; and comforters without number have been of no avail to withdraw him from tears and groans. But on the approach of night, conquered by the despotic power of sleep, he hath closed his eyelids in slumber, and received some small relief from the miseries of the day time.

2. And now, I pray you, let us proceed to the subject which hath given rise to these observations. For

well I know, that ye are all eagerly awaiting this matter; and that each one of you is in pain till he learn on what account this Book was not given from the beginning. But even now I do not see that the time is fit for a discourse on this subject. And why so? Because the week hath nearly arrived at its close with us, and I fear to touch upon a subject, the exposition of which I should presently afterwards be obliged to cut short. For the subject requires of us several days in succession, and a continuous effort of memory: wherefore we must again defer it. But take it not amiss! We will assuredly pay you the debt with interest; for thus it is expedient both for you, and for us who are to discharge it. Meanwhile, however, let us now speak on that subject which we left out yesterday. And what was it we left out yesterday? "God was walking," it says, "in Paradise in the cool of the day." What is here meant, I ask? "God was walking!" God was not walking; for how should He do this who is everywhere present and fills all things? But He caused a perception of this sort in Adam, in order that he might collect himself; that he might not be careless; that in flying and in hiding himself, he might present beforehand some portion of the excuse, even before any words had passed. For even as those who are about to be led to the tribunal, to sustain the charges respecting the crimes they have committed, present themselves before those who are to try them with a squalid, begrimed, sad, and subdued visage, in order that from their appearance, they may incline them to loving-kindness, mercy, and forgiveness, so also did it happen in the case of Adam. For it was necessary that he should be led to this Tribunal in a subdued state. Therefore God took him beforehand, and humbled him. But that someone was walking there, he perceived; but whence came he to suppose that God was walking there? Such is the habitual custom of those who have committed sin. They are suspicious of all things; they tremble at shadows; they are in terror at every sound, and they imagine that everyone is approaching them in a hostile manner. Often therefore the guilty, when they observe people running on another business, suppose that they are come against them; and when others are conversing one with another on quite a different subject, they that are conscious of sin suppose they are conversing about them.

3. For such is the nature of sin, that it betrays whilst no one finds fault; it condemns whilst no one accuses; it makes the sinner a timid being; one that trembles at a sound; even as righteousness has the contrary effect. Hear, at least, how the Scripture describes this cowardice of the former, and this boldness of the latter. "The wicked flee when no man pursues." How doth he flee when no man pursues? He hath that within which drives him on—an accuser in his conscience; and this he carries about everywhere; and just as it would be impossible to flee from himself, so neither can he escape the persecutor within; but wherever he goes, he is scourged, and hath an incurable wound! But not such is the righteous man. Of what nature then is he? Hear: "The righteous is bold as a lion!" Such a man was Elias. He saw, for instance, the king coming towards him, and when he said, "Why is it that thou perverts Israel?" he answered, "I pervert not Israel, but thou and thy father's house." Truly, the just man is bold as a lion; for he stood up against the king just as a lion doth against some vile cur. Although the one had the purple, the other had the sheepskin, which was the more venerable garment of the two; for that purple brought forth the grievous famine; but

this sheepskin effected a liberation from that calamity! It divided the Jordan! It made Elisha a two-fold Elias! O how great is the virtue of the Saints! Not only their words; not only their bodies, but even their very garments are always esteemed venerable by the whole creation. The sheepskin of this man divided the Jordan! The sandals of the Three Children trampled down the fire! The word of Elisha changed the waters, so that it made them to bear the iron on their surface! The rod of Moses divided the Red Sea and cleft the rock! The garments of Paul expelled diseases! The shadow of Peter put death to flight! The ashes of the holy Martyrs drive away demons! For this reason they do all things with authority, even as Elias did. For he looked not on the diadem, nor the outward pomp of the king, but he looked on the soul clad in rags, squalid, begrimed, and in a more wretched condition than that of any criminal; and seeing him the captive and slave of his passions, he despised his power. For he seemed to see a king but in a scene, and not a real one. For what was the advantage of outward abundance, when the poverty within was so great? And what harm could outward poverty do, when there was such a treasure of wealth within? Such a lion also was the blessed Paul; for when he had entered into the prison, and only raised his voice, he shook all the foundations; he gnawed in pieces the fetters, employing not his teeth, but words; on which account it were fitting to call such men not merely lions, but something more than lions; for a lion ofttimes, after he hath fallen into a net, is taken; but the Saints when they are bound, become still more powerful; just as this blessed man did then in the prison, having loosed the prisoners, shaken the walls, and bound the keeper, and overcome him by the word of godliness. The lion utters his voice, and puts all the wild beasts to flight. The Saint utters his voice, and drives away the demons on every side! The weapons of the lion are a hairy mane, pointed claws, and sharp teeth. The weapons of the righteous man are spiritual wisdom, temperance, patience, contempt of all present things. Whoever hath these weapons shall not only be able to deride wicked men, but even the adverse powers themselves.

4. Study then, O man, the life according to God, and no one shall conquer thee at any time; and although thou maybe accounted the most insignificant of men, thou shalt be more powerful than all. On the other hand, if thou art indifferent about virtue of soul, though thou wert the most powerful of men, thou wilt easily be worsted by all that assail thee. And the examples already quoted proved this. But if thou art desirous, I will also endeavor to teach thee by actual facts the unconquerableness of the righteous, and the vulnerable condition of sinners. Hear then how the prophet intimates both these particulars. "The ungodly," says he, "are not so, but are like the chaff which the wind scattered away from the face of the earth." For even as chaff lies exposed to the gusts of wind, and is easily caught up and swept along, so is also the sinner driven about by every temptation; for whilst he is at war with himself, and bears the warfare about with him, what hope of safety does he possess; betrayed as he is at home, and carrying with him that conscience, which is a constant enemy? Such, however, is not the nature of the righteous man. But what manner of man is he? Hear the same prophet, saying, "They that trust in the Lord are as Mount Zion." What means then, "As Mount Zion?" "He shall not be shaken," says he, "forever." For whatever engines thou brings up, whatever darts thou

hurls, desiring to overturn a mountain, thou wilt never be able to prevail; for how canst thou? Thou wilt break in pieces all thine engines, and exhaust thine own strength. Such also is the righteous man. Whatever blows he may receive, he suffered no evil therefrom; but destroyed the power of those who take counsel against him, and not of men only, but of demons. Thou hast heard often what engines the Devil brought up against Job; but not only did he fail to overthrow that mountain, but drew back exhausted, his darts broken to pieces, and his engines rendered useless, by that assault!

5. Knowing these things, let us take heed to our life; and let us not be earnest as to the goods that perish; neither as to the glory that goes out; nor as to that body which growth old; nor as to that beauty which is fading; nor as to that pleasure which is fleeting; but let us expend all our care about the soul; and let us provide for the welfare of this in every way. For to cure the body, when diseased, is not an easy matter to everyone; but to cure a sick soul is easy to all; and the sickness of the body requires medicines, as well as money, for its healing; but the healing of the soul is a thing that is easy to procure, and devoid of expense. And the nature of the flesh is with much labor delivered from those wounds which are troublesome; for very often the knife must be applied, and medicines that are bitter; but with respect to the soul there is nothing of this kind. It suffices only to exercise the will, and the desire, and all things are accomplished. And this hath been the work of God's providence. For inasmuch as from bodily sickness no great injury could arise, (for though we were not diseased, yet death would in any case come, and destroy and dissolve the body); but everything depends upon the health of our souls; this being by far the

more precious and necessary, He hath made the medicating of it easy, and void of expense or pain. What excuse therefore, or what pardon shall we obtain, if when the body is sick, and money must be expended on its behalf, and physicians called in, and much anguish endured, we make this so much a matter of our care (though what might result from that sickness could be no great injury to us), and yet treat the soul with neglect? And this, when we are neither called upon to pay down money; nor to give others any trouble; nor to sustain any sufferings; but without any of all these things, by only choosing and willing, have it in our power to accomplish the entire amendment of it; and knowing assuredly that if we fail to do this, we shall sustain the extreme sentence, and punishments, and penalties, which are inexorable! For tell me, if any one promised to teach thee the healing art in a short space of time, without money or labor, would you not think him a benefactor? Would you not submit both to do and to suffer all things, whatsoever he who promised these things commanded? Behold, now, it is permitted thee without labor to find a medicine for wounds, not of the body, but of the soul, and to restore it to a state of health, without any suffering! Let us not be indifferent to the matter! For pray what is the pain of laying aside anger against one who hath aggrieved thee? It is a pain, indeed, to remember injuries, and not to be reconciled! What labor is it to pray, and to ask for a thousand good things from God, who is ready to give? What labor is it, not to speak evil of anyone? What difficulty is there in being delivered from envy and ill-will? What trouble is it to love one's neighbor? What suffering is it not to utter shameful words, nor to revile, nor to insult another? What fatigue is it not to swear? For again I return to this same admonition. The labor of swearing is indeed exceedingly great. Oftentimes, whilst under the influence of anger or wrath, we have sworn, perhaps, that we would never be reconciled to those who have injured us. Yet afterwards, when our wrath was quenched, and our anger allayed, desiring to be reconciled, and restrained by the obligation of these oaths, we have suffered the same anguish, as if we were in a snare, and held fast by indissoluble bonds. Of which fact the Devil being aware, and understanding clearly that anger is a fire; that it is easily extinguished, and that when it is extinguished, then reconciliation and love follows; wishing this fire to remain unquenched, he often binds us by an oath; so that although the anger should cease, the obligation of the oath remaining may keep up the fire within us; and that one of these two things may take place, either that being reconciled we are forsworn, or that not being reconciled we subject ourselves to the penalties of cherishing malice.

6. Knowing these things then, let us avoid oaths; and let our mouth continually practice the saying, "Believe me;" and this will be to us a foundation for all pious behavior; for the tongue, when it has been disciplined to use this one expression, is ashamed, and would blush to utter words that are disgraceful and ugly; and should it at any time be drawn away by habit, it will be checked again, by having many accusers. For when any one observes him who is not a swearer giving utterance to foul words, he will take his advantage over him, and ridicule, and exclaim tauntingly, "Thou who says in all affairs, 'Believe me,' and ventures not to utter an oath, dost thou disgrace thy tongue with these shameful expressions?" So that being forcibly urged by

those who are with us, even if unwilling, we shall return again to a pious behavior. "But what," says one, "if it be necessary to take an oath?" Where there is a transgression of the law, there is no such thing as necessity. "Is it possible then," it is replied, "not to swear at all?" What says thou? Hath God commanded, and dares thou to ask if it be possible for His law to be kept? Why, truly it is a thing impossible that His law should not be kept; and I am desirous to persuade you from present circumstances of this; that so far from its being impossible not to swear, it is impossible to swear. For behold, the inhabitants of the city were commanded to bring in a payment of gold, such as it might have seemed beyond the power of many to do; yet the greater part of the sum has been collected; and you may hear the tax gatherers saying, "Why delay, man? Why put us off from day to day? It is not possible to avoid it. It is the law of the Emperor, which admits of no delay." What says thou, I ask? The Emperor hath commanded thee to bring in thy money, and it is impossible not to bring it in! God hath commanded thee to avoid oaths! And how says thou, it is impossible to avoid them!

7. I am now for the sixth day admonishing you in respect of this precept. Henceforth, I am desirous to take leave of you, meaning to abstain from the subject, that ye may be on your guard. There will no longer be any excuse or allowance for you; for of right, indeed, if nothing had been said on this matter, it ought to have been amended of yourselves, for it is not a thing of an intricate nature, or that requires great preparation. But since ye have enjoyed the advantage of so much admonition and counsel, what excuse will ye have to offer, when ye stand accused before that dread tribunal, and are required to give

account of this transgression. It is impossible to invent any excuse; but of necessity you must either go hence amended, or, if you have not amended, be punished, and abide the extremest penalty! Thinking, therefore, upon all these things, and departing hence with much anxiety about them, exhort ye one another, that the things spoken of during so many days may be kept with all watchfulness in your minds, so that whilst we are silent, ye instructing, edifying, exhorting one another, may exhibit great improvement; and having fulfilled all the other precepts, may enjoy eternal crowns; which God grant we may all obtain, through the grace and lovingkindness of our Lord Jesus Christ, by whom and with whom be glory, to the Father, together with the Holy Ghost, for ever and ever. Amen.

Homily IX.

Commendation of those who had laid aside the practice of swearing. It is shown that no one need scruple about hearing the divine oracles in the Church after a meal. Answer to the question, Why it was so long before the Holy Scriptures were given? Comment on the passage, "The heavens declare the glory of God," with a description of the natural world. And finally, an admonition against swearing.

1. It was but lately that I spoke to you as I do now to you again! And O that I could be always with you,— yea, rather am I always with you, though not by bodily presence, yet by the power of love! For I have no other life but you, and the care of your salvation. As the husbandman hath no other anxiety, but about his seeds

and his harvests; and the pilot about the waves and the harbors; so the preacher is anxious with respect to his auditors and their progress, even as I am at the present time! Wherefore I bear you all upon my mind, not only here, but also at home. For if the multitude be great, and the measure of my heart be narrow, yet love is wide; and "ye are not straitened in us." I will not add what follows next, for neither are we straitened with you. Whence is this apparent? Because I have met with many who have said, "We have performed the precept, by making rules for each other, defining penalties for those who swear, and enforcing punishment upon those who transgress this law." A punishment which is indeed well becoming you, and which is a sign of the greatest charity. For I am not ashamed of making myself busy in these matters, since this love of interference does not proceed from idle curiosity but from tender care. For if it be no reproach to the physician to make enquiry concerning the patient, neither is it any fault in us to be ever asking about your salvation; since thus being informed what has been accomplished, and what has been left undone, we shall be able to apply the further remedies with the requisite knowledge. These things we have ascertained by enquiry; and we give thanks to God that we have not sown our seed upon rocks, nor dropped it amidst thorns; and that we have neither needed much time, nor long delay, in order that we might reap the harvest. On this account I have you continually upon my heart. On this account I do not feel the labors of teaching, being eased of the burden by the profit of the hearer. This reward is, indeed, sufficient to recruit our strength, to give us wings, to elevate us, and to persuade us to undergo the utmost toil on your behalf.

2. Since therefore ye have manifested much generosity of feeling, suffer us to discharge the further debt of which we gave a promise the other day; although indeed I see not all present who were here when I made the promise. What, I would ask, can be the cause of this? What hath repelled them from our table? He that hath partaken of a bodily meal, it would seem, has thought it an indignity after receiving material food, to come to the hearing of the divine oracles. But not rightly do they think thus. For if this were improper, Christ would not have gone through His large and long discourses after that mystic supper; and if this had been unsuitable, He would not, when He had fed the multitude in the desert, have communicated His discourses to them after that meal. For (if one must say something startling on this point), the hearing of the divine oracles at that time is especially profitable. For when thou hast made up thy mind that after eating and drinking thou must repair also to the assembly, thou wilt assuredly be careful, though perchance with reluctance, of the duty of sobriety; and wilt neither be led away at any time into excess of wine, or gluttony. For the thought, and the expectation of entering the church, schools thee to partake of food and drink with becoming decency; lest, after thou hast entered there, and joined thy brethren, you should appear ridiculous to all present, by smelling of wine, and unmannerly eructation. These things I now speak not to you who are now present, but to the absent; that they may learn them through your means. For it is not having eaten that hinders one's hearing, but listlessness. But thou whilst deeming it to be a condemnation not to fast, then adds another fault, which is far greater and heavier, in not being a partaker of this sacred food; and having nourished

the body, thou consumes the soul with famine. Yet what kind of apology hast thou for doing this? For in the matter of fasting thou hast, perhaps, bodily weakness to plead, but what hast thou to say with respect to hearing? For surely weakness of body is no impediment to thy partaking of the divine oracles! If I had said, "Let no one who has breakfasted mix with us;" "let no one who has eaten be a hearer," you would have had some kind of excuse; but now, when we would fain drag, entice, and beseech you to come, what apology can ye have for turning away from us? The unfit hearer is not he that hath eaten and drunk; but he who gives no heed to what is said, who yawns, and is slack in attention, having his body here, but his mind wandering elsewhere, and such a one, though he may be fasting, is an unprofitable hearer. On the other hand, the man who is in earnest, who is watchful and keeps his mind in a state of attention, though he may have eaten and drunk, will be our most suitable hearer of all. For this rule, indeed, very properly prevails with relation to the secular tribunals and councils. Inasmuch as they know not how to be spiritually wise, therefore they eat not to nourishment, but to bursting; and they drink often to excess. For this reason, as they render themselves unfit for the management of their affairs, they shut up the court-houses and council-chambers in the evening and at midday. But here there is nothing of this sort,—God forbid! But he who has eaten will rival him who fasts, as far as regards sobriety of soul; for he eats and drinks, not so as to distend the stomach, or to darken the reason, but in such a way as to recruit the strength of the body when it has become weakened.

3. But enough of this admonition. It is time now to deal with our subject; although our mind holds back and

shrinks from giving this instruction, on account of those who are not come. And just as an affectionate mother when she is about to spread out her table, grieves and laments when all her children are not there, thus also do I now suffer; and when I think of the absence of our brethren, I am reluctant to discharge my debt. But ye have it in your power to rid me of this tardiness. For if ye promise me that ye will convey to them an exact report of all I say, we shall readily pay you down the whole; for thus the instructions, charitably afforded on your part, will make up to them for their absence; and ye will hear me the more attentively, knowing that you must necessarily give an account of these things to others. In order then that our subject may be made the clearer, let us take it up and repeat it from the beginning. We were enquiring, then, the other day, "On what account the Scriptures were delivered after so many years. For this Book was delivered neither in the time of Adam, nor of Noah, nor of Abraham, but in that of Moses. And I hear many who say, that if the Book was profitable, it ought to have been delivered from the very beginning; but if it was useless, it ought not to have been delivered afterwards. But this is an obsolete argument; for it is not quite true that anything which is profitable ought to have been delivered from the beginning, nor if anything was delivered from the beginning, is it quite necessary that the same should continue afterwards. For example; Milk is useful, yet it is not always given; but it is given to us only when we are children; and solid food is useful; but no one ever gives it us in the beginning of our life, but when we have passed out of the age of childhood. Again, the summer season is useful; but it does not show itself constantly; and the winter season is advantageous; yet this too makes room for others. What then? Do they say that the Scriptures are not useful? I reply; they are most useful and most necessary. And if so useful, for what reason then, say they, were they not delivered to us from the beginning? It was because God was desirous of instructing the nature of man, not by letters, but by things. But what does the expression "by things" signify? By means of the Creation itself.

4. Observe then, how the Apostle, alighting upon this same topic, and directing himself to those very Greeks who said, that they had not from the beginning learnt the knowledge of God from the Scriptures, frames his answer. Having said that, "the wrath of God is revealed from heaven against all ungodliness and unrighteousness of men, who hold the truth in unrighteousness;" when he saw that he was met by an objection; and that many would still enquire, from whence the Gentiles knew the truth of God, he goes on to add, "Because that which may be known of God is manifest in them." But how is it manifest in them? How were they able to know God, and who hath shewed? Declare this. "God," says he, "hath shewed it unto them." In what manner? By the sending of what kind of prophet? What evangelist? What kind of teacher? If the holy Scriptures were not yet given. "The invisible things of Him," says he, "from the creation of the world are clearly seen, being understood by the things that are made, even His eternal Power and Godhead."1408 But what he means is just this, He hath placed His Creation in the midst, before the eyes of all men; in order that they may guess at the Creator from His works; which, indeed, another writer has referred to; "For from the greatness and beauty of the creatures, proportionably the Maker of them is seen." See

the greatness? Marvel at the power of Him that made it! See the beauty? Be astonished at the wisdom which adorned it! This it was which the prophet signified when he said, "The heavens declare the glory of God." How then, tell me, do they declare it? Voice they have none; mouth they possess not; no tongue is theirs! How then do they declare? By means of the spectacle itself. For when thou sees the beauty, the breadth, the height, the position, the form, the stability thereof during so long a period; hearing as it were a voice, and being instructed by the spectacle, thou adores Him who created a body so fair and strange! The heavens may be silent, but the sight of them emits a voice, that is louder than a trumpet's sound; instructing us not by the ear, but through the medium of the eyes; for the latter is a sense which is more sure and more distinct than the former.

5. For if God had given instruction by means of books, and of letters, he who knew letters would have learnt what was written; but the illiterate man would have gone away without receiving any benefit from this source, unless someone else had introduced him to it; and the wealthy man would have purchased the Bible, but the poor man would not have been able to obtain it. Again, he who knew the language that was expressed by the letters, might have known what was therein contained; but the Scythian, and the Barbarian, and the Indian, and the Egyptian, and all those who were excluded from that language, would have gone away without receiving any instruction. This however cannot be said with respect to the heavens; but the Scythian, and Barbarian, and Indian, and Egyptian, and every man that walks upon the earth, shall hear this voice; for not by means of the ears, but through the sight, it reaches our understanding. And of the

things that are seen, there is one uniform perception; and there is no difference, as is the case with respect to languages. Upon this volume the unlearned, as well as the wise man, shall be alike able to look; the poor man as well as the rich man; and wherever any one may chance to come, there looking upwards towards the heavens, he will receive a sufficient lesson from the view of them: and the prophet himself intimated and indicated this fact, that the creation utters this voice so as to be intelligible to barbarians, and to Greeks, and to all mankind without exception, when he spoke on this wise; "There is no speech, nor language, where there voice is not heard." What he means is to this effect, that there is no nation or tongue which is unable to understand this language; but that such is their utterance, that it may be heard of all mankind. And that not merely of the heavens, but of the day and night. But how of the day and night? The heavens, indeed, by their beauty and magnitude, and by all the rest, astonish the beholder, and transport him to an admiration of the Creator; but as to the day and night, what can these show us of the same kind? Nothing certainly of the same kind, but other things which are not inferior to them; as for example; the harmony, and the order which they so accurately observe. For when thou considers how they distribute between them the whole year, and mutually divide the length of the whole space, even as if it were by a beam and scales, thou wilt be astonished at Him who hath ordered them! For just as certain sisters dividing their father's inheritance among themselves with much affection, and not insulting one another in the smallest degree, even so too the day and the night distribute the year with such an equality of parts, with the utmost accuracy; and keep to their own boundaries, and never push one another aside. Never hath the day been long in winter; and in like manner never hath the night been long in summer, whilst so many generations have passed away; but during so great an interval and length of time one hath not defrauded the other even in the smallest degree; not of half an hour's space, no, nor of the twinkling of an eye!

6. Therefore also the Psalmist, struck with astonishment at the equality of this distribution, exclaimed, "Night unto night showed knowledge." If thou knows how to meditate wisely on these matters, thou wilt admire the Being who fixed these immoveable boundaries even from the beginning. Let the avaricious hear these things; and those who are coveting the wealth of others; and let them imitate the equality of the day and night. Let those who are puffed up and high-minded also hear; and those who are unwilling to concede the first places to others! The day gives place to the night, and does not invade the territory of others! But thou, whilst always enjoying honor, canst thou not bear to share it with thy brethren? Consider also with me the wisdom of the Lawgiver. In winter He hath ordered that the night should be long; when the germs are tender, and require more coolness; and are unable to sustain the hotter rays of the sun; but when they are somewhat grown, the day again increases with them, and becomes then the longest, when the fruit has now attained ripeness. And this is a beneficial arrangement not only for seeds, but for our bodies. For since during winter, the sailor, and the pilot, and the traveler, and the soldier, and the farmer, sit down for the most part at home, fettered by the frost; and the season is one of idleness; God hath appointed that the greater part of this time should be consumed in night, in

order that the length of the day might not be superfluous, when men were unable to do anything. Who can describe the perfect order of the seasons; and how these, like some virgins dancing in a circle, succeed one another with the happiest harmony; and how those who are in the middle cease not to pass over to the opposite ones with a gradual and noiseless transition? Therefore, neither are we overtaken by the summer immediately after winter; nor by the winter immediately after the summer; but mid-way the spring is interposed; that while we gently and gradually take up one season after the other, we may have our bodies hardened to encounter the summer heat without uneasiness. For since sudden changes to opposite extremes are productive of the worst injury and disease, God hath contrived that after winter we should take up the spring, and after the spring the summer; and after the summer the autumn; and thus transport us to winter, so that these changes from seasons which are opposite, should come upon us harmlessly and by degrees, through the aid of intermediate ones. Who then is so wretched and pitiable, that beholding the heavens; and beholding sea, and land; and beholding this exact adjustment of the seasons, and the unfailing order of day and night, he can think that these things happen of their own accord, instead of adoring Him who hath arranged them all with a corresponding wisdom!

    7. But I have yet somewhat more to say on this head. For not only, indeed, does the magnitude and beauty of the creation, but also the very manner of it, display a God who is the artificer of the universe. For since we were not present at the beginning, whilst he was engaged in the work of forming and creating all things; nor had we been present, could we have known how they came into

being, the power that disposed them being invisible; He hath made the mode of this creation to become our best teacher, by compounding all things in a manner which transcends the course of nature. Perhaps what I have said, is not sufficiently clear. Therefore it is necessary that I should again repeat it in a clearer manner. All men, then, must admit that it is the course of nature for water to be supported on the earth, and not the earth on the waters. For the earth being a certain dense, hard, unyielding, and solid substance, is easily able to support the nature of water; but the water, which is fluid, and rare, and soft, and diffusive, and giving way to all it meets with, must be unable to support any solid body, though it were of the lightest kind. Often indeed when a small pebble fails upon it, it yields, and makes way, and sends it down to the bottom. When therefore thou beholds not a small pebble, but the whole earth borne upon the waters, and not submerged, admire the power of Him who wrought these marvelous things in a supernatural manner! And whence does this appear, that the earth is borne upon the waters? The prophet declares this when he says, "He hath founded it upon the seas, and prepared it upon the floods." And again: "To him who hath founded the earth upon the waters." What says thou? The water is not able to support a small pebble on its surface, and yet bears up the earth, great as it is; and mountains, and hills, and cities, and plants, and men, and brutes; and it is not submerged! What do I say? Is not submerged? How comes it to pass, that since the water has been in close contact with it below, during so long a period, it has not been dissolved, and the whole of it become mud? For the substance of wood, when soaked in water but a little time, is rotted and dissolved; and why do I say of wood? What can be firmer than iron? Yet often this is softened, when it remains a long time in water; and well it may. For it derives its substance from the earth. Therefore many run-away servants, when they make their escape, dragging their shackles and chains along with them, go to brooks of water, and thrust their shackled feet therein, and after making the iron softer by this means, they easily break it by striking it with a stone. Iron, forsooth, is softened, and wood is rotted, and stones are worn away by the nature of water; yet so great a mass as the earth hath remained such a length of time lying upon the waters, without being either submerged, or dissolved, and destroyed!

8. And who is there that must not feel astonished and amazed at these things; and confidently pronounce that they are not the works of nature, but of that Providence which is above nature? Therefore one speaks thus: "Who hanged the earth upon nothing." And another observes, "In His hands are the corners of the earth." And again: "He hath laid the foundation of it upon the seas." And these declarations, though they seem contrary to one another, have yet an entire agreement. For he that said, "He hath laid the foundation of it upon the seas," meant the same thing as he did who declared, "He hath hung it upon nothing." For its standing upon the waters is just the same thing as hanging upon nothing. Where then is it suspended and placed? Hear the same one saying, "In His hands are the corners of the earth." Not that God hath hands, but that thou may know that His power it is, providing for all things which holds together and supports the body of the earth! But if thou believes not what I now say, believe what thou beholds! For even in another element it is possible to find this admirable workmanship. For it is the nature of fire to tend upwards, and to be

always mounting aloft; and although you force and constrain it never so much, it cannot submit to have its course directed downwards. For often, when we are carrying a lighted torch, although we incline its head downwards, we cannot compel the force of the flame to direct itself to the ground; but still it turns upward, and passes from below toward that which is above. But with respect to the sun, God hath made it quite the contrary. For He hath turned his beams toward the earth, and made his light to direct itself downward, all but saying to him by the very shape (of the heavens), "Look downward.— Shine upon men, for thou wert made for them!" The light, indeed, of a candle cannot be made to submit to this; but this star, great and marvelous as it is, bends downward, and looks toward the earth, which is contrary to the nature of fire; owing to the power of Him who hath commanded it. Would you have me speak of another thing of the like kind? Waters embrace the back of the visible heaven on all parts; and yet they neither flow down, nor are moved out of their place, although the nature of water is not of this kind. For it easily runs together into what is concave; but when the body is of a convex form, it glides away on all sides; and not even a small portion is capable of standing upon such a figure. But, lo! This wonder is found to exist in the heavens; and the prophet, again, to intimate this very circumstance, observes, "Praise the Lord, ye waters that are above the heavens." Besides, the water hath not quenched the sun; nor hath the sun, which hath gone on his way beneath for so long a time, dried up the water that lies above.

9. Do you desire that we should lead thee down again to the earth, and point out the marvel? See not this sea abounding with waves, and fierce winds; yet this sea,

spacious, and large, and furious as it is, is walled in with a feeble sand! Mark also the wisdom of God, He permitted it not to be at rest, nor tranquil, lest you should suppose its good order to be of mere natural regulation; but remaining within its limits, it lifts up its voice, and is in tumult, and roars aloud, and raises its waves to a prodigious height. But when it comes to the shores, and beholds the sand, it breaks up, and returns back again within itself; teaching thee, by both these things, that it is not the work of nature that it remains within its boundaries, but the work of Him whose power restrains it! For this cause accordingly He hath made the wall feeble; and hath not encompassed these shores with wood, or stone, or mountains, lest you should impute the regulation of the elements to such things. And, therefore, God Himself, upbraiding the Jews with this very circumstance, said, "Fear ye not Me, which have placed the sand for the bound of the sea that it cannot pass it." But the marvelous thing is not this only, that He hath made a great and admirable world; and that He hath compacted it in a way above the usual course of nature; but that He hath also constituted it out of opposite things; such as hot and cold, dry and moist, fire and water, earth and air, and that these contrary elements, of which this whole universe consists, though continually at strife one with another, are not consumed of one another. The fire hath not overrun and burnt up all things; the water hath not overflowed and drowned the whole earth. With respect to our bodies, however, these effects really take place; and upon the increase of the bile, fever is generated; and the whole animal frame sustains an injury; and when there is a superabundance of phlegm, many diseases are produced which destroy the animal. But in the case of the universe, nothing of this kind happens; but each thing remains held as it were by a kind of bridle and band; preserving, by the will of the Creator, its own boundaries; and their strife becomes a source of peace to the whole. Are not these things evident even to a blind man? And are not even the simple easily able to comprehend, that they were made, and are upheld, by some Providence? For who is so silly and senseless, that beholding such a mass of substances, such beauty, such combination, the continual strife of such vast elements, their opposition, and yet durability, would not reason with himself and say, "If there were not some Providence to uphold the mass of these bodies, not permitting the universe to fall to pieces, it could not remain; it could not have been lasting. So perfect is the order of the seasons, such the harmony of the day and night, so many the kinds of brute animals, and plants, and seeds, and herbs, that preserve their course, and yet, to the present day, none has ever fallen into decay or sudden dissolution.

10. We might continue to speak not only of these things, but also of many others, which are even more profound; and might moralize even upon the Creation itself; but reserving these subjects for the morrow, let us earnestly endeavor to retain what has been said, and to convey it to the rest. I know indeed, that the abstruseness of these speculations has seemed strange to your ears; but if we be a little vigilant, and accustom ourselves to them, we shall easily be able to teach others. Meanwhile, it is necessary farther to say this to your Charity. Even as God hath given us glory by means of this great creation, so let us also glorify Him by a pure conversation! "The heavens declare the glory of God," though only seen; and we therefore should declare God's glory not only in speaking, but in silence, and in astonishing all men by the

brightness of our life. For He says, "Let your light so shine before men, that they may see your good works, and glorify your Father which is in heaven." For when an unbeliever beholds thee, who art a believer, subdued, modest, and orderly in manners, he will wonder and say, "Truly great is the God of the Christians! What manner of men hath He formed? What, and from what hath He made them? Hath He turned them from men into angels? If anyone treats them contemptuously, they revile not! If anyone beats them, they are not enraged! If anyone does them an injury, they pray for him who has put them in pain! They have no enemy! They know nothing of cherishing malice! They are guiltless of vain babbling! They have not learnt to utter a falsehood! They cannot endure a false oath, or rather, they swear not at all, but would prefer to have their tongue cut out, rather than to let an oath proceed out of their mouth!" Such are the things which we should give them cause to say of us; and we should exterminate our evil habit of oaths, and pay at least as much honor to God, as we do to our more valuable garments. For how truly absurd is it, that when we have one garment better than the rest, we do not suffer ourselves to be continually wearing it; and yet everywhere we draggle about the name of God without concern, or ceremony! Let us not, I earnestly pray and beseech you, let us not thus despise our own salvation; but the care which we have used respecting this precept from the beginning, let us carry on even to the end. For I thus continually exhort you on the subject of oaths, not as though condemning you of listlessness, but inasmuch as I have seen that ye are for the most part reformed, I press you, and am urgent, that the whole work should be finished off, and come to its perfection. Even so act the spectators of public games. They excite those who are near the prize, with the more vehemence. Let us, then, by no means become weary; for we have nearly reached the completion of this amendment; and the difficulty was at the beginning. But now that the greater part of the evil habit has been cut away, and less remains to correct, no labor is necessary, but we only need a moderate degree of watchfulness, and diligence for some short time, in order that we ourselves being amended, may also become instructors to others; and that we may behold the Holy Passover with much confidence, and that with much pleasure we may reap a double or treble measure of the customary gladness of the festival. For not so much does it delight us to be delivered from the toil and fatigue of fasting, as to meet that holy season with an illustrious and well-earned crown; a crown indeed that is never to fade!

11. But in order that the amendment may take place the more quickly, do this which I tell thee. Inscribe upon the wall of thy house, and upon the wall of thy heart, that "flying sickle;" and think that it is flying forth on occasion of the curse, and constantly remember it. And if thou observes another person swearing, restrain, forbid, and be careful for him, and be careful for thine own domestics. For if we would look to this, that we might not merely correct ourselves, but also bring others to the same point, we shall ourselves quickly arrive at the goal; since while we undertake to instruct others, we shall be ashamed and blush, should we in our own case seem to leave those things unperformed, which we enjoin upon them. There is no need to say more; for much has been already spoken on these matters; and these things are now said only by way of remembrance. But may God, who is more sparing of our souls than we are, make us perfect in

this, and every good work; that so having completed the whole fruit of righteousness, we may be found worthy of the kingdom of heaven, through the grace and lovingkindness of our Lord Jesus Christ, through Whom, and with Whom, to the Father, with the Holy Ghost, be glory, for ever and ever. Amen.

Homily X.
Commendation of those who came to hear after taking a meal.—Observations on the physiology of the natural world; and against those who deify the creation; and on the duty of not swearing.

1. I joy, and rejoice with you all, that ye have actually put in practice that admonition of ours, which we lately made with respect to those who were absent, for the reason that they were not fasting. For I think that many of those who have dined are to-day present; and go to fill up this goodly assemblage; and that this is the fact, I conjecture from the more brilliant spectacle that I see around me, and the greater concourse of hearers. Not in vain, it seems, did I lately spend so many words on their account, appealing to your Charity, to draw them to their Mother;1436 and to persuade them that it is lawful, even after bodily nourishment, to partake also of that which is spiritual. And in which case, beloved, I ask, did ye act for the better; at the time of the last assembly when after your meal ye turned to your slumbers; or now, when after the meal ye have presented yourselves at the hearing of the divine laws? Was it best when ye loitered about in the forum, and took part in meetings which were no wise profitable; or now, when ye stand with your own brethren, and hear the prophetic oracles? It is no disgrace, beloved,

to have eaten, but after eating to remain at home, and so to be deprived of this sacred banquet. For whilst thou remains at home, thou wilt be more slothful and supine; but coming here thou wilt shake off all slumber and listlessness; and laying aside not only listlessness, but also all sadness, thou wilt be more at ease, and in better heart in all the events that may happen.

2. What need then is there to say more? Stand only nigh the man who fasts, and thou wilt straightway partake of his good odor; for fasting is a spiritual perfume; and through the eyes, the tongue, and every part, it manifests the good disposition of the soul. I have said this, not for the purpose of condemning those who have dined, but that I may shew the advantage of fasting. I do not, however, call mere abstinence from meats, fasting; but even before this, abstinence from sin; since he who, after he has taken a meal, has come hither with suitable sobriety, is not very far behind the man who fasts; even as he who continues fasting, if he does not give earnest and diligent heed to what is spoken, will derive no great benefit from his fast. He who eats, and yet takes a part in the sacred assembly with suitable earnestness, is in much better case than he who eats not at all, and remains absent. This abstinence will by no means be able to benefit us as much as the participation in spiritual instruction conveyed to us benefit and advantage. Where indeed, besides, wilt thou hear the things upon which thou meditates here? Wert thou to go to the bench of justice? Quarrels and contentions are there! Or into the council-chamber? There is anxious thought about political matters! Or to thine home? Solicitude on the subject of thy private affairs afflicts thee in every direction! Or wert thou to go to the conferences and debates of the forum? Everything there is

earthly and corruptible! For all the words that pass among those assembled there, are concerning merchandize, or taxes, or the sumptuous table, or the sale of lands, or other contracts, or wills, or inheritances, or some other things of that kind. And should you enter even into the royal halls, there again you would hear in the same way all discoursing of wealth, or power, or of the glory which is held in honor here, but of nothing that is spiritual. But here on the contrary everything relates to heaven, and heavenly things; to our soul, to our life, the purpose for which we were born, and why we spend an allotted time upon earth, and on what terms we migrate from hence, and into what condition we shall enter after these things, and why our body is of clay, what also is the nature of death, what, in short, the present life is, and what the future. The discourses that are here made by us contain nothing at all of an earthly kind, but are all in reference to spiritual things. Thus, then, it is that we shall have made great provision for our salvation, and shall depart hence with a good hope.

3. Since, therefore, we did not scatter the seed in vain, but ye hunted out all who were absent, as I exhorted you; suffer us now to return you a recompense; and having reminded you of a few things that were said before, to repay you again what remains. What then were those matters that were before treated of? We were enquiring how, and in what manner, before the giving of the Scriptures, God ordered His dispensation toward us; and we said, that by means of the creation He instructed our race, stretching out the heavens, and there openly unfolding a vast volume, useful alike to the simple and the wise, to the poor and to the rich, to Scythians and to barbarians, and to all in general who dwell upon the earth;

a volume which is much larger than the multitude of those instructed by it. We discoursed also at length concerning the night, and the day, and the order of these, as well as of the harmony which is strictly preserved by them; and much was said respecting the measured dance of the seasons of the year, and of their equality. For just as the day defrauded not the night even of half an hour throughout the whole year, so also do these distribute all the days among themselves equally. But, as I said before, not only does the greatness and beauty of the creation shew forth the Divine Architect, but the very manner likewise in which it is compacted together, and the method of operation, transcending as it does, the ordinary course of nature. For it would have been in accordance with nature for water to be borne upon the earth; but now we see, on the contrary, that the earth is supported by the waters. It would have been in accordance with nature that fire should tend upwards; but now on the contrary we see the beams of the sun directed towards the earth; and the waters to be above the heavens, yet not falling away; and the sun running below them, yet not quenched by the waters, nor dispelling their moisture. Besides these things we said that this whole universe consists of four elements, these being adverse to and at strife with one another; yet one does not consume the other, although they are mutually destructive. Whence it is evident that some invisible power bridles them, and the will of God becomes their bond.

4. To-day, I wish to dwell a little more on this subject. Arouse yourselves, however, and give earnest heed unto us! And that the wonder may appear more clearly, I will draw the lesson concerning these things from our own bodies. This body of ours, so short, and

small, consists of four elements; viz. of what is warm, that is, of blood; of what is dry, that is, of yellow bile; of what is moist, that is, of phlegm; of what is cold, that is, of black bile. And let no one think this subject foreign to that which we have in hand. "For He that is spiritual judges all things; yet He Himself is judged of no man." Thus also Paul touched upon principles of agriculture, whilst discoursing to us of the Resurrection; and said, "Thou fool; that which thou sows is not quickened, except it die." But if that blessed man brought forward questions of agriculture, neither should anyone blame us if we handle matters pertaining to medical science. For our discourse is now respecting the Creation of God; and this groundwork of ideas will be necessary for our purpose. As, therefore, I said before, this body of ours consists of four elements; and if either revolts against the whole, death is the result of this revolt. As for instance, by a superabundance "of bile" fever is produced; and should this proceed beyond a certain measure, it effects a rapid dissolution. Again, when there is an excess of the cold element, paralyses, agues, apoplexies, and an infinite number of other maladies are generated. And every form of disease is the effect of an excess of these elements; when either of them overpassing its own bounds, acts the part of a tyrant against the rest, and mars the symmetry of the whole. Interrogate then him who says, that all things are spontaneous and self-produced. If this little and diminutive body, having the advantage of medicines, and of medical skill, and of a soul within which regulates it, and of much moral wisdom, as well as innumerable other helps, be not always able to continue in a state of order, but often perishes, and is destroyed, when some disturbance takes place within it; how could a world like this, containing substances of such vast bulk and compounded of those same elements, remain during so long a time without any disturbance, unless it enjoyed the advantage of a manifold providence? Neither would it be reasonable to suppose that this body, which has the benefit of superintendence both without and within, should scarcely be sufficient for its own preservation; and that a world such as this is, enjoying no such superintendence, should during so many years suffer nothing of that sort which our body suffers. For how, I ask, is it that not one of these elements hath gone beyond its own boundaries, nor swallowed up all the rest? Who hath brought them together from the beginning? Who hath bound? Who hath bridled? Who hath held them together during so long a period? For if the body of the world were simple and uniform, what I speak of would not have been so impossible. But when there hath been such a strife between the elements, even from the beginning; who so senseless as to think that these things would have come together, and remained together when united, without One to effect this conjunction? For if we who are evil-affected towards one another not by nature, but by will, cannot come spontaneously to an agreement as long as we remain at variance, and hold ourselves ungraciously towards one another; if we have yet need of someone else to bring us into a state of conjunction; and after this conjunction further to clench us, and persuade us to abide by our reconciliation, and not again to be at variance; how could the elements, which neither partake of sense nor reason, and which are naturally adverse, and inimical to each other, have come together, and agreed and remained with one another, if there were not some ineffable Power which effected this conjunction; and after this conjunction, always restrained them by the same bond?

5. Do you not perceive how this body wastes away, withers, and perishes after the secession of the soul, and each of the elements thereof returns to its own appointed place? This very same thing, indeed, would also happen to the world, if the Power which always governs it had left it devoid of Its own providence. For if a ship does not hold together without a pilot, but soon founders, how could the world have held together so long a time if there was no one governing its course? And that I may not enlarge, suppose the world to be a ship; the earth to be placed below as the keel; the sky to be the sail; men to be the passengers; the subjacent abyss, the sea. How is it then that during so long a time, no shipwreck has taken place? Now let a ship go one day without a pilot and crew, and thou wilt see it straightway foundering! But the world, though subsisting now five thousand years, and many more, hath suffered nothing of the kind. But why do I talk of a ship? Suppose one hath pitched a small hut in the vineyards; and when the fruit is gathered, leaves it vacant; it stands, however, scarce two or three days, but soon goes to pieces, and tumbles down! Could not a hut, forsooth, stand without superintendence? How then could the workmanship of a world, so fair and marvelous; the laws of the night and day; the interchanging dances of the seasons; the course of nature chequered and varied as it is in every way throughout the earth, the sea, the sky; in plants, and in animals that fly, swim, walk, creep; and in the race of men, far more dignified than any of these, continue yet unbroken, during so long a period, without some kind of providence? But in addition to what has been said, follow me whilst I enumerate the meadows, the

gardens, the various tribes of flowers; all sorts of herbs, and their uses; their odors, forms, disposition, yea, but their very names; the trees which are fruitful, and which are barren; the nature of metals,—and of animals,—in the sea, or on the land; of those that swim, and those that traverse the air; the mountains, the forests, the groves; the meadow below, and the meadow above; for there is a meadow on the earth, and a meadow too in the sky; the various flowers of the stars; the rose below, and the rainbow above! Would you have me point out also the meadow of birds? Consider the variegated body of the peacock, surpassing every dye, and the fowls of purple plumage. Contemplate with me the beauty of the sky; how it has been preserved so long without being dimmed; and remains as bright and clear as if it had been only fabricated to-day; moreover, the power of the earth, how its womb has not become effete by bringing forth during so long a time! Contemplate with me the fountains; how they burst forth and fail not, since the time they were begotten, to flow forth continually throughout the day and night! Contemplate with me the sea, receiving so many rivers, yet never exceeding its measure! But how long shall we pursue things unattainable! It is fit, indeed, that over every one of these which has been spoken of, we should say, "O Lord, how hast Thou magnified Thy works; in wisdom hast Thou made them all."

6. But what is the sapient argument of the unbelievers, when we go over all these particulars with them; the magnitude, the beauty of the creation, the prodigality, the munificence everywhere displayed? This very thing, say they, is the worst fault, that God hath made the world so beautiful and so vast. For if He had not made it beautiful and vast, we should not have made a

god of it; but now being struck with its grandeur, and marveling at its beauty, we have thought it to be a deity. But such an argument is good for nothing. For that neither the magnitude, nor beauty of the world is the cause of this impiety, but their own want of understanding, is what we are prepared to show, proved by the case of ourselves, who have never been so affected. Why then have "we" not made a deity of it? Do we not see it with the same eyes as themselves? Do we not enjoy the same advantage from the creation with themselves? Do we not possess the same soul? Have we not the same body? Do we not tread the same earth? How comes it that this beauty and magnitude hath not persuaded us to think the same as they do? But this will be evident not from this proof only, but from another besides. For as a proof that it is not for its beauty they have made a deity of it, but by reason of their own folly, why do they adore the ape, the crocodile, the dog, and the vilest of animals? Truly, "they became vain in their imaginations, and their foolish heart was darkened. Professing themselves to be wise, they became fools."

7. Nevertheless, we will not frame our answer from these things only, but will also say something yet further. For God, foreseeing these things of old, destroyed, in His wisdom, this plea of theirs. On this account He made the world not only wonderful and vast, but also corruptible and perishable; and placed therein many evidences of its weakness; and what He did with respect to the Apostles, He did with respect to the whole world. What then did He with respect to the Apostles? Since they used to perform many great and astonishing signs and wonders, He suffered them constantly to be scourged, to be expelled, to inhabit the dungeon, to

encounter bodily infirmities, to be in continual tribulations, lest the greatness of their miracles should make them to be accounted as gods amongst mankind. Therefore when He had bestowed so great favor upon them, He suffered their bodies to be mortal, and in many cases obnoxious to disease; and did not remove their infirmity, that He might give full proof of their nature. And this is not merely my assertion, but that of Paul himself, who says, "For though I would desire to glory, I shall not be a fool; but now I forbear, lest any man should think of me above that which he sees me to be, or that he hears of me." And again, "But we have this treasure in earthen vessels." But what is meant by "earthen vessels?" In this body, he means, which is mortal and perishable. For just as the earthen vessel is formed from clay and fire, so also the body of these saints being clay, and receiving the energy of the spiritual fire, becomes an earthen vessel. But for what reason was it thus constituted, and so great a treasure, and such a plentitude of graces entrusted to a mortal and corruptible body? "That the excellency of the power may be of God, and not of us." For when thou sees the Apostles raising the dead, yet themselves sick, and unable to remove their own infirmities, thou may clearly perceive, that the resurrection of the dead man was not effected by the power of him who raised him, but by the energy of the Spirit. For in proof, that they were frequently sick, hear what Paul says respecting Timothy, "Use a little wine for thy stomach's sake, and thine often infirmities." And again, of another he says, "But Trophimus I have left at Miletus sick." And writing to the Philippians, he said, "Epaphroditus was sick nigh unto death." For if, when this was the case, they accounted them to be gods, and prepared to do sacrifice unto them, saying, "The gods are come down to us in the likeness of men;" had such infirmities not existed, to what extent of impiety might not men have proceeded, when they beheld their miracles? As then in this case, because of the greatness of these signs, He suffered their nature to remain in a state of infirmity, and permitted those repeated trials, in order that they might not be thought to be gods, thus likewise He did with respect to the creation, a thing nearly parallel to this. For He fashioned it beautiful and vast; but on the other hand corruptible.

8. And both of these points the Scriptures teach, for one in treating of the beauty of the heavens thus speaks; "The heavens declare the glory of God." And again, "Who hath placed the sky as a vault, and spread it out as a tent over the earth." And again, "Who holds the circle of heaven." But another writer, shewing that although the world be great and fair, it is yet corruptible, thus speaks; "Thou, Lord, in the beginning hast laid the foundation of the earth, and the heavens are the works of Thine hands. They shall perish, but Thou remains, and they all shall wax old as doth a garment, and as a vesture shalt Thou fold them up, and they shall be changed." And again, David says of the sun, that "he is as a bridegroom coming out of his chamber, and rejoices as a giant to run his course." See how he places before thee the beauty of this star, and its greatness? For even as a bridegroom when he appears from some stately chamber, so the sun sends forth his rays under the East; and adorning the heaven as it were with a saffron-colored veil, and making the clouds like roses, and running unimpeded all the day; he meets no obstacle to interrupt his course. Beholds thou, then, his beauty? Beholds thou his greatness? Look also at the proof of his weakness! For a certain wise man, to

make this plain, said, "What is brighter than the sun, yet the light thereof suffers eclipse." Nor is it only from this circumstance that his infirmity is to be perceived, but also in the concourse of the clouds. Often, at least, when a cloud passes underneath him, though emitting his beams, and endeavoring to pierce through it, he has not strength to do so; the cloud being too dense, and not suffering him to penetrate through it. "He nourishes the seeds, however," replies someone—Yes—still he does not nourish them by himself, but requires the assistance of the earth, and of the dew, and of the rains, and of the winds, and the right distribution of the seasons. And unless all these things concur, the sun's aid is but superfluous. But this would not seem to be like a deity, to stand in need of the assistance of others, for that which he wishes to do; for it is a special attribute of God to want nothing; He Himself at least did not in this manner bring forth the seeds from the ground; He only commanded, and they all shot forth. And again, that thou may learn that it is not the nature of the elements, but His command which effects all things; He both brought into being these very elements which before were not; and without the need of any aid, He brought down the manna for the Jews. For it is said, "He gave them bread from heaven." But why do I say, that in order to the perfection of fruits, the sun requires the aid of other elements for their sustenance; when he himself requires the assistance of many things for his sustenance, and would not himself be sufficient for himself. For in order that he may proceed on his way, he needs the heaven as a kind of pavement spread out underneath him; and that he may shine, he needs the clearness and rarity of the air; since if even this become unusually dense, he is not able to show his light; and, on the other hand, he requires coolness and moisture, lest his rays should be intolerable to all, and burn up everything. When, therefore, other elements overrule him, and correct his weakness (overrule as for example, clouds, and walls, and certain other bodies that intercept his light:—or correct his excess, as the dews, and fountains, and cool air), how can such a one be a Deity? For God must be independent, and not stand in need of assistance, be the source of all good things to all, and be hindered by nothing; even as Paul, as well as the prophet Isaiah, says of God; the latter thus making Him speak in His own Person, "I fill heaven and earth, says the Lord." And again, "Am I a God nigh at hand, and not a God afar off?" And again, David says, "I have said unto the Lord, Thou art my Lord, for Thou hast no need of my good things." But Paul, demonstrating this independence of help, and shewing that both these things especially belong to God; to stand in need of nothing, and of Himself to supply all things to all; speaks on this wise, "God that made the heaven, and the earth, and the sea, Himself needed not anything, giving to all life and all things."

9. It would indeed be easy for us to take a survey of the other elements, the heaven, the air, the earth, the sea, and to shew the imbecility of these, and how each requires the assistance of his neighbor, and without this assistance, is lost and destroyed. For as it regards the earth, if the fountains fail it, and the moisture infused from the sea and the rivers, it quickly perishes by being parched. The remaining elements too stand in need of one another, the air of the sun, as well as the sun of the air. But not to protract this discourse; in what has been said, having given a sufficient supply of reasons to start from for those who are willing to receive them, we shall be

content. For if the sun, which is the most surprising part of the whole creation, hath been proved to be so feeble and needy, how much more the other parts of the universe? What then I have advanced (offering these things for the consideration of the studious), I will myself again shew you in discourse from the Scriptures; and prove, that not only the sun, but also the whole universe is thus corruptible. For since the elements are mutually destructive, and when much cold intervenes, it chastens the force of the sun's rays; and on the other hand, the heat prevailing, consumes the cold; and since the elements are both the causes and subjects of contrary qualities, and dispositions, in one another; it is very evident that these things offer a proof of great corruptibility; and of the fact, that all these things which are visible, are a corporeal substance.

10. But since this subject is too lofty for our simplicity, permit me now to lead you to the sweet fountain of the Scriptures, that we may refresh your ears. For we will not discourse to you of the heaven and the earth separately, but will exhibit the Apostle declaring this very thing to us concerning the whole creation, in these plain terms, that the whole creation is now in bondage to corruption; and why it is thus in bondage, and at what time it shall be delivered from it, and unto what condition it shall be translated. For after he had said, "The sufferings of this present time are not worthy to be compared with the glory that shall be revealed in us;" he goes on to add; "For the earnest expectation of the creature waited for the manifestation of the sons of God. For the creature was made subject to vanity, not willingly, but by reason of Him who hath subjected the same in hope." But what he intends is to this effect; "The

creature," he says, "was made corruptible;" for this is implied in the expression, "being made subject to vanity." For it was made corruptible by the command of God. But God so commanded it for the sake of our race; for since it was to nurture a corruptible man, it was necessary itself should also be of the same character; for of course corruptible bodies were not to dwell in an incorruptible creation. But, nevertheless, he tells us, it will not remain so. "The creature also itself shall be delivered from the bondage of corruption;" and afterwards, for the purpose of shewing when this event shall take place, and through whom, he adds, "Into the glorious liberty of the sons of God." For when we are raised, his meaning is, and assume incorruptible bodies; then also this body of the heaven, the earth, and the whole creation, shall be incorruptible, and imperishable. When, therefore, thou beholds the sun arising, admire the Creator; when thou beholds him hiding himself and disappearing, learn the weakness of his nature, that thou may not adore him as a Deity! For God hath not only implanted in the nature of the elements this proof of their weakness, but hath also bidden His servants, that were but men, command them; so that although you should not know their servitude from their aspect, thou may learn, from those who have commanded them, that they are all thy fellow-servants. Therefore it was, that Joshua, the son of Nave, said, "Let the sun stand still in Gibeon, and the moon over against the valley of Ajalon." And again the prophet Isaiah made the sun to retrace his steps, under the reign of Hezekiah; and Moses gave orders to the air, and the sea, the earth, and the rocks. Elisha changed the nature of the waters; the Three Children triumphed over the fire. Thou sees how God hath provided for us on either hand; leading us by the beauty of the elements to the knowledge of His divinity; and, by their feebleness, not permitting us to lapse into the worship of them.

11. For the sake of all these things then, let us glorify Him, our Guardian; not only by words, but also by deeds; and let us shew forth an excellent conversation, not only in general, but in particular with regard to abstinence from oaths. For not every sin brings the same penalty; but those which are easiest to be amended, bring upon us the greatest punishment: which indeed Solomon intimated, when he said, "It is not wonderful if anyone be taken stealing; for he steals that he may satisfy his soul that is hungry; but the adulterer, by the lack of understanding, destroys his own soul." But what he means is to this effect. The thief is a grievous offender, but not so grievous a one as the adulterer: for the former, though it be a sorry reason for his conduct, yet at the same time has to plead the necessity arising from indigence; but the latter, when no necessity compels him, by his mere madness rushes into the gulf of iniquity. This also may be said with regard to those who swear. For they have not any pretext to allege, but merely their contempt.

12. I know, indeed, that I may seem to be too tedious and burdensome; and that I may be thought to give annoyance by continuing this admonition. But nevertheless, I do not desist, in order that ye may even be shamed by my shamelessness to abstain from the custom of oaths. For if that unmerciful and cruel judge, paying respect to the importunity of the widow, changed his custom, much more will ye do this; and especially when he who is exhorting you, doth it not for himself, but for your salvation. Or rather, indeed, I cannot deny that I do this for myself; for I consider your benefit as my own

success. But I could wish that you, even as I labor, and weary myself for your safety, would in like manner make your own souls a matter of anxiety to yourselves; and then assuredly this work of reformation would be perfected. And what need is there to multiply words? For if there were no hell, neither punishment for the contumacious, nor reward for the obedient; and I had come to you, and asked this in the way of a favor, would ye not have consented? Would ye not have granted my petition, when I asked so trifling a favor? But when it is God who asks this favor, and for the sake of yourselves, who are to grant it, and not for Himself, Who is to receive it; who is there so ungracious, who is there so miserable and wretched, that he will not grant this favor to God, when He asks it; and especially when he himself who grants it, is in future to enjoy the benefit of it? Considering these things then, repeat over to yourselves, when ye depart hence, all that has been said; and correct in every way those who take no heed to it; to the end that we may receive the recompense of other men's good actions, as well as our own, through the grace and lovingkindness of our Lord Jesus Christ, by Whom, and with Whom be glory to the Father, with the Holy Ghost, for ever and ever. Amen.

St. John Chrysostom

Homily XI.

Thanksgiving to God for deliverance from the evils expected owing to the sedition; and recollection of the events which took place at the time. Also against those who find fault with the structure of the human body, and in general concerning the creation of man; and, in conclusion, on success in avoiding oaths.

1. When I think of the past tempest, and of the present calm, I cease not saying, "Blessed be God, who makes all things, and changes them; who hath brought light out of darkness; who leads to the gates of hell, and brings back; who chastises, but kills not." And this I desire you too to repeat constantly, and never to desist. For if He hath benefitted us by deeds, what pardon shall we deserve, if we do not requite Him even by words. Therefore, I exhort that we never cease to give Him thanks; since if we are grateful for the former benefits, it is plain that we shall enjoy others also, which are greater. Let us say, then, continually, Blessed be God, who hath permitted us to spread before you in security the accustomed table, whilst He hath also granted you to hear our word with assurance of safety! Blessed be God, that we no longer run hither flying from the danger without, but only from desire to hear; that we no longer meet one another with agony, trembling, and anxious thoughts; but with much confidence, having shaken off all our fear. Our condition, indeed, on former days was nothing better than that of those who are tossed up and down in the midst of the deep; and expecting shipwreck every hour. We were scared all day long by innumerable rumors, and disturbed

and agitated on every side; and were every day busy and curious to know who had come from the court? What news he had brought? And whether what was reported was true or false? Our nights too we passed without sleep, and whilst we looked upon the city, we wept over it, as if it were on the eve of its destruction.

2. For this cause yourselves too kept silence on those former days, because the whole city was empty, and all had migrated to the deserts, and because those who were left behind were overshadowed by the cloud of despondency. For the soul when once it is filled with despondency, is not apt to hear anything that may be said. For this cause, when the friends of Job came, and saw that tragedy of his house, and the just man sitting down upon the dunghill, and covered with sores, they rent their garments, and groaned and sat down by him in silence; making it manifest that nothing is so suitable to the afflicted at first, as quiet and silence. For the calamity was too great for consolation. Therefore also the Jews, whilst they were in bondage to work in clay and the brick-making, when they saw Moses come to them, were not able to give heed to his words, by reason of their failure of spirit, and their affliction. And what marvel is it that faint-hearted men have felt this, when we find that the Disciples also fell into the same infirmity. For after that mystic Supper, when Christ took them apart and discoursed with them, the disciples at first asked Him more than once, "Whither goes Thou?" But when He had told them what evils they should in a little while afterwards encounter, the wars, and the persecutions, and the universal enmity, the stripes, the prisons, the tribunals, the appearance before magistrates; then, their souls oppressed as by a heavy burthen with the dread of the

things He had spoken, and with the sadness of these approaching events, remained henceforth in a state of stupor. Christ, therefore, perceiving their consternation, reproved it by saying, "I go to My Father, and no one among you asked Me, Whither goes Thou? But because I have said these things unto you, sorrow hath filled your hearts." For this reason also we were silent for some time past, awaiting the present opportunity. For if a person who is about to ask a favor of any one, though the request be a reasonable one, waits a fitting occasion to propose it, that he may find him who is to grant the petition in a mild and well-disposed frame of mind; and that receiving assistance from the favorable opportunity, he may obtain the benefit; how much rather is it necessary that the speaker should seek a fit season, so that he may address his discourse to an auditor well affected, and free from all care and despondency; which accordingly we have done.

3. Inasmuch, then, as ye have now shaken off despondency, we are desirous to recall you to the recollection of former matters; so that our discourse may be rendered the clearer to you. For what we said of the creation, that God not only made it beautiful, and wonderful, and vast, but also weak and corruptible; and moreover that He hath established divers proofs of this; ordering both these circumstances for our advantage; leading us on by its beauty to admiration of Him who framed it: and by its weakness leading us away from the worship of the creature; this we may see, take place also in the case of the body. For with respect to this too there are many among the enemies to the truth, as well as among those who belong to our own ranks, who make it a subject of enquiry, why it was created corruptible and frail? Many also of the Greeks and heretics affirm, that it

was not even created by God. For they declare it to be unworthy of God's creative art, and enlarge upon its impurities, its sweat, its tears, its labors, and sufferings, and all the other incidents of the body. But, for my part, when such things are talked of, I would first make this reply. Tell me not of man, fallen, degraded and condemned. But if you would learn what manner of body God formed us with at the first, let us go to Paradise, and survey the Man that was created at the beginning. For that body was not thus corruptible and mortal; but like as some statue of gold just brought from the furnace, that shines splendidly, so that frame was free from all corruption. Labor did not trouble it, nor sweat deface it. Cares did not conspire against it; nor sorrows besiege it; nor was there any other affection of that kind to distress it. But when man did not bear his felicity with moderation, but threw contempt upon his Benefactor, and thought a deceiving demon more worthy of credit than God who cared for him, and who had raised him to honor, and when he expected to become himself a god, and conceived thoughts above his proper dignity, then,—then indeed it was that God, to humble him by decisive acts, made him mortal, as well as corruptible; and fettered him with such varied necessities; not from hatred or aversion, but in care for him, and to repress at the very outset that evil and destructive pride; and instead of permitting it to proceed any further, He admonished Him by actual experience, that he was mortal and corruptible; thus to convince him that he must never again think or dream of such things as he had done. For the devil's suggestion, was, "Ye shall be as gods." Desiring then utterly to eradicate this idea, God made the body subject to much suffering and disease; to instruct him by its very nature that he must never again entertain such a thought. And that this is true, is really most evident from what befell him; for after such an expectation, he was condemned to this punishment. Consider also with me the wisdom of God in this matter. He did not allow him to be the first to die, but permitted his son to suffer this death; in order that seeing before his eyes the body corrupting and decaying, he might receive a striking lesson of wisdom from that spectacle; and learn what had come to pass, and be duly chastened before he departed hence.

4. Really then, as I said, this point is apparent from what has already taken place; but it will be made no less clear from what yet remains to be stated. For if whilst we are fettered with such necessities of the body; and whilst it is the lot of all men to die, to suffer corruption, to molder in the sight of all, and to dissolve into dust, so that the Gentile philosophers made one and the same comprehensive definition of the human race (for when asked what man was, they answered, he is an animal, rational and mortal); if, forsooth, whilst all admitted this, there were some who dared in the opinion of the multitude to immortalize themselves; and notwithstanding that the very sense of sight bore witness to their mortality, were ambitious to be called gods, and were honored as such; to what a length of impiety would not many men have proceeded, if death had not gone on teaching all men the mortality and corruptibility of our nature? Hear, for instance, what the prophet says of a barbarian king, when seized with this frenzy. "I will exalt," says he, "my throne above the stars of heaven; and I will be like unto the Most High." Afterwards, deriding him, and speaking of his death, he says, "Corruption is under thee, and the worm is thy covering;" but his meaning is, "Do you dare, O man,

whom such an end is awaiting, to entertain such imaginations?" Again, of another, I mean the king of the Tyrians, when he conceived the like aims, and was ambitious to be considered as a God, he says, "Thou art not a God, but a man, and they that pierce thee shall say so." Thus God, in making this body of ours as it is, hath from the beginning utterly taken away all occasion of idolatry.

5. But why dost thou marvel if this hath happened in respect to the body, when even with respect to the soul it is plain, that a similar thing hath taken place. For God made it not mortal, but permitted it to be immortal; He constituted it however subject to forgetfulness, to ignorance, to sadness, and to care; and this, lest regarding its own nobility of birth, it might take up a conceit too high for its proper dignity. For if, even while the case stands thus, some have dared to aver, that it is of the Divine essence; to what a pitch of frenzy would they not have reached, if it had been devoid of these imperfections? What, however, I affirmed respecting the creation, I affirm also respecting the body, that both these things alike excite my admiration of God; that He hath made it corruptible; and that in its very corruptibility, He hath manifested His own power and wisdom. For that He could have made it of some better material, He hath evidenced from the celestial and the solar substance. For He that made those such as they are, could have made this also like them, had He thought proper to do so. But the cause of its imperfection is what I before adverted to. This circumstance by no means lowers the admiration due to the Creator's workmanship, but rather increases it; for the meanness of the substance, manifests the resource and adaptiveness of His art; since He hath introduced such a

harmony of parts in clay and ashes, and senses so various and manifold and capable of such spiritual wisdom.

6. In proportion, therefore, as you find fault with the meanness of the substance, be so much the more astonished at the greatness of the art displayed. For this reason also, I do not so much admire the statuary who forms a beautiful figure out of gold, as him who, by the resources of art, is able, even in crumbling clay, to exhibit a marvelous and inimitable mold of beauty. In the former case, the material gives some aid to the artist, but in the latter, there is a naked display of his art. Would you learn then, how great the wisdom of the Creator is, consider what it is that is made out of clay? What else is there but brick and tile? Nevertheless, God, the Supreme Artist, from the same material of which only the brick and tile is formed, hath been able to make an eye so beautiful, as to astonish all who behold it, and to implant in it such power, that it can at once survey the high aerial expanse, and by the aid of a small pupil embrace the mountains, forests, hills, the ocean, yea, the heaven, by so small a thing! Tell me not then of tears and rheums, for these things are the fruit of thy sin; but consider its beauty, and visual power; and how it is that whilst it ranges over such an expanse of air, it experiences no weariness or distress! The feet indeed become tired and weakened even after going but a small distance; but the eye, in traversing a space so lofty and so wide, is not sensible of any infirmity. For since this is the most necessary to us of all our members, He has not suffered it to be oppressed with fatigue; in order that the service it renders us might be free and unfettered.

7. But rather, I should say, what language is fully adequate to set forth the whole excellency of this

member? And why do I speak of the pupil and the visual faculty? For if you were to investigate that which seems the meanest of all the members, I mean the eyelashes, you would behold even in these the manifold wisdom of God the Creator! For as it is with respect to the ears of corn; the beards, standing forth as a sort of spears, repel the birds, and do not suffer them to settle upon the fruits, and to break the stalk, which is too tender to bear them; so also is it with regard to the eyes. The hairs of the eyelids are ranged in front, and answer the purpose of beards and spears; keeping dust and light substances at a distance from the eyes, and anything that might incommode the sight; and not permitting the eyelids to be annoyed. Another instance of wisdom, no less remarkable, is to be observed in eyebrows. Who can help being struck by their position? For they do not project to an immoderate degree, so as to obscure the sight; nor do they retire farther back than is fitting; but in the same manner as the eaves of a house, they stand out above, receiving the perspiration as it descends from the forehead, and not permitting it to annoy the eyes. For this purpose too there is a growth of hair upon them, which serves by its roughness to stay what descends from above, and affords the exact protection that is needed, and contributes also much appearance of beauty to the eyes. Nor is this the only matter of wonder! There is another thing also which is equally so. How is it, I ask, that the hairs of the head increase, and are cut off; but those of the eyebrows, not so? For not even this has happened undesignedly, or by chance, but in order that they might not darken the sight too much by becoming very long; an inconvenience from which those suffer who have arrived at extreme old age.

8. And who could possibly trace out all the wisdom which is manifested by means of the brain! For, in the first place, He made it soft, since it serves as a fountain to all the senses. Next, in order that it might not suffer injury owing to its peculiar nature, He fortified it on every side with bones. Further; that it might not suffer from friction, by the hardness of the bones, He interposed a middle membrane: and not only a single one, but also a second; the former being spread out on the underside of the skull, but the latter enveloping the upper substance of the brain, and the first being the harder of the two. And this was done, both for the cause that has been mentioned, and in order that the brain might not be the first to receive the blows inflicted upon the head; but that these membranes first encountering them, might free it from all injury, and preserve it unwounded. Moreover, that the bone which covers the brain is not a single and continuous one, but has many sutures on every side, is a circumstance which contributes much to its security. For a ventilation of the vapors that surround it may easily take place outward through these sutures, so as to prevent it from being suffocated; and if a blow should be inflicted upon it, on any particular point, the damage does not extend to the whole. For if the bone had been one and continuous, the stroke even when it fell upon one part, only, would have injured the whole; but now, by its being divided into many parts, this can never happen. For if one part should chance to be wounded, only the bone that is situated near that part receives injury, but all the rest remain unhurt; the continuity of the stroke being intercepted by the division of the bones, and being unable to extend itself to the adjacent parts. By reason of this God hath constructed a covering for the brain of many bones; and just as when

one builds a house, he lays on a roof, and tiles upon the upper part, so God hath placed these bones above upon the head, and hath provided that the hairs should shoot forth, and serve as a kind of cap for it.

9. The very same thing also He hath done with regard to the heart. For inasmuch as the heart has preeminence over all the members in our body, and that the supreme power over our whole life is entrusted to it, and death happens when it receives but a slight blow; He hath fenced it about on every side with stiff and hard bones, surrounding it by the protection of the breast-bone before, and the blade-bones behind. And what He did with respect to the membranes of the brain, He hath done in this instance also. For in order that it might not be rubbed and pained in striking against the hard bones which encompass it, in the throbbing and quick pulsation to which it is subject in anger and similar affections, He both interposed many membranes there, and placed the lungs by the side of it to act the part of a soft bed to these pulsations, so that the heart may break its force on these without sustaining injury or distress.

But why do I speak of the heart, and of the brain, when if anyone will investigate even the very nails, he will see the manifold wisdom of God displayed in these; as well by their form, as by their substance and position. I might also have mentioned why our fingers are not all equal, and many other particulars besides; but to those who are inclined to attend, the wisdom of God Who created us, will be sufficiently clear from what has been said. Wherefore, leaving this department to be investigated with diligence by those who are desirous of the task, I shall turn myself to another objection.

10. There are many forsooth, who, besides what has been already referred to, bring forward this objection. If man be the king of the brutes, why have many animals an advantage over him in strength, agility, and fleetness? For the horse is swifter, the ox is more enduring, the eagle is lighter, and the lion stronger, than man. What then have we to reply to this argument? Thus much; that from that circumstance we may especially discern the wisdom of God and the honor which He has put upon us. A horse, it is true, is swifter than man, but for making dispatch on a journey, the man is better fitted than the horse. For a horse, though the very swiftest and strongest that may be, can scarcely travel two hundred stadia in a day; but a man, harnessing a number of horses in succession, will be able to accomplish a distance of two thousand stadia. Thus, the advantage which swiftness affords to the horse, intelligence and art afford to the man in a much greater excess. The man, it is true, has not feet so strong as the other, but then he has those of the other which serve him as well as his own. For not one of the brutes has ever been able to subjugate another to his own use; but man has the range of them all; and by that variety of skill which is given him of God, makes each of the animals subservient to the employment best suited to him. For if the feet of men had been as strong as those of horses, they would have been useless for other purposes, for difficult ground, for the summits of mountains, for climbing trees; for the hoof is usually an impediment to treading in such places. So that although the feet of men are softer than theirs, they are still adapted to more various uses, and are not the worse for their want of strength, while they have the power of the horse ministering to their aid, and at the same time they have the advantage over him in variety of

tread. Again, the eagle has his light pinion; but I have reason and art, by which I am enabled to bring down and master all the winged animals. But if you would see my pinion too, I have one much lighter than he; one which can soar, not merely ten or twenty stadia, or even as high as heaven, but above heaven itself, and above the heaven of heavens; even to "where Christ sits at the right hand of God!"

11. Again, the irrational animals have their weapons in their own body; thus, the ox has his horns; the wild boar his tusks; the lion his claws. But God hath not furnished the nature of my body with weapons, but hath made these to be extraneous to it, for the purpose of shewing that man is a gentle animal; and that I have not always occasion to use my weapons, for from time to time I lay these aside, and from time to time resume them. In order then that I might be free and unfettered in this matter, not being at all times compelled to carry my weapons, He hath made these to be separate from my nature. For it is not only in our possessing a rational nature that we surpass the brutes, but we also excel them in body. For God has made this to correspond with the soul's nobility, and fitted to execute its commands. He has not, indeed, made the body such as it is, without reason; but such as it ought to be, as having to minister to a rational soul; so that if it were not such as it is, the operations of the soul would be greatly impeded: and this is manifest from diseases. For if this nice adjustment of the body be diverted from its proper condition in ever so small a degree, many of the soul's energies are impeded; as, for instance, if the brain should become too hot, or too cold. So that from the body it is easy to see much of the Divine Providence, not only because He made it at first

better than it is at present; nor because even now He hath changed it for a useful purpose, but also because He will raise it again to much greater glory.

12. But, if thou art desirous to learn in a different way what wisdom God hath shewn respecting the body, I will mention that by which Paul seems most especially to be constantly struck. But what is this? That He hath made the members to excel one another, though not in the same things? Some He hath appointed to surpass the rest in beauty, and some in strength. Thus, the eye is beautiful, but the feet are stronger. The head is honorable, but it cannot say to the feet, "I have no need of you." And this may be seen too with regard to irrational animals; and the same in all the relations of life. The king, for instance, has need of his subjects, and the subjects of the king; just as the head has need of the feet. And again, as to brutes; some are more powerful than the rest; and some more beautiful. Some there are that delight us; some that nourish; and some that clothe us. Thus the peacock delights; and fowls and swine nourish; sheep and goats provide us clothing; and the ox and ass share our labors. There are also others which provide us with none of these, but which call our powers into active exercise. Thus the wild animals increase the strength of the hunters; and instruct our race by the fear which they inspire, and render us more cautious; and for medical purposes, they supply no small contributions from their bodies. So that if anyone say to thee, "How art thou a lord of the brutes, whilst afraid of the lion?" Answer him, "Things were not ordered in this manner at the beginning, when I was in favor with God, when I dwelt in Paradise. But when I had offended my Master, I fell under the power of those who were my servants! Yet not even now entirely; since I

possess an art by which I overcome the wild animals." So also it happens in great houses; the sons, while they are yet under age, are afraid of many of the servants; but when they have done amiss, their dread is greatly heightened. And this we may say also of serpents, and scorpions, and vipers; that they are formidable to us by reason of sin.

13. And not only as it regards our body, and the various states of life, is this diversity observable; nor is it confined to brutes; but it may be seen also in trees; and the meanest of them may be observed to have an excellence above those which are greater; so that all things are not alike in all, that all may be necessary to us; and that we may perceive the manifold wisdom of the Lord. Do not then lay blame on God on account of the body's corruptibleness, but for this the rather do Him homage, and admire Him for His wisdom and His tender care; His wisdom, that in so corruptible a body He hath been able to display such harmony; His tender care that for the benefit of the soul He hath made it corruptible, that He might repress her vanity, and subdue her pride! Why then did He not make it thus from the beginning, asks someone? It was, I reply, to justify Himself before thee by these very works; and as much as to say by the result itself, "I called thee to greater honor, but thou didst constitute thyself unworthy of the gift, banishing thyself from Paradise! Nevertheless, I will not even now despise thee, but I will correct thy sin, and bring thee back to heaven. Therefore for thine own sake, I have permitted thee so long to decay and suffer corruption, that in the fullness of time the discipline of thy humility might be established; and that thou mightiest never more resume thy former conceit.

14. For all these things then let us give thanks to God who loves man; and for His tender care over us, render Him a recompense, that will also be profitable to ourselves; and as regards the commandment which I so frequently discourse of to you, let us use our utmost diligence! For I will not desist from the exhortation until ye are amended: seeing that what we aim at is not that we may address you seldom or frequently, but that we may continue speaking till we have persuaded you. To the Jews when God said by the prophet, "If ye fast for strife and debate, to what purpose do ye fast for me?" And by us He says to you, "If ye fast unto oaths and perjuries, to what purpose do ye fast? For how shall we behold the sacred Passover? How shall we receive the holy Sacrifice? How shall we be partakers of those wonderful mysteries by means of the same tongue with which we have trampled upon God's law, the same tongue with which we have contaminated the soul? For if no one would dare to receive the royal purple with filthy hands, how shall we receive the Lord's Body with a tongue that has become polluted! For the oath is of the wicked one, but the Sacrifice is of the Lord. "What communion then hath light with darkness, and what concord hath Christ with Belial?"

15. That ye are desirous, indeed, to be rid of this impiety, I know well; but since each man may not be able easily to accomplish this by himself, let us enter into fraternities and partnerships in this matter; and as the poor do in their feasts, when each one alone would not be able to furnish a complete banquet; when they all meet together, they each bring their contribution to the feast; so also let us act. Inasmuch as we are of ourselves too listless, let us make partnerships with each other, and

pledge ourselves to contribute counsel, and admonition, and exhortation, and rebuke and reminiscence, and threatening; in order that from the diligence of each we may all be amended. For seeing that we observe the affairs of our neighbor more sharply than we do our own, let us be watchful of the safety of others, and commit the guardianship of ourselves to them; and let us engage in this pious rivalry, to the end that thus becoming superior to such an evil habit, we may come with boldness to this holy feast; and be partakers of the holy Sacrifice, with a favorable hope and a good conscience; through the grace and lovingkindness of our Lord Jesus Christ, by whom and with whom, be glory to the Father, with the Holy Spirit, for ever and ever. Amen.

Homily XII.

Thanksgiving to God for the pardon granted to the offenders against the Emperor. Physical discourse on the Creation. Proof that God, in creating man, implanted in him a natural law. Duty of avoiding oaths with the utmost diligence.

1. Yesterday I said "Blessed be God!" and to-day again I say the very same thing. For although the evils we dreaded have passed away, we should not suffer the memory of them to disappear; not indeed that we may grieve, but that we may give thanks. For if the memory of these terrors abide with us, we shall never be overtaken by the actual experience of such terrors. For what need have we of the experience, whilst our memory acts the part of a monitor? Seeing then that God hath not permitted us to be overwhelmed in the flood of those

troubles when upon us, let us not permit ourselves to become careless when these are passed away. Then, when we were sad, He consoled us, let us give thanks to Him now that we are joyful. In our agony He comforted us, and did not forsake us; therefore let us not betray ourselves in prosperity by declining into sloth. "Forget not," says one, "the time of famine in the day of plenty." Therefore let us be mindful of the time of temptation in the day of relief; and with respect to our sins let us also act in the same manner. If thou hast sinned, and God hath pardoned thy sin, receive thy pardon, and give thanks; but be not forgetful of the sin; not that you should fret thyself with the thought of it, but that thou may school thy soul, not to grow wanton, and relapse again into the same snares.

2. Thus also Paul did; for having said, "He counted me faithful, putting me into the ministry," he goes on to add, "who was before a blasphemer, a persecutor, and injurious." "Let the life of the servant," says he, "be openly exposed, so that the lovingkindness of the Master be apparent. For although I have received the remission of sins, I do not reject the memory of those sins." And this not only manifested the lovingkindness of the Lord, but made the man himself the more illustrious. For when thou hast learnt who he was before, then thou wilt be the more astonished at him; and when thou sees out of what he came to be what he was, then thou wilt commend him the more; and if thou hast greatly sinned, yet upon being changed thou wilt conceive favorable hopes from this instance. For in addition to what has been said, such an example comforts those who are in despair, and causes them again to stand erect. The same thing also will be the case with regard to our city; for all the events

that have happened serve to shew your virtue, who by means of repentance have prevailed to ward off such wrath, whilst at the same time they proclaim the lovingkindness of God, who has removed the cloud that was so threatening, in consequence of a small change of conduct, and so raises up again all those who are sunk in despair, when they learn, from our case, that he who looks upward for the Divine help, is not to be overwhelmed, though innumerable waves should encompass him on all sides.

3. For who hath seen, who hath ever heard of sufferings such as were ours? We were every day in expectation that our city would be overturned from its foundations together with its inhabitants. But when the Devil was hoping to sink the vessel, then God produced a perfect calm. Let us not then be unmindful of the greatness of these terrors, in order that we may remember the magnitude of the benefits received from God. He who knows not the nature of the disease will not understand the physician's art. Let us tell these things also to our children; and transmit them to the remotest generations, that all may learn how the Devil had endeavored to destroy the very foundation of the city; and how God was able visibly to raise it up again, when it was fallen and prostrate; and did not permit even the least injury to befall it, but took away the fear; and dispelled with much speed the peril it had been placed in. For even through the past week we were all expecting that our substance would be confiscated; and that soldiers would have been let loose upon us; and we were dreaming of a thousand other horrors. But lo! All these things have passed away, even like a cloud or a flitting shadow; and we have been punished only in the expectation of what is dreadful; or

rather we have not been punished, but we have been disciplined, and have become better; God having softened the heart of the Emperor. Let us then always and every day say, "Blessed be God!" and with greater zeal let us give heed to our assembling, and let us hasten to the church, from whence we have reaped this benefit. For ye know whither ye fled at the first; whither ye flocked together; and from what quarter our safety came. Let us then hold fast by this sacred anchor; and as in the season of danger it did not betray us, so now let us not leave it in the season of relief; but let us await with exact attention the stated assemblies and prayers; and let us every day give a hearing to the divine oracles. And the leisure which we spent in busily running about after those who came from the court, whilst we were laboring under anxiety in respect to the evils that threatened us; this let us consume wholly in hearing the divine laws, instead of unseasonable and senseless pastimes; lest we should again reduce ourselves to the necessity of that sort of occupation.

4. On the three foregoing days, then, we have investigated one method of acquiring the knowledge of God, and have brought it to a conclusion; explaining how "the heavens declare the glory of God;" and what the meaning of that is, which is said by Paul; viz. "That the invisible things of Him from the creation of the world are clearly seen, being understood by the things that are made." And we shewed how from the creation of the world, and how by heaven, and earth, the sea, the Creator is glorified. But to-day, after briefly philosophizing on that same subject, we will proceed to another topic. For He not only made it, but provided also that when it was made, it should carry on its operations; not permitting it to be all immoveable, nor commanding it to be all in a state

of motion. The heaven, for instance, hath remained immoveable, according as the prophet says, "He placed the heaven as a vault, and stretched it out as a tent over the earth." But, on the other hand, the sun with the rest of the stars, runs on his course through every day. And again, the earth is fixed, but the waters are continually in motion; and not the waters only, but the clouds, and the frequent and successive showers, which return at their proper season. The nature of the clouds is one, but the things which are produced out of them are different. For the rain, indeed, becomes wine in the grape, but oil in the olive. And in other plants is changed into their juices; and the womb of the earth is one, and yet bears different fruits. The heat, too, of the sun-beams is one, but it ripens all things differently; bringing some to maturity more slowly, and others more quickly. Who then but must feel astonishment and admiration at these things?

5. Nay, this is not the only wonder, that He hath formed it with this great variety and diversity; but farther, that He hath spread it before all in common; the rich and the poor, sinners as well as the righteous. Even as Christ also declared: "He makes His sun to rise upon the evil and the good, and sends His rain upon the just and unjust." Moreover, when He stocked the world with various animals, and implanted divers dispositions in the creatures, He commanded us to imitate some of these, and to avoid others. For example; the ant is industrious, and performs a laborious task. By giving heed then, thou wilt receive the strongest admonition from this animal not to indulge in sloth, nor to shun labor and toil. Therefore also the Scripture has sent the sluggard to the ant, saying, "Go to the ant, thou sluggard, emulate his ways, and be wiser than he." Art thou unwilling, he means, to learn from the

Scriptures, that it is good to labor, and that he who will not work, neither ought he to eat? Learn it from the irrationals! This also we do in our families, when those who are older, and who are considered superior, have done amiss, we bid them to attend to thoughtful children. We say, "Mark such an one, who is less than you, how earnest and watchful he is." Do thou then likewise receive from this animal the best exhortation to industry; and marvel at thy Lord, not only because He hath made heaven and the sun, but because He hath also made the ant. For although the animal be small, it affords much proof of the greatness of God's wisdom. Consider then how prudent the ant is, and consider how God hath implanted in so small a body, such an unceasing desire of working! But whilst from this animal thou learns industry; take from the bee at once a lesson of neatness, industry, and social concord! For it is not more for herself than for us, that the bee labors, and toils every day; which is indeed a thing especially proper for a Christian; not to seek his own things, but the things of others. As then she traverses all the meadows that she may prepare a banquet for another, so also, O man, do thou likewise; and if thou hast accumulated wealth, expend it upon others; if thou hast the faculty of teaching, do not bury the talent, but bring it out publicly for the sake of those who need it! Or if thou hast any other advantage, become useful to those who require the benefit of thy labors! See not that for this reason, especially, the bee is more honored than the other animals; not because she labors, but because she labors for others? For the spider also labors, and toils, and spreads out his fine textures over the walls, surpassing the utmost skill of woman; but the creature is without estimation, since his work is in no way profitable to us;

such are they that labor and toil, but for themselves! Imitate too the simplicity of the dove! Imitate the ass in his love to his master, and the ox also! Imitate the birds in their freedom from anxiety! For great, great indeed is the advantage that may be gained from irrational creatures for the correction of manners.

6. From these animals Christ also instructs us, when He says, "Be ye wise as serpents, and harmless as doves." And again; "Behold the fowls of the air, for they sow not, neither do they reap, nor gather into barns; yet your heavenly Father feeds them." The prophet also, to shame the ungrateful Jews, thus speaks; "The ox knows his owner, and the ass his master's crib; but Israel doth not know me." And again; "The turtle and the swallow and the crane observe the time of their coming, but my people knows not the judgment of the Lord his God." From these animals, and such as these, learn to achieve virtue, and be instructed to avoid wickedness by the contrary ones. For as the bee follows good, so the asp is destructive. Therefore shun wickedness, lest thou hear it said, "The poison of asps is under their lips." Again, the dog is devoid of shame. Hate, therefore, this kind of wickedness. The fox also is crafty, and fraudulent. Emulate not this vice; but as the bee, in flying over the meadows, does not choose every sort of flower; but selecting that which is useful, leaves the rest; so also do thou; and whilst surveying the whole race of irrational animals, if anything profitable may be drawn from these, accept it; the advantages which they have naturally, make it thy business to practice of thine own free choice. For in this respect also thou hast been honored of God; that what they have as natural advantages He hath permitted thee to achieve of thy own free choice, in order that thou may

also receive a reward. For good works with them spring not from free will, and reason, but from nature only. In other words, the bee makes honey, not because it has learnt this by reason and reflection, but because it is instructed by nature. Because if the work had not been natural, and allotted to the race, some of them assuredly would have been unskilled in their art; whereas from the time that the world was first made, even to the present day, no one hath observed bees resting from labor, and not making honey. For such natural characteristics are common to the whole race. But those things which depend on our free choice are not common; for labor is necessary that they may be accomplished.

7. Take then all the best things, and clothe thyself with them; for thou art indeed king of the irrationals; but kings, if there be any thing excellent possessed by their subjects, be it gold or silver, or precious stones, or sumptuous vestments, usually possess the same in greater abundance. From the creation also, learn to admire thy Lord! And if any of the things thou sees exceed thy comprehension, and thou art not able to find the reason thereof, yet for this glorify the Creator, that the wisdom of these works surpasses thine understanding. Say not, wherefore is this? Or, to what end? For everything is useful, even if we know not the reason of it. As therefore, if thou goes into a surgery, and sees many instruments lying before thee, thou wonder at the variety of the implements though ignorant of their use; so also act with respect to the creation. Although thou sees many of the animals, and of the herbs, and plants, and other things, of which thou knows not the use, admire the variety of these; and feel astonishment for this reason at the perfect workmanship of God; that He hath neither made all things

manifest to thee, nor permitted all things to be unknown. For He hath not permitted all things to be unknown, lest you should say, that the things that exist are not of providence. He hath not permitted all things to be known to thee, lest the greatness of thy knowledge should excite thee to pride. Thus at least it was that the evil demon precipitated the first man headlong and by means of the hope of greater knowledge, deprived him of that he already possessed. Therefore also, a certain wise man exhorts, saying, "Seek not out the things that are too hard for thee; neither search the things that are too deep for thee. But what is commanded thee, think thereupon with reverence; for the greater part of His works are done in secret." And again; "More things are shewed unto thee than men understand." But this he speaks for the purpose of consoling the man who is sad and vexed, because he does not know all things; for even those things he observes, which thou art permitted to know, greatly surpass thine understanding; for you could not have found them by thyself, but thou hast been taught them of God. Wherefore be content with the wealth given thee, and do not seek more; but for what thou hast received give thanks; and do not be angry on account of those things which thou hast not received. And, for what thou knows, give glory, and do not stumble at those things of which thou art ignorant. For God hath made both alike profitably; and hath revealed some things, but hidden others, providing for thy safety.

  8. One mode, then, of knowing God, is that by the creation, which I have spoken of, and which might occupy many days. For in order that we might go over the formation of man only with exactness, (and I speak of exactness such as is possible to us, not of real exactness;

since many as are the reasons we have already given for the works of creation, many more of these there are, ineffable, which God who made them knows, for of course we do not know them all); in order then, I say, that we might take an exact survey of the whole modelling of man; and that we might discover the skill there is in every member; and examine the distribution and situation of the sinews, the veins, and the arteries, and the molding of every other part; not even a whole year would suffice for such a disquisition.

9. For this reason, here dismissing this subject; and having given to the laborious and studious an opportunity, by what has been said, of going over likewise the other parts of Creation; we shall now direct our discourse to another point which is itself also demonstrative of God's providence. What then is this second point? It is, that when God formed man, he implanted within him from the beginning a natural law. And what then was this natural law? He gave utterance to conscience within us; and made the knowledge of good things, and of those which are the contrary, to be self-taught. For we have no need to learn that fornication is an evil thing, and that chastity is a good thing, but we know this from the first. And that you may learn that we know this from the first, the Lawgiver, when He afterwards gave laws, and said, "Thou shalt not kill," did not add, "since murder is an evil thing," but simply said, "Thou shall not kill;" for He merely prohibited the sin, without teaching. How was it then when He said, "Thou shalt not kill," that He did not add, "because murder is a wicked thing." The reason was, that conscience had taught this beforehand; and He speaks thus, as to those who know and understand the point. Wherefore when He speaks to

us of another commandment, not known to us by the dictate of consciences He not only prohibits, but adds the reason. When, for instance, He gave commandment respecting the Sabbath; "On the seventh day thou shalt do no work;" He subjoined also the reason for this cessation. What was this? "Because on the seventh day God rested from all His works which He had begun to make." And again; "Because thou wert a servant in the land of Egypt." For what purpose then I ask did He add a reason respecting the Sabbath, but did no such thing in regard to murder? Because this commandment was not one of the leading ones. It was not one of those which were accurately defined of our conscience, but a kind of partial and temporary one; and for this reason it was abolished afterwards. But those which are necessary and uphold our life, are the following; "Thou shalt not kill; Thou shalt not commit adultery; Thou shalt not steal." On this account then He adds no reason in this case, nor enters into any instruction on the matter, but is content with the bare prohibition.

10. And not only from thence, but from another consideration also, I will endeavor to shew you how man was self-taught with respect to the knowledge of virtue. Adam sinned the first sin; and after the sin straightway hid himself; but if he had not known he had been doing something wrong, why did he hide himself? For then there were neither letters, nor law, nor Moses. Whence then doth he recognize the sin, and hide himself? Yet not only does he so hide himself, but when called to account, he endeavors to lay the blame on another, saying, "The woman, whom Thou gives me, she gave me of the tree, and I did eat." And that woman again transfers the accusation to another, viz. the serpent. Observe also the

wisdom of God; for when Adam said, "I heard Thy voice, and I was afraid, for I was naked, and I hid myself," God does not at once convict him of what he had done, nor say, "Why hast thou eaten of the tree?" But how? "Who told thee," He asks, "that thou was naked, unless thou hast eaten of that Tree of which alone I commanded thee not to eat?" He did not keep silence, nor did He openly convict him. He did not keep silence, that He might call him forth to the confession of his crime. He did not convict him openly, lest the whole might come from Himself, and the man should so be deprived of that pardon which is granted us from confession. Therefore he did not declare openly the cause from whence this knowledge sprung, but he carried on the discourse in the form of interrogation, leaving the man himself to come to the confession.

11. Again, in the case of Cain and Abel, the same proceeding is observable. For, in the first place, they set apart the fruits of their own labors to God. For we would shew not from his sin only, but also from his virtue, that man was capable of knowing both these things. Wherefore that man knew sin to be an evil thing, Adam manifested; and that he knew that virtue was a good thing, Abel again made evident. For without having learnt it from any one, without having heard any law promulgated respecting the first fruits, but having been taught from within, and from his conscience, he presented that sacrifice. On this account I do not carry the argument down to a later period; but I bring it to bear upon the time of these earlier men, when there were as yet no letters, as yet no law, nor as yet prophets and judges; but Adam only existed with his children; in order that thou may learn, that the knowledge of good and evil had been previously

implanted in their natures. For from whence did Abel learn that to offer sacrifice was a good thing; that it was good to honor God, and in all things to give thanks? "Why then?" replies someone, "did not Cain bring his offering?" This man also did offer sacrifice, but not in like manner. And from thence again the knowledge of conscience is apparent. For when, envying him who had been honored, he deliberated upon murder, he conceals his crafty determination. And what says he; "Come, let us go forth into the field." The outward guise was one thing, the presence of love; the thought another, the purpose of fratricide. But if he had not known the design to be a wicked one, why did he conceal it? And again, after the murder had been perpetrated, being asked of God, "Where is Abel thy brother?" he answers, "I know not; Am I my brother's keeper?" Wherefore does he deny the crime? Is it not evidently because he exceedingly condemns himself. For as his father had hid himself, so also this man denies his guilt, and after his conviction, again says, "My crime is too great to obtain pardon."

12. But it may be objected, that the Gentile allows nothing of this sort. Come then, let us discuss this point, and as we have done with respect to the creation, having carried on the warfare against these objectors not only by the help of the Scriptures, but of reason, so also let us now do with respect to conscience. For Paul too, when he was engaged in controversy with such persons, entered upon this head. What then is it that they urge? They say, that there is no self-evident law seated in our consciences; and that God hath not implanted this in our nature. But if so, whence is it, I ask, that legislators have written those laws which are among them concerning marriages, concerning murders, concerning wills, concerning trusts, concerning

abstinence from encroachments on one another, and a thousand other things. For the men now living may perchance have learned them from their elders; and they from those who were before them, and these again from those beyond? But from whom did those learn who were the originators and first enactors of laws among them? Is it not evident that it was from conscience? For they cannot say, that they held communication with Moses; or that they heard the prophets. How could it be so when they were Gentiles? But it is evident that from the very law which God placed in man when He formed him from the beginning, laws were laid down, and arts discovered, and all other things. For the arts too were thus established, their originators having come to the knowledge of them in a self-taught manner.

13. So also came there to be courts of justice, and so were penalties defined, as Paul accordingly observes. For since many of the Gentiles were ready to controvert this, and to say, "How will God judge mankind who lived before Moses? He did not send a lawgiver; He did not introduce a law; He commissioned no prophet, nor apostle, nor evangelist; how then can He call these to account?" Since Paul therefore wished to prove that they possessed a self-taught law; and that they knew clearly what they ought to do; hear how he speaks; "For when the Gentiles who have not the law, do by nature the things contained in the law, these having not the law, are a law unto themselves; which shew the work of the law written in their hearts." But how without letters? "Their conscience also bearing witness, and their thoughts the meanwhile accusing, or else excusing one another. In the day when God shall judge the secrets of men by Jesus Christ according to my gospel." And again; "As many as

have sinned without law, shall perish without law; and as many as have sinned in the law, shall be judged by the law." What means, "They shall perish without law?" The law not accusing them, but their thoughts, and their conscience; for if they had not a law of conscience, it were not necessary that they should perish through having done amiss. For how should it be so if they sinned without a law? But when he says, "without a law," he does not assert that they had no law, but that they had no written law, though they had the law of nature. And again; "But glory, honor, and peace, to every man that works good, to the Jew first, and also to the Gentile."

14. But these things he spoke in reference to the early times, before the coming of Christ; and the Gentile he names here is not an idolater, but one who worshipped God only; unfettered by the necessity of Judaical observances, (I mean Sabbaths, and circumcision, and divers purifications,) yet exhibiting all manner of wisdom and piety. And again, discoursing of such a worshipper, he observes, "Wrath and indignation, tribulation and anguish, upon every soul of man that doeth evil, of the Jew first, and also of the Gentile." Again he here calls by the name of Greek one who was free from the observance of Judaic customs. If, then, he had not heard the law, nor conversed with the Jews, how could there be wrath, indignation and tribulation against him for working evil? The reason is, that he possessed a conscience inwardly admonishing him, and teaching him, and instructing him in all things. Whence is this manifest? From the way in which he punished others when they did amiss; from the way in which he laid down laws; from the way in which he set up the tribunals of justice. With the view of making this more plain, Paul spoke of those who were living in

wickedness. "Who, knowing the ordinance of God, that they which commit such things are worthy of death, not only do the same, but also consent with them that practice them." "But from whence," says someone, "did they know, that it is the will of God, that those who live in iniquity should be punished with death?" From whence? Why, from the way in which they judged others who sinned. For if thou deems not murder to be a wicked thing, when thou hast gotten a murderer at thy bar, you should not punish him. So if thou deems it not an evil thing to commit adultery, when the adulterer has fallen into thy hands, release him from punishment! But if thou records laws, and prescribes punishments, and art a severe judge of the sins of others; what defense canst thou make, in matters wherein thou thyself does amiss, by saying that thou art ignorant what things ought to be done? For suppose that thou and another person have alike been guilty of adultery. On what account dost thou punish him, and deem thyself worthy of forgiveness? Since if thou didst not know adultery to be wickedness, it were not right to punish it in another. But if thou punishes, and thinks to escape the punishment thyself, how is it agreeable to reason that the same offences should not pay the same penalty?

15. This indeed is the very thing which Paul rebukes, when he says, "And thinks thou this, O man, that judges them which do such things, and does the same, that thou shalt escape the judgment of God?" It is not, it cannot be possible; for from the very sentence, he means, which thou pronounces upon another, from this sentence God will then judge thee. For surely thou art not just, and God unjust! But if thou overlooks not another suffering wrong, how shall God overlook? And if thou corrects the

sins of others, how will not God correct thee? And though He may not bring the punishment upon thee instantly, be not confident on that account, but fear the more. So also Paul bade thee, saying, "Despises thou the riches of His goodness, and forbearance, and longsuffering, not knowing that the goodness of God leaded thee to repentance?" For therefore, says he, doth he bear with thee, not that thou may become worse, but that thou may repent. But if thou wilt not, this longsuffering becomes a cause of thy greater punishment; continuing, as thou dost, impenitent. This, however, is the very thing he means, when he says, "But after thy hardness and impenitent heart treasures up to thyself wrath against the day of wrath, and revelation of the righteous judgment of God. Who will render to every man according to his deeds." Since, therefore, He rendered to every man according to his works; for this reason He both implanted within us a natural law, and afterwards gave us a written one, in order that He might demand an account of sins, and that He might crown those who act rightly. Let us then order our conduct with the utmost care, and as those who have soon to encounter a fearful tribunal; knowing that we shall enjoy no pardon, if after a natural as well as written law, and so much teaching and continual admonition, we neglect our own salvation.

16. I desire then to address you again on the subject of oaths; but I feel ashamed. For to me, indeed, it is not wearisome both by day and by night to repeat the same things to you. But I am afraid, lest, having followed you up so many days, I should seem to condemn you of great listlessness, that you should require continual admonition respecting so easy a matter. And I am not only ashamed, but also in fear for you! for frequent

instruction to those who give heed, is salutary and profitable; but to those who are listless, it is injurious, and exceedingly perilous; for the oftener any one hears, the greater punishment does he draw upon himself, if he does not practice what is told him. With this accordingly God reproached the Jews, speaking thus: "I have sent my prophets, rising up early, and sending them; and even then ye did not hearken." We therefore do this of our great care for you. But we fear, lest, on that tremendous Day, this admonition and counsel should rise up against you all. For when the point to be attained is easy, and he whose office it is continually to admonish, desists not from his task, what defense shall we have to offer? Or what argument will save us from punishment? Tell me, if a sum of money chance to be due to you, do you not always, when you meet the debtor, remind him of the loan? Do thou too act thus; and let everyone suppose that his neighbor owes him money, viz., the fulfilling of this precept; and upon meeting him, let him put him in mind of the payment, knowing that no small danger lies at our door, whilst we are unmindful of our brethren. For this cause I too cease not to make mention of these things. For I fear, lest by any means I should hear it said on that day, "O wicked and slothful servant, thou oughtest to have put my money to the exchangers." Behold, however, I have laid it down, not once, or twice, but oftentimes. It is left then for you to discharge the usury of it. Now the usury of hearing is the manifestation of it by deeds, for the deposit is the Lord's. Therefore let us not negligently receive that with which we are entrusted; but let us keep it with diligence, that we may restore it with much interest on That Day. For unless thou bring others to the performance of the same good works, thou shalt hear that voice, which he who buried the talent heard. But God forbid it should be this! But may you hear that different voice which Christ uttered, saying to him who had made profit, "Well done, good and faithful servant; thou hast been faithful over a few things, I will make thee ruler over many things."

17. And this voice we shall hear, if we shew the same earnestness as he did. And we shall shew this earnestness, if we do this which I say. When you depart, whilst what you have heard is yet warm within you, exhort one another! And just as ye each salute at parting, so let everyone go from hence with an admonition, and say to his neighbor, "Observe and remember that thou keep the commandment;" and thus shall we assuredly get the mastery. For when friends also dismiss one with such counsel; and on one's return home, one's wife again admonishes one to the same effect; and our word keeps its hold on you when alone; we shall soon shake off this evil habit. I know, indeed, that ye marvel why I am so earnest respecting this precept. But discharge the duty enjoined, and then I will tell you. Meanwhile, this I say; that this precept is a divine law; and it is not safe to transgress it. But if I shall see it rightly performed, I will speak of another reason, which is not less than this, that ye may learn that it is with justice I make so much ado about this law. But it is now time to conclude this address in a prayer. Wherefore, let us all say in common, "O God, Who wills not the death of a sinner, but that he should be converted and live; grant that we, having discharged this and every other precept, may be found worthy so to stand at the tribunal of Thy Christ, that having enjoyed great boldness, we may attain the kingdom to Thy glory. For to Thee belongs glory, together with Thine only begotten

Son, and the Holy Ghost, now and ever, and world without end." Amen.

Homily XIII.

A further thanksgiving to God for the change in the late melancholy aspect of affairs. Reminiscence of those who were dragged away, and punished because of the sedition. Exposition on the subject of the creation of man, and of his having received a natural law. Of the complete accomplishment of abstinence from oaths.

1. With the same introduction and prelude that I began yesterday and the day before, I shall begin to-day. Now again I will say, "Blessed be God!" What a day did we see last Wednesday! And what in the present! On that day how heavy was the gloom! How bright the calm of the present! That was the day when that fearful tribunal was set in the city, and shook the hearts of all, and made the day to seem no better than night; not because the beams of the sun were extinguished, but because that despondency and fear darkened your eyes. Wherefore, that we may reap the more pleasure, I wish to relate a few of the circumstances which then occurred; for I perceive that a narrative of these things will be serviceable to you, and to all who shall come afterwards. Besides, to those who have been delivered from shipwreck, it is sweet to remember the waves, and the tempest, and the winds, when they are come into port. And to those who have fallen into sickness, it is an agreeable thing, when the sickness is over, to talk over with others the fevers by which they were nearly brought to the grave. When terrors have passed away, there is a pleasure in relating

those terrors; the soul no longer fearing them, but deriving therefrom more cheerfulness. The remembrance of past evils always makes the present prosperity to appear more strikingly.

2. When the greater portion of the city had taken refuge from the fear and danger of that occasion, in secret places, in deserts, and in hollows; terror besetting them in all directions; and the houses were empty of women, and the forum of men, and scarce two or three appeared walking together across it, and even these going about as if they had been animated corpses: at this period, I proceeded to the tribunal of justice, for the purpose of seeing the end of these transactions; and there, beholding the fragments of the city collected together, I marveled most of all at this, that although a multitude was around the doors, there was the profoundest silence, as though there had been no man there, all looking upon one another; not one daring to enquire of his neighbor, nor to hear anything from him; for each regarded his neighbor with suspicion; since many already, having been dragged away, beyond all expectation, from the midst of the forum, were now confined within. Thus we all alike looked up to heaven, and stretched out our hands in silence, expecting help from above, and beseeching God to stand by those who were brought to judgment, to soften the hearts of the judges, and to make their sentence a merciful one. And just as when some persons on land, beholding others suffering shipwreck, cannot indeed go near to them, and reach out the hand, and relieve their distress, being kept back from them by the waves; yet away on the shore, with outstretched hands and tears, they supplicate God that He may help the drowning; so there in like manner, did all silently and mentally call upon God,

pleading for those at the tribunal, as for men surrounded by the waves, that He would stretch out His hand, and not suffer the vessel to be overwhelmed, nor the judgment of those under trial to end in an utter wreck. Such was the state of things in front of the doors; but when I entered within the court, other sights I saw which were still more awful; soldiers armed with swords and clubs, and strictly keeping the peace for the judges within. For since all the relatives of those under trial, whether wives, or mothers, or daughters, or fathers, stood before the doors of the seat of justice; in order that if anyone happened to be led away to execution, yet no one inflamed at the sight of the calamity might raise any tumult or disturbance; the soldiers drove them all afar off; thus preoccupying their mind with fear.

3. One sight there was, more pitiable than all; a mother, and a sister of a certain person, who was among those under trial within, sat at the very vestibule of the court of justice, rolling themselves on the pavement, and becoming a common spectacle to all the bystanders; veiling their faces, and shewing no sense of shame, but that which the urgency of the calamity permitted. No maid servant, nor neighbor, nor female friend, nor any other relative accompanied them. But hemmed in by a crowd of soldiers, alone, and meanly clad, and groveling on the ground, about the very doors, they were in more pitiable case than those who were undergoing judgment within, and hearing as they did the voice of the executioners, the strokes of the scourge, the wailing of those who were being scourged, the fearful threats of the judges, they themselves endured, at every scourging, sharper pains than those who were beaten. For since, in the confessions of others, there was a danger of

accusations being proved, if they heard anyone scourged that he might mention those who were guilty, and uttering cries, they, looking up to heaven, besought God to give the sufferer some strength of endurance, lest the safety of their own relations should be betrayed by the weakness of others, while incapable of sustaining the sharp anguish of the strokes. And again, the same thing occurred as in the case of men who are struggling with a tempest. For just as when they perceive the violence of a wave lifting up its head from afar, and gradually increasing, and ready to overwhelm the vessel, they are almost dead with terror, before it comes near the ship; so also was it with these. If at any time they heard voices, and cries that reached them, they saw a thousand deaths before their eyes, being in terror, lest those who were urged to bear witness, giving way to their torments, should name some one of those who were their own relatives. And thus, one saw tortures both within and without. Those within the executioners were tormenting; these women, the despotic force of nature, and the sympathy of the affections. There was lamentation within, and without! Inside, on the part of those who were found guilty, and outside on the part of their relatives. Yea, rather not these only, but their very judges inwardly lamented, and suffered more severely than all the rest; being compelled to take part in so bitter a tragedy.

 4. As for me, while I sat and beheld all this, how matrons and virgins, wont to live in seclusion, were now made a common spectacle to all; and how those who were accustomed to lie on a soft couch, had now the pavement for their bed; and how they who had enjoyed so constant an attendance of female servants and eunuchs, and every sort of outward distinction, were now bereft of all these

things; and groveling at the feet of every one, beseeching him to lend help by any means in his power to those who were undergoing examination, and that there might be a kind of general contribution of mercy from all; I exclaimed, in those words of Solomon, "Vanity of vanities, all is vanity." For I saw both this and another oracle fulfilled in every deed, which says, "All the glory of man is as the flower of grass. The grass withered, and the flower falls away." For then indeed, wealth, and nobility, and notoriety, and the patronage of friends, and kinship and all worldly things, were found worthless; the sin, and transgression of the law which had taken place, having put all these succors to flight. And just as the mother of young birds, when the nestlings have been carried away, coming and finding her nest empty, is unable to rescue her captive brood; but by hovering around the hands of the fowler, in this way displays her grief; even so did these women then do, when their children were snatched away from their dwellings, and shut up within, as it were in a net, or a trap. They could not indeed come in and deliver the prisoners, but they manifested their anguish by wallowing on the ground near the very doors; by lamentation and groans; and by endeavoring to approach as near as possible to those who had captured them. These things then beholding, I cast in my mind That Dread Tribunal; and I said within myself, "If now, when men are the judges, neither mother, nor sister, nor father, nor any other person, though guiltless of the deeds which have been perpetrated, can avail to rescue the criminals; who will stand by us when we are judged at the dread Tribunal of Christ? Who will dare to raise his voice? Who will be able to rescue those who shall be led away to those unbearable punishments. Notwithstanding they were the first men of the city who were then brought to trial, and the very chief of the nobility, yet they would have been glad if it could be granted them to lose all their possessions, yea, if need were, their liberty itself, so that they might continue to enjoy this present life.

5. But to proceed. The day now hastening to its close, and late evening arriving, and the final sentence of the court being expected, all were in still greater agony, and besought God that He would grant some delay and respite; and incline the soul of the judges to refer the facts that had been investigated to the decision of the Emperor; since perchance some advantage might arise from this reference. Moreover, by the people general supplications were sent up to the Merciful God; imploring that He would save the remnants of the city; and not suffer it entirely to be razed from its foundations. Nor could one see any one joining in this cry but with tears. Nevertheless, none of these things then moved the judges within, although they heard. One thing only they considered, that there might be a rigid enquiry into the deeds that had been perpetrated.

6. At last having loaded the culprits with chains, and bound them with iron, they sent them away to the prison through the midst of the forum. Men that had kept their studs of horses, who had been presidents of the games, who could reckon up a thousand different offices of distinction which they had held, had their goods confiscated, and seals might be seen placed upon all their doors. Their wives also being ejected from their parents' home, each had literally to play the part of Job's wife. For they went "wandering from house to house and from place to place, seeking a lodging." And this it was not easy for them to find, everyone fearing and trembling to

receive, or to render assistance in any way to the relatives of those who were under impeachment. Nevertheless, though such events had happened, the sufferers were patient under all; since they were not deprived of the present life. And neither the loss of wealth, nor dishonor, nor so much public exposure, nor any other matter of that nature, caused them vexation. For the greatness of the calamity, and the circumstance of their having expected still worse things, when they suffered these, had prepared the soul for the exercise of a wise fortitude. And now they learnt, how simple a thing is virtue for us, how easy and expeditious of performance, and that from our neglect only it seems to be laborious. They who before this time could not bear the loss of a little money with meekness, now they were subject to a greater fear, although they had lost all their substance, felt as if they had found a treasure, because they had not lost their lives. So that if the sense of a future hell took possession of us, and we thought of those intolerable punishments, we should not grieve, even though for the sake of the law of God we were to give both our substance, and our bodies and lives too, knowing that we should gain greater things; deliverance from the terrors that are hereafter.

7. Perchance the tragedy of all I have told you, has greatly softened your hearts. Do not however take it amiss. For since I am about to venture upon some more subtle thoughts and require a more sensitive state of mind on your part, I have done this intentionally, in order that by the terror of the description your minds might have shaken off all listlessness, and withdrawn themselves from all worldly cares, and might with the more readiness convey the force of the things about to be spoken into the depths of your soul.

Sufficiently indeed, then, our discourse of late evinced to you, that a natural law of good and evil is seated within us. But that our proof of it may be more abundantly evident, we will again to-day apply ourselves strenuously to the same subject of discourse. For that God from the beginning, when He formed man, made him capable of discriminating both these, all men make evident. Hence when we sin, we are all ashamed at the presence of our inferiors; and oftentimes a master, on his way to the house of a harlot, if he then perceives any one of his more respectable servants, turns back, reddening with shame, from this untoward path. Again, when others reproach us, fixing on us the names of particular vices, we call it an insult; and if we are aggrieved, we drag those who have done the wrong to the public tribunal. Thus we can understand what vice is and what virtue is. Wherefore Christ, for the purpose of declaring this, and shewing that He was not introducing a strange law, or one which surpassed our nature, but that which He had of old deposited beforehand in our conscience, after pronouncing those numerous Beatitudes, thus speaks; "All things whatsoever ye would that men should do to you, do ye even so to them." "Many words," says He, "are not necessary, nor laws of great length, nor a diversity of instruction. Let thine own will be the law. Do you wish to receive kindness? Be kind to another. Do you wish to receive mercy? Show mercy to thy neighbor. Do you wish to be applauded? Applaud another. Do you wish to be beloved? Exercise love. Do you wish to enjoy the first rank? First concede that place to another. Become thyself the judge, thyself the lawgiver of thine own life. And again; "Do not to another what thou hates." By the latter precept, he would induce to a departure from iniquity; by the former, to the exercise of virtue. "Do not thou to another," he says, "what thou hates." Do you hate to be insulted? Do not insult another. Do you hate to be envied? Envy not another. Do you hate to be deceived? Do not deceive another. And, in a word, in all things, if we hold fast these two precepts, we shall not need any other instruction. For the knowledge of virtue He hath implanted in our nature; but the practice of it and the correction He hath entrusted to our moral choice.

8. Perhaps what is thus said, is obscure; wherefore I will again endeavor to make it more plain. In order to know that it is a good thing to exercise temperance, we need no words, nor instruction; for we ourselves have the knowledge of it in our nature, and there is no necessity for labor or fatigue in going about and enquiring whether temperance is good and profitable; but we all acknowledge this with one consent, and no man is in doubt as to this virtue. So also we account adultery to be an evil thing, and neither is there here any need of trouble or learning, that the wickedness of this sin may be known; but we are all self-taught in such judgments; and we applaud virtue, though we do not follow it; as, on the other hand, we hate vice, though we practice it. And this hath been an exceeding good work of God; that He hath made our conscience, and our power of choice already, and before the action, claim kindred with virtue, and be at enmity with wickedness.

9. As I said then, the knowledge of each of these things resides within the conscience of all men, and we require no teacher to instruct us in these things; but the regulation of our conduct is left to our choice, and earnestness, and efforts. And why was this? but because if He had made everything to be of nature, we should have

departed uncrowned and destitute of reward; and even as the brutes, who receive no reward nor praise for those advantages which they have naturally, so neither should we enjoy any of these things; for natural advantages are not the praise and commendation of those who have them, but of the Giver. For this reason, then, He did not commit all to nature; and again, He did not suffer our will to undertake the whole burden of knowledge, and of right regulation; lest it should despair at the labor of virtue. But conscience suggests to it what ought to be done; and it contributes its own exertions for the accomplishment. That it is a good thing to be temperate, we all understand without difficulty; for the knowledge is of nature: but we should not be able without difficulty, without bridling lust, and employing much exertion, to practice the rule of temperance; for this does not come to us by nature as the knowledge does, but requires also a willing mind and earnestness. And not only in this respect has He made the burden lighter for us, but also in another way again, by letting even some good dispositions exist naturally within us. For we are all naturally disposed to feel indignation along with those who are contemptuously treated, (whence it arises that we become the enemies of those who are insolent, though we ourselves may have suffered no part of the grievance,) and to sympathize in the pleasure of those who enjoy assistance and protection; and we are overcome by the calamities of others, as well as by mutual tenderness. For although calamitous events may seem to induce a certain pusillanimity, we entertain nevertheless a common fondness for each other. And to this effect a certain wise man speaks significantly; "Every animal loves his like, and man his neighbor."

10. But God hath provided many other instructors for us besides conscience; viz., fathers for children, masters for servants, husbands for wives, teachers for pupils, law-givers and judges for those who are to be governed, and friends for friends. And frequently too we gain no less from enemies than friends; for when the former reproach us with our offences, they stir us up, even against our will, to the amendment of them. So many teachers hath He set over us, in order that the discovery of what is profitable, and the regulation of our conduct, might be easy to us, the multitude of those things which urge us on toward it not permitting us to fall away from what is expedient for us. For although we should despise parents, yet while we fear magistrates, we shall in any case be more submissive than otherwise. And though we may set them at naught when we sin, we can never escape the rebuke of conscience: and if we dishonor and repel this, yet whilst fearing the opinion of the many, we shall be the better for it. And though we are destitute of shame with regard to this, the fear of the laws will press on us so as to restrain us, however reluctantly.

11. Thus fathers and teachers take the young in hand, and bring them into order; and lawgivers and magistrates, those who are grown up. And servants, as being more inclined to listlessness, in addition to what has been previously mentioned, have their masters to constrain them to temperance; and wives have their husbands. And many are the walls which environ our race on all sides, lest it should too easily slide away, and fall into wickedness. Beside all these too; sicknesses and calamities instruct us. For poverty restrains, and losses sober us, and danger subdues us, and there are many other things of this sort. Doth neither father, nor teacher, nor

prince, nor lawgiver, nor judge make thee fear? Doth no friend move thee to shame, nor enemy sting thee? Doth no master chastise? Doth no husband instruct? Doth no conscience correct thee? Still, when bodily sickness comes, it often sets all right; and a loss has made the audacious man to become gentle. And what is more than this, heavy misfortunes, which befall not only ourselves but others too, are often of great advantage to us; and we who ourselves suffered nothing, yet beholding others enduring punishment, have been no less sobered by it than they.

12. And with respect to right deeds, any one may see that this happens; for as when the bad are punished others become better, so whenever the good achieve anything right, many are urged onward to a similar zeal: a thing which hath also taken place with respect to the avoiding of oaths. For many persons, observing that others had laid aside the evil practice of oaths, took a pattern from their diligence, and got the better of the sin; wherefore we are the more disposed to touch again on the subject of this admonition. For let no one tell me that "many" have accomplished this; this is not what is desired, but that "all" should do so; and until I see this I cannot take breath. That Shepherd had a hundred sheep, and yet when one of them had wandered away, he took no account of the safety of the ninety and nine, until he found the one that was lost, and restored it again to the flock. See not that this also happens with respect to the body; for if by striking against any obstacle, we have only turned back a nail, the whole body sympathizes with the member. Say not this; that only a certain few have failed; but consider this point, that these few being unreformed, will corrupt many others. Although there was but one who

had committed fornication among the Corinthians, yet Paul so groaned as if the whole city were lost. And very reasonably, for he knew that if that member were not chastened, the disease progressing onward would at length attack all the rest. I saw, but lately, in the court of justice, those distinguished men bound and conducted through the forum; and while some were wondering at this extraordinary degradation, others said there was nothing to wonder at; for that, where there is matter of treason, rank must go for nothing. Is it not then much more true that rank must be of no avail where is impiety?

13. Thinking therefore of these things, let us arouse ourselves; for if ye bring not your own endeavors to the task, everything on our part is to no purpose. And why so? Because it is not with the office of teaching, as it is with other arts. For the silversmith, when he has fabricated a vessel of any kind, and laid it aside, will find it on the morrow just as he left it. And the worker in brass, and the stone-cutter, and every other artificer, will each again take his own work in hand, whatever it is, just in the state he quitted it. But it is not so with us, but altogether the reverse; for we have not lifeless vessels to forge, but reasonable souls. Therefore we do not find you such as we leave you, but when we have taken you, and with manifold labor molded, reformed you and increased your ardor on your departing from this place, the urgency of business, besetting you on every side, again perverts you, and causes us increased difficulty. Therefore, I supplicate and beseech you to put your own hand to the work; and when ye depart hence, to shew the same earnest regard for your own safety, that I have here shewn for your amendment.

14. Oh! That it were possible that I could perform good works as your substitute, and that you could receive the rewards of those works! Then I would not give you so much trouble. But how can I do this? The thing is impossible; for to every man will He render according to his own works. Wherefore as a mother, when she beholds her son in a fever, while she witnesses his sufferings from choking and inflammation, frequently bewails him, and says to him, "O my son, would that I could sustain thy fever, and draw off its flame upon myself!" so now I say, Oh! That by laboring as your substitute, I could do good works for you all! But no, this is not to be done. But of his own doings must each man give the account, and one cannot see one person suffer punishment in the room of another. For this reason I am pained and mourn, that on That Day, when ye are called to judgment, I shall not be able to assist you, since, to say the truth, no such confidence of speech with God belongs to me. But even if I had much confidence, I am not holier than Moses, or more righteous than Samuel; of whom it is said, that though they had attained to so great virtue, they could not in any way avail to assist the Jews; inasmuch as that people had given themselves over to excessive negligence. Since, then, from our own works we shall be punished or saved; let us endeavor, I beseech you, in conjunction with all the other precepts, to fulfill this one; that, finally departing this life with a favorable hope, we may obtain those good things which are promised, through the grace and lovingkindness of our Lord Jesus Christ, through Whom and with Whom, to the Father, with the Holy Ghost, be glory both now and ever, world without end. Amen.

Homily XIV.

After the whole people had been freed from all distress, and had become assured of safety, certain persons again disturbed the city by fabricating false reports, and were convicted. Wherefore this Homily refers to that subject; and also to the admonition concerning oaths; for which reason also, the history of Jonathan, and Saul, and that of Jephthah, is brought forward; and it is shewn how many perjuries result from one oath.

1. Not a little did the devil yesterday disturb our city; but God also hath not a little comforted us again; so that each one of us may seasonably take up that prophetic saying, "In the multitude of the sorrows that I had in my heart, thy comforts have refreshed my soul." And not only in consoling, but even in permitting us to be troubled, God hath manifested His tender care towards us. For to-day I shall repeat what I have never ceased to say, that not only our deliverance from evils, but also the permission of them arises from the benevolence of God. For when He sees us falling away into listlessness, and starting off from communion with Him, and making no account of spiritual things, He leaves us for a while; that thus brought to soberness, we may return to Him the more earnestly. And what marvel is it, if He does this towards us, listless as we are; since even Paul declares that with regard to himself and his disciples, this was the cause of their trials? For inditing his second Epistle to the Corinthians, he speaks thus: "We would not, brethren, have you ignorant of our trouble which came to us in Asia, that we were pressed out of measure, above strength, insomuch that we despaired even of life; but we had the sentence of death in

ourselves." As though he would say, "Dangers so great hung over us, that we gave up ourselves for lost; and no longer hoped that any favorable change would take place, but were altogether in expectation of death." For such is the sense of that clause, "We had the sentence of death in ourselves." But nevertheless, after such a state of desperation, God dispelled the tempest, and removed the cloud, and snatched us from the very gates of death. And afterwards, for the purpose of shewing that his being permitted to fall into this danger also was the result of much tender care for him, he mentions the advantage which resulted from the temptations, which was, that he might continually look to Him, and be neither high-minded, nor confident. Therefore having said this, "We had the sentence of death in ourselves;" he adds also the reason; "That we should not trust in ourselves, but in God which quickened the dead." For it is in the nature of trials to arouse us when we are dozing, or falling down, and to stir us up, and make us more religious. When, therefore, O beloved! Thou sees a trial at one time extinguished, and at another time kindled again, be not cast down! Do not despond, but retain a favorable hope, reasoning thus with thyself, that God does not deliver us into the hands of our enemies either because He hates or abandons us, but because He is desirous to make us more in earnest, and more intimate with Himself.

2. Let us not then be desponding; nor let us despair of a change for the better; but let us hope that speedily there will be a calm; and, in short, casting the issue of all the tumults which beset us upon God, let us again handle the customary points; and again bring forward our usual topic of instruction. For I am desirous to discourse to you further concerning the same subject, to

the end that we may radically extirpate from your souls the wicked practice of oaths. Wherefore it is necessary for me again to have recourse to the same entreaty that I made before. For lately I besought you, that each one taking the head of John, just cut off, and the warm blood yet dripping from it, you would thus go home, and think that you saw it before your eyes, while it emitted a voice, and said, "Abhor my murderer, the oath!" What a rebuke did not effect, this an oath effected; what a tyrant's wrath was insufficient for, this the necessity of keeping an oath brought about! And when the tyrant was publicly rebuked in the hearing of all, he bore the censure nobly; but when he had thrown himself into the fatal necessity caused by oaths, then he cut off that blessed head. This same thing, therefore, I entreat; and cease not entreating, that wherever we go, we go bearing this head; and that we shew it to all, crying aloud, as it does, and denouncing oaths. For although we were never so listless and remiss, yet beholding the eyes of that head fearfully glaring upon us, and threatening us if we swear, we should be more powerfully kept in check by this terror, than by any curb; and be easily able to restrain and avert the tongue from its inclination toward oaths.

3. There is not only this great evil in an oath, that it punishes those who are guilty of it, both when violated, and when kept; a thing we do not see take place with any other sin; but there is another equally great evil attending it. And what is that? Why that ofttimes it is utterly impossible even for those who are desirous, and even make a point of it, to keep their oath. For, in the first place, he who is continually swearing, whether willingly or unwillingly; knowingly or unknowingly; in jest or in earnest; being frequently carried away by anger and by

many other things, will most surely become perjured. And no one can gainsay this; so evident and generally allowed is the fact, that the man who swears frequently, must also be a perjurer. Secondly, I affirm, that although he were not carried away by passion, and did not become the victim of perjury unwillingly and unwittingly, yet by the very nature of the case he will assuredly be necessitated both consciously and voluntarily to perjure himself. Thus, oftentimes when we are dining at home, and one of the servants happens to do amiss, the wife swears that he shall be flogged, and then the husband swears the contrary, resisting, and not permitting it. In this case, whatever they may do, perjury must in any case be the result; for however much they may wish and endeavor to keep their oaths, it is no longer possible; but whatever happens, one or other of these will be ensnared in perjury; or rather both in any case.

4. And how, I will explain; for this is the paradox. He who hath sworn that he would flog the man-servant or maid-servant, yet hath afterwards been prohibited from this, hath perjured himself, not having done what he hath sworn to do: and also, he hath involved in the crime of perjury the party forbidding and hindering the oath from being kept. For not only they who take a false oath, but they who impose that necessity on others, are liable to the same accusation. And not merely in houses, but also in the forum we may see that this takes place; and especially in fights, when those who box with one another swear things that are contrary. One swears that he will beat, the other that he will not be beaten. One swears that he will carry off the cloak, the other that he will not suffer this. One that he will exact the money, the other that he will not pay it. And many other such contradictory things,

those who are contentious take an oath to do. So also in shops, and in schools, it may generally be observed that the same thing occurs. Thus the workman hath often sworn that he will not suffer his apprentice to eat or drink, before he has finished all his assigned task. And so also the pedagogue has often acted towards a youth; and a mistress towards her maidservant; and when the evening hath overtaken them, and the work hath remained unfinished, it is necessary either that those who have not executed their task should perish with hunger, or that those who have sworn should altogether forswear themselves. For that malignant demon, who is always lying in wait against our blessings, being present and hearing the obligation of the oaths, impels those who are answerable to indifference; or works some other difficulty; so that the task being unperformed, blows, insults, and perjuries, and a thousand other evils, may take place. And just as when children drag with all their might a long and rotten cord in directions opposite to each other; if the cord snaps in the middle, they all fall flat upon their backs, and some strike their heads, and some another part of the body; so also they who each engage with an oath to perform things that are contrary, when the oath is broken by the necessity of the case, both parties fall into the same gulf of perjury: these by actually perjuring themselves, and those by affording the occasion of perjury to the others.

    5. That this also may be rendered evident, not only from what happens every day in private houses, and the places of public concourse, but from the Scriptures themselves, I will relate to you a piece of ancient history, which bears upon what has been said. Once, when the Jews had been invaded by their enemies, and Jonathan

(now he was the son of Saul) had slaughtered some, and put the rest to flight; Saul, his father, being desirous to rouse the army more effectually against the remainder; and in order that they might not desist until he had subjugated them all, did that which was altogether opposite to what he desired, by swearing that no one should eat any food until evening, and until vengeance was taken of his enemies. What, I ask, could have been more senseless than this? For when it was needful that he should have refreshed those who were fatigued and exhausted, and have sent them forth with renewed vigor against their enemies, he treated them far worse than he had done their enemies, by the constraint of an oath, which delivered them over to excessive hunger. Dangerous, indeed, it is for anyone to swear in a matter pertaining to himself; for we are forcibly impelled to do many things by the urgency of circumstances. But much more dangerous is it by the obligation of one's own oath, to bind the determination of others; and especially where any one swears, not concerning one, or two, or three, but an unlimited multitude, which Saul then inconsiderately did, without thinking that it was probable that, in so vast a number, one at least might transgress the oath; or that soldiers, and soldiers too on campaign, are very far removed from moral wisdom, and know nothing of ruling the belly; more especially when their fatigue is great. He, however, overlooking all these points, as if he were merely taking an oath about a single servant, whom he was easily able to restrain, counted equally on his whole army. In consequence of this he opened such a door for the devil, that in a short time he framed, not two, three, or four, but many more perjuries out of this oath. For as when we do not swear at all, we close the whole entrance against him, so if we utter but a single oath, we afford him great liberty for constructing endless perjuries. And just as those who twist skeins, if they have one to hold the end, work the whole string with nicety, but if there is no one to do this, cannot even undertake the commencement of it; in the same manner too the devil, when about to twist the skein of our sins, if he could not get the beginning from our tongues, would not be able to undertake the work; but should we only make a commencement, while we hold the oath on our tongue, as it were a hand, then with full liberty he manifests his malignant art in the rest of the work, constructing and weaving from a single oath a thousand perjuries.

6. And this was just what he did now in the case of Saul. Observe, however, what a snare is immediately framed for this oath: "The army passed through a wood, that contained a nest of bees, and the nest was in front of the people, and the people came upon the nest, and went along talking." See what a pit-fall was here? A table ready spread, that the easiness of access, the sweetness of the food, and the hope of concealment, might entice them to a transgression of the oath. For hunger at once, and fatigue, and the hour, (for "all the land," it is said, "was dining,") then urged them to the transgression. Moreover, the sight of the combs invited them from without to relax the strain on their resolution. For the sweetness, as well as the present readiness of the table, and the difficulty of detecting the stealth, were sufficient to ensnare their utmost wisdom. If it had been flesh, which needed boiling or roasting, their minds would not have been so much bewitched; since while they were delaying in the cookery of these, and engaged in preparing them for food, they might expect to be discovered. But now there was nothing

of this kind; there was honey only, for which no such labor was required, and for which the dipping of the tip of the finger sufficed to partake of the table, and that with secrecy. Nevertheless, these persons restrained their appetite, and did not say within themselves, "What does it concern us? Hath any one of us sworn this? He may pay the penalty of his inconsiderate oath, for why did he swear?" Nothing of this sort did they think; but religiously passed on; and though there were so many enticements, they behaved themselves wisely. "The people went on talking." What is the meaning of this word "talking?" Why, that for the purpose of soothing their pain with words, they held discourse with one another.

7. What then, did nothing more come of this, when all the people had acted so wisely? Was the oath, forsooth, observed? Not even so was it observed. On the contrary, it was violated! How, and in what way? Ye shall hear forthwith, in order that ye may also thoroughly discern the whole art of the devil. For Jonathan, not having heard his father take the oath, "put forth the end of the rod that was in his hand, and dipped it in the honeycomb, and his eyes saw clearly." Observe, who it was whom he impelled to break the oath; not one of the soldiers, but the very son of him who had sworn it. For he did not only desire to effect perjury, but was also plotting the slaughter of a son, and making provision for it beforehand; and was in haste to divide nature against her own self. And what he had done aforetime in the case of Jephthah, that he hoped now again to accomplish. For he likewise, when he had promised that the first thing that met him, after a victorious battle, he would sacrifice, fell into the snare of child-murder; for his daughter first

meeting him, he sacrificed her and God did not forbid it. And I know, indeed, that many of the unbelievers impugn us of cruelty and inhumanity on account of this sacrifice; but I should say, that the concession in the case of this sacrifice was a striking example of providence and clemency; and that it was in care for our race that He did not prevent that sacrifice. For if after that vow and promise He had forbidden the sacrifice, many also who were subsequent to Jephthah, in the expectation that God would not receive their vows, would have increased the number of such vows, and proceeding on their way would have fallen into child-murder. But now, by suffering this vow to be actually fulfilled, He put a stop to all such cases in future. And to shew that this is true, after Jephthah's daughter had been slain, in order that the calamity might be always remembered, and that her fate might not be consigned to oblivion, it became a law among the Jews, that the virgins assembling at the same season should bewail during forty days the sacrifice which had taken place; in order that renewing the memory of it by lamentation, they should make all men wiser for the future; and that they might learn that it was not after the mind of God that this should be done, for in that case He would not have permitted the virgins to bewail and lament her. And that what I have said is not conjectural, the event demonstrated; for after this sacrifice, no one vowed such a vow unto God. Therefore also He did not indeed forbid this; but what He had expressly enjoined in the case of Isaac, that He directly prohibited; plainly shewing through both cases, that He doth not delight in such sacrifices.

8. But the malignant demon was laboring hard now again to produce such a tragedy. Therefore he impelled Jonathan to the trespass. For if any one of the

soldiers had transgressed the law, it seemed to him no great evil that would have been done; but now being insatiate of human ills, and never able to get his fill of our calamities, he thought it would be no grand exploit if he effected only a simple murder. And if he could not also pollute the king's right hand with the murder of his child, he considered that he had achieved no great matter. And why do I speak of child-murder? For he, the wicked one, thought that by this means he should compass a slaughter even more accursed than that. For if he had sinned wittingly, and been sacrificed, this would only have been child-murder; but now sinning ignorantly, (for he had not heard of the oath), if he had been slain, he would have made the anguish of his father double; for he would have had both to sacrifice a son, and a son who had done no wrong. But now to proceed with the rest of the history; "When he had eaten," it is said, "His eyes saw clearly." And here it condemns the king of great folly; shewing that hunger had almost blinded the whole army, and diffused much darkness over their eyes. Afterwards some one of the soldiers, perceiving the action, says, "Thy father swore an oath upon all the people, saying, cursed be the man who eats any food today. And the people were faint. And Jonathan said, My father hath made away with the land." What does he mean by the word, "made away with?" Why, that he had ruined, or destroyed them all. Hence, when the oath was transgressed, all kept silence, and no one dared to bring forth the criminal; and this became afterwards no small matter of blame, for not only are those who break an oath, but those also who are privy to it and conceal it, partakers of the crime.

9. But let us see what follows; "And Saul said, Let us go down after the strangers, and spoil them. And the

priest said, Let us draw near hither unto God." For in old times God led forth the people to battle; and without His consent no one dared to engage in the fight, and war was with them a matter of religion. For not from weakness of body, but from their sins they were conquered, whenever they were conquered; and not by might and courage, but by favor from above they prevailed, whenever they did prevail. Victory and defeat were also to them a means of training, and a school of virtue. And not to them only, but to their adversaries; for this was made evident to them too, that the fate of battle with the Jews was decided not by the nature of their arms, but by the life and good works of the warriors. The Midianites at least perceiving this, and knowing that people to be invincible, and that to have attacked them with arms and engines of war would have been fruitless, and that it was only possible to conquer them by sin, having decked out handsome virgins, and set them in the array, excited the soldiers to lasciviousness, endeavoring by means of fornication to deprive them of God's assistance; which accordingly happened. For when they had fallen into sin, they became an easy prey to all; and those whom weapons, and horses, and soldiers, and so many engines availed not to capture, sin by its nature delivered over bound to their enemies. Shields, and spears, and darts were all alike found useless; but beauty of visage and wantonness of soul overpowered these brave men.

10. Therefore one gives this admonition; "Observe not the beauty of a strange woman, and meet not a woman addicted to fornication. For honey distils from the lips of an harlot, which at the time may seem smooth to thy throat, but afterward thou wilt find it more bitter than gall, and sharper than a two-edged sword." For the harlot

knows not how to love, but only to ensnare; her kiss hath poison, and her mouth a pernicious drug. And if this does not immediately appear, it is the more necessary to avoid her on that account, because she veils that destruction, and keeps that death concealed, and suffers it not to become manifest at the first. So that if anyone pursues pleasure, and a life full of gladness, let him avoid the society of fornicating women, for they fill the minds of their lovers with a thousand conflicts and tumults, setting in motion against them continual strifes and contentions, by means of their words, and all their actions. And just as it is with those who are the most virulent enemies, so the object of their actions and schemes is to plunge their lovers into shame and poverty, and the worst extremities. And in the same manner as hunters, when they have spread out their nets, endeavor to drive thither the wild animals, in order that they may put them to death, so also is it with these women. When they have spread out on every side the wings of lasciviousness by means of the eyes, and dress, and language, they afterwards drive in their lovers, and bind them; nor do they give over until they have drunk up their blood, insulting them at last, and mocking their folly, and pouring over them a flood of ridicule. And indeed such a man is no longer worthy of compassion but deserves to be derided and jeered, since he is found more irrational than a woman, and a harlot besides. Therefore the Wise Man gives this word of exhortation again, "Drink waters from thine own cistern, and from the fountain of thine own well." And again; "Let the hind of thy friendship, and the foal of thy favors, consort with thee." These things he speaks of a wife associated with her husband by the law of marriage. Why leaves thou her who is a helpmate, to run to one who is a plotter against thee? Why dost thou turn away from her who is the partner of thy living, and court her who would subvert thy life? The one is thy member and body, the other is a sharp sword. Therefore, beloved, flee fornication; both for its present evils, and for its future punishment.

11. Perchance we may seem to have fallen aside from the subject; but to say thus much, is no departure from it. For we do not wish to read you histories merely for their own sake, but that you may correct each of the passions which trouble you: therefore also we make these frequent appeals, preparing our discourse for you in all varieties of style; since it is probable that in so large an assembly, there is a great variety of distempers; and our task is to cure not one only, but many different wounds; and therefore it is necessary that the medicine of instruction should be various. Let us however return thither from whence we made this digression: "And the Priest said, Let us draw near unto God. And Saul asked counsel of God. Shall I go down after the strangers? Wilt Thou deliver them into my hands? But on that day the Lord answered him not." Observe the benignity and mildness of God who loves man. For He did not launch a thunderbolt, nor shake the earth; but what friends do to friends, when treated contemptuously, this the Lord did towards the servant. He only received him silently, speaking by His silence, and by it giving utterance to all His wrath. This Saul understood, and said, as it is recorded, "Bring near hither all the tribes of the people, and know and see in whom this sin hath been this day. For as the Lord lives, Who hath saved Israel, though the answer be against Jonathan my son, he shall surely die." See his rashness? Perceiving that his first oath had been

transgressed, he does not even then learn self-control, but adds again a second. Consider also the malignity of the devil. For since he was aware that frequently the son when discovered, and publicly arraigned, is able by the very sight at once to make the father relent, and might soften the king's wrath, he anticipated his sentence by the obligation of a second oath; holding him by a kind of double bond, and not permitting him to be the master of his own determination, but forcing him on every side to that iniquitous murder. And even whilst the offender was not yet produced, he hath passed judgment, and whilst ignorant of the criminal, he gave sentence. The father became the executioner; and before the enquiry declared his verdict of condemnation! What could be more irrational than this proceeding?

12. Saul then having made this declaration, the people were more afraid than before, and all were in a state of great trembling and terror. But the devil rejoiced, at having rendered them all thus anxious. There was no one, we are told, of all the people, who answered. "And Saul said, Ye will be in bondage, and I, and Jonathan my son, will be in bondage." But what he means is to this effect; "You are aiming at nothing else, than to deliver yourselves to your enemies, and to become slaves instead of free men; whilst you provoke God against you, in not delivering up the guilty person." Observe also another contradiction produced by the oath. It had been fitting, if he wished to find the author of this guilt, to have made no such threat, nor to have bound himself to vengeance by an oath; that becoming less afraid, they might more readily bring the offender to light. But under the influence of anger, and great madness, and his former unreasonableness, he again does that which is directly

contrary to what he desires. What need is there to enlarge? He commits the matter to a decision by lot; and the lot falls upon Saul, and Jonathan; "And Saul said, Cast ye the lot between me and Jonathan; and they cast the lot, and Jonathan was taken. And Saul said to Jonathan, Tell me, what hast thou done? And Jonathan told him, saying, I only tasted a little honey on the top of the rod which is in my hand, and, lo! I must die." Who is there that these words would not have moved and turned to pity? Consider what a tempest Saul then sustained, his bowels being torn with anguish, and the most profound precipice appearing on either hand! But nevertheless he did not learn self-control, for what does he say? "God do so to me, and more also; for thou shalt surely die this day." Behold again the third oath, and not simply the third, but one with a very narrow limit as to time; for he does not merely say, "Thou shalt die;" but, "this day." For the devil was hurrying, hurrying him on, constraining him and driving him to this impious murder. Wherefore he did not suffer him to assign any future day for the sentence, lest there should be any correction of the evil by delay. And the people said to Saul, "God do so to us, and more also, if he shall be put to death, who hath wrought this great salvation in Israel. As the Lord lives, there shall not an hair of his head fall to the ground; because he hath wrought a merciful thing from God today." Behold how, in the second place, the people also swore, and swore contrary to the king.

13. Now recollect, I pray, the cord pulled by the children, and breaking, and throwing on their backs those who pull it. Saul swore not once or twice, but several times. The people swore what was contrary, and strained in the opposite direction. Of necessity then it followed,

that the oath must in any wise be broken through. For it were impossible that all these should keep their oaths. And now tell me not of the event of this transaction; but consider how many evils were springing from it; and how the devil from thence was preparing the tragedy and usurpation of Absalom. For if the king had chosen to resist, and to proceed to the execution of his oath, the people would have been in array against him; and a grievous rebellion would have been set on foot. And again, if the son consulting his own safety had chosen to throw himself into the hands of the army, he would straightway have become a parricide. See not, that rebellion, as well as child-murder, and parricide, and battle, and civil war, and slaughter, and blood, and dead bodies without number, are the consequences of one oath. For if war had perchance broken out, Saul might have been slain, and Jonathan perchance too, and many of the soldiers would have been cut to pieces; and after all the keeping of the oath would not have been forwarded. So that it is not for thee to consider that these events did not occur, but to mark this point, that it was the nature of the case to necessitate the occurrence of such things. However, the people prevailed. Come then, let us reckon up the perjuries that were the consequence. The oath of Saul was first broken by his son; and again a second and a third, concerning the slaying of his son, by Saul himself. And the people seemed to have kept their oath. Yet if anyone closely examines the matter, they too all became liable to the charge of perjury. For they compelled the father of Jonathan to perjure himself, by not surrendering the son to the father. See how many persons one oath made obnoxious to perjury, willingly and unwillingly; how many evils it wrought, how many deaths it caused?

14. Now in the commencement of this discourse I promised to shew that perjury would in any case result from opposite oaths; but truly the course of the history has proved more than I was establishing. It has exhibited not one, two, or three individuals, but a whole people, and not one, two, or three oaths, but many more transgressed. I might also make mention of another instance, and shew from that, how one oath caused a still greater and more grievous calamity. For one oath entailed upon all the Jews the capture of their cities, as well as of their wives and children; the ravages of fire, the invasion of barbarians, the pollution of sacred things, and ten thousand other evils yet more distressing. But I perceive that the discourse is running to a great length. Therefore, dismissing here the narration of this history, I beseech you, together with the beheading of John, to tell one another also of the murder of Jonathan, and the general destruction of a whole people (which did not indeed take place, but which was involved in the obligation of the oaths); and both at home, and in public, and with your wives, and friends, and with neighbors, and with all men in general, to make an earnest business of this matter, and not to think it a sufficient apology that we can plead custom.

15. For that this excuse is a mere pretext, and that the fault arises not from custom but from listlessness, I will endeavor to convince you from what has already occurred. The Emperor has shut up the baths of the city, and has given orders that no one shall bathe; and no one has dared to transgress the law, nor to find fault with what has taken place, nor to allege custom. But even though in weak health perchance, men and women, and children and old men; and many women but recently eased from the pangs of childbirth; though all requiring this as a

necessary medicine; bear with the injunction, willingly or unwillingly; and neither plead infirmity of body, nor the tyranny of custom, nor that they are punished, whereas others were the offenders, nor any other thing of this kind, but contentedly put up with this punishment, because they were in expectation of greater evils; and pray daily that the wrath of the Emperor may go no further. See that where there is fear, the bond of custom is easily relaxed, although it be of exceedingly long standing, and great necessity? To be denied the use of the bath is certainly a grievous matter. For although we be never so philosophic, the nature of the body proves incapable of deriving any benefit for its own health, from the philosophy of the soul. But as to abstinence from swearing, this is exceedingly easy, and brings no injury at all; none to the body, none to the mind; but, on the contrary, great gain, much safety, and abundant wealth. How then is it anything but absurd, to submit to the greatest hardships, when an Emperor enjoins it; but when God commands nothing grievous nor difficult, but what is very tolerable and easy, to despise or to deride it, and to advance custom as an excuse? Let us not, I entreat, so far despise our own safety, but let us fear God as we fear man. I know that ye shudder at hearing this, but what deserves to be shuddered at is that ye do not pay even so much respect to God; and that whilst ye diligently observe the Emperor's decrees, ye trample under foot those which are divine, and which have come down from heaven; and consider diligence concerning these a secondary object. For what apology will there be left for us, and what pardon, if after so much admonition we persist in the same practices. For I began this admonition at the very commencement of the calamity which has taken hold of the city, and that is now on the point of coming to an end; but we have not as yet thoroughly put in practice even one precept. How then can we ask a removal of the evils which still beset us, when we have not been able to perform a single precept? How can we expect a change for the better? How shall we pray? With what tongue shall we call upon God? For if we perform the law, we shall enjoy much pleasure, when the Emperor is reconciled to the city. But if we remain in the transgression, shame and reproach will be ours on every hand, inasmuch as when God hath freed us from the danger we have continued in the same listlessness.

16. Oh! That it were possible for me to undress the souls of those who swear frequently, and to expose to view the wounds and the bruises which they receive daily from oaths! We should then need neither admonition nor counsel; for the sight of these wounds would avail more powerfully than all that could be said, to withdraw from their wickedness even those who are most addicted to this wicked practice. Nevertheless, if it be not possible to spread before the eyes the shameful state of their soul, it may be possible to expose it to the thoughts, and to display it in its rottenness and corruption. For as it says, "As a servant that is continually beaten will not be clear of a bruise, so he that swears and names God continually will not be purified of his sin." It is impossible, utterly impossible, that the mouth which is practiced in swearing, should not frequently commit perjury. Therefore, I beseech you all, by laying aside this dreadful and wicked habit, to win another crown. And since it is everywhere sung of our city, that first of all the cities of the world, she bound on her brow the name of Christians, so let all have to say, that Antioch alone, of all the cities throughout the world, hath expelled all oaths from her own borders. Yea,

rather, should this be done, she will not be herself crowned alone, but will also carry others along with her to the same pitch of zeal. And as the name of Christians having had its origin here, hath as it were from a kind of fountain overflown all the world, even so this good work, having taken its root and starting-point from hence, will make all men that inhabit the earth your disciples; so that a double and treble reward may arise to you, at once on account of your own good works, and of the instruction afforded to others. This will be to you the brightest of diadems! This will make your city a mother city, not on earth, but in the heavens! This will stand by us at That Day, and bring us the crown of righteousness; which God grant that we may all obtain, through the grace and lovingkindness of our Lord Jesus Christ, with Whom to the Father, together with the Holy Spirit, be glory, now and ever, and world without end. Amen.

Homily XV.

Again on the calamity of the city of Antioch. That fear is every way profitable. That sorrow is more useful than laughter. And upon the saying, "Remember that thou walks in the midst of snares." And that it is worse to exact an oath, than to commit murder.

1. To-day, and on the former Sabbath, it had behooved us to enter on the subject of fasting; nor let anyone suppose that what I said was unseasonable. For on the days of the fast, counsel and admonition on that subject are indeed not at all necessary; the very presence of these days exciting even those who are the most remiss to the effort of fasting. But since many men, both when about to enter upon the fast, as if the belly were on the point of being delivered over to a sort of lengthened siege, lay in beforehand a stock of gluttony and drunkenness; and again, on being set at liberty, going forth as from a long famine and a grievous prison, run to the table with unseemly greediness, just as if they were striving to undo again the advantage gained through the fast, by an excess of gluttony; it might have been needful, that then as well as now, we should agitate the subject of temperance. Nevertheless, we have neither lately said anything of that kind, neither shall we now speak upon it. For the fear of the impending calamity suffices, instead of the strongest admonition and counsel, to sober the soul of everyone. For who is there so miserable and degraded, as to be drunken in such a tempest? Who is there so insensible, when the city is thus agitated, and such a shipwreck is threatened, as not to become abstemious and watchful, and more thoroughly reformed by this distress than by

any other sort of admonition and counsel? For discourse will not be able to effect as much as fear does. And this very thing it is now possible to shew from the events which have taken place. How many words then did we spend before this in exhorting many that were listless, and counselling them to abstain from the theatres, and the impurities of these places! And still they did not abstain; but always on this day they flocked together to the unlawful spectacles of the dancers; and they held their diabolical assembly in opposition to the full congregation of God's Church; so that their vehement shouts, borne in the air from that place, resounded against the psalms which we were singing here. But behold, now whilst we were keeping silence, and saying nothing on the subject, they of themselves have shut up their orchestra; and the Hippodrome has been left deserted! Before this, many of our own people used to hasten to them; but now they are all fled hither from thence to the church, and all alike join in praising our God!

2. See what advantage is come of fear? If fear were not a good thing, fathers would not have set tutors over their children; nor lawgivers magistrates for cities. What can be more grievous than hell? Yet nothing is more profitable than the fear of it; for the fear of hell will bring us the crown of the kingdom. Where fear is, there is no envy; where fear is, the love of money does not disturb; where fear is, wrath is quenched, evil concupiscence is repressed, and every unreasonable passion is exterminated. And even as in a house, where there is always a soldier under arms, no robber, nor housebreaker, nor any such evil doer will dare to make his appearance; so also while fear holds possession of our minds, none of the base passions will readily attack us,

but all fly off and are banished, being driven away in every direction by the despotic power of fear. And not only this advantage do we gain from fear, but also another which is far greater. For not only, indeed, does it expel our evil passions, but it also introduces every kind of virtue with great facility. Where fear exists, there is zeal in alms-giving, and intensity of prayer, and tears warm and frequent, and groans fraught with compunction. For nothing so swallows up sin, and makes virtue to increase and flourish, as a perpetual state of dread. Therefore it is impossible for him who does not live in fear to act aright; as, on the other hand, it is impossible that the man who lives in fear can go wrong.

3. Let us not then grieve, beloved, let us not despond on account of the present tribulation, but let us admire the well-devised plan of God's wisdom. For by these very means through which the devil hoped to overturn our city, hath God restored and corrected it. The devil animated certain lawless men to treat the very statues of the Emperor contemptuously, in order that the very foundations of the city might be razed. But God employed this same circumstance for our greater correction; driving out all sloth by the dread of the expected wrath: and the thing has turned out directly opposite to what the devil wished, by the means which he had himself prepared. For our city is being purified every day; and the lanes and crossings, and places of public concourse, are freed from lascivious and voluptuous songs; and turn where we will there are supplications, and thanksgivings, and tears, instead of rude laughter; there are words of sound wisdom instead of obscene language, and our whole city has become a Church, the workshops being closed, and all being engaged throughout the day in

these general prayers; and calling upon God in one united voice with much earnestness. What preaching, what admonition, what counsel, what length of time had ever availed to accomplish these things?

4. For this then let us be thankful, and let us not be petulant or discontented; for that fear is a good thing, what we have said hath made manifest. But hear Solomon thus uttering a lesson of wisdom concerning it; Solomon, who was nourished in every luxury, and enjoyed much security. What then does he say? "It is better to go to the house of mourning than to the house of laughter." What say you, I ask? Is it better to go where there is weeping, lamentation, and groans, and anguish, and so much sadness, than where there is the dance, the cymbals, and laughter, and luxury, and full eating and drinking? Yes, verily, he replies. And tell me why is it so, and for what reason? Because, at the former place, insolence is bred, at the latter, sobriety. And when a person goes to the banquet of one more opulent, he will no longer behold his own house with the same pleasure, but he comes back to his wife in a discontented mood; and in discontent he partakes of his own table; and is peevish towards his own servants, and his own children, and everybody in his house; perceiving his own poverty the more forcibly by the wealth of others. And this is not the only evil; but that he also often envies him who hath invited him to the feast, and returns home having received no benefit at all. But with regard to the house of mourning, nothing of this sort can be said. On the contrary, much spiritual wisdom is to be gained there, as well as sobriety. For when once a person hath passed the threshold of a house which contains a corpse, and hath seen the departed one lying speechless, and the wife tearing her hair, mangling her

cheeks, and wounding her arms, he is subdued; his countenance becomes sad; and every one of those who sit down together can say to his neighbor but this, "We are nothing, and our wickedness is inexpressible!" What can be more full of wisdom than these words, when we both acknowledge the insignificance of our nature, and accuse our own wickedness, and account present things as nothing? Giving utterance, though in different words, to that very sentiment of Solomon—that sentiment which is so marvelous and pregnant with Divine wisdom—"Vanity of vanities, all is vanity." He who enters the house of mourning, weeps forthwith for the departed, even though he be an enemy. See how much better that house is than the other? For there, though he be a friend, he envies; but here, though he be an enemy, he weeps. This is a thing which God requires of us above all, that we should not insult over those who have occasioned us grief. And not only may we gather these advantages, but others also which are not less than these. For each one is also put in mind of his own sins, and of the fearful Tribunal; of the great Account, and of the Judgment; and although he may have been suffering a thousand evils from others, and have a cause for sadness at home, he will receive and take back with him the medicine for all these things. For reflecting that he himself, and all those who swell with pride, will in a little while suffer the same thing; and that all present things, whether pleasant or painful, are transitory; he thus returns to his house, disburdened of all sadness and envy, with a light and buoyant heart; and hence he will hereafter be more meek, and gentle, and benignant to all; as well as more wise; the fear of things to come having made its way into his soul, and consumed all the thorns.

6. All this Solomon perceived when he said, "It is better to go to the house of mourning than to the house of drinking." From the one grows listlessness, from the other an earnest anxiety. From the one, contempt; from the other, fear; a fear which conducts us to the practice of every virtue. If fear were not a good thing, Christ would not have expended such long and frequent discourses on the subject of punishment, and vengeance to come. Fear is nothing less than a wall, and a defense, and an impregnable tower. For indeed we stand in need of much defense, seeing that there are many ambushes on every side. Even as this same Solomon again says admonishingly, "Perceive that thou goes in the midst of snares, and that thou walks on the battlements of cities." Oh with how many good things is this saying pregnant! Yea, not less than the former! Let us then, write it, each of us, upon our minds, and carry it about ever in our memories, and we shall not easily commit sin. Let us write it there, having first learnt it with the utmost exactness. For he does not say, "Observe" that thou goes in the midst of snares; but, "Perceive!" And for what reason did he say, "Discern?" He tells us that the snare is concealed; for this is indeed a snare, when the destruction does not appear openly, and the injury is not manifest, which lies hidden on all sides. Therefore he says, "Perceive!" Thou needs much reflection and diligent scrutiny. For even as boys conceal traps with earth, so the devil covers up our sins with the pleasures of this life.

7. But "perceive;" scrutinizing diligently; and if any kind of gain falls in thy way, look not only at the gain, but inspect it carefully, lest somewhere death and sin lurk within the gain; and should you perceive this, fly from it. Again, when some delight or pleasure may

chance to present itself, look not only at the pleasure; but lest somewhere in the depth of the pleasure some iniquity should lie enveloped, search closely, and if thou discovers it, hasten away! And should anyone counsel, or flatter, or cajole, or promise honors, or any other such thing whatever, let us make the closest investigation; and look at the matter on all sides, lest something pernicious, something perilous, should perchance befall us through this advice, or honor, or attention, and we run upon it hastily and unwittingly. For if there were only one or two snares, the precaution would be easy. But now, hear how Solomon speaks when he wishes to set forth the multitude of these; "Perceive that thou goes in the midst of snares;" he does not say, that thou "goes by" snares, but "in the midst" of snares. On either side are the pit-falls; on either side the deceits. One goes into the forum; one sees an enemy; one is inflamed by the bare sight of him! One sees a friend honored; one is envious! One sees a poor man; one despises and takes no notice of him! One sees a rich man; one envies him! One sees someone injuriously treated; one recoils in disgust! One sees someone acting injuriously; one is indignant! One sees a handsome woman, and is caught! See beloved, how many snares there are? Therefore it is said, "Remember that thou goes in the midst of snares." There are snares in the house, snares at the table, and snares in social intercourse. Very often a person unwittingly, in the confidence of friendship, gives utterance to some particular of those matters which ought not to be repeated again, and so great a peril is brought about, that the whole family is thereby ruined!

8. On every side then let us search closely into these matters. Often has a wife, often have children, often

have friends, often have neighbors, proved a snare to the unheeding! And why, it is asked, are there so many snares? That we may not fly low, but seek the things that are above. For just as birds, as long as they cleave the upper air, are not easily caught; so also thou, as long as thou looks to things above, wilt not be easily captured, whether by a snare, or by any other device. The devil is a fowler. Soar, then, too high for his arrows. The man who hath mounted aloft will no longer admire anything in the affairs of this life. But as when we have ascended to the top of the mountains, the city and its walls seem to us to be but small, and the men appear to us to be going along upon the earth like ants; so when thou hast ascended to the heights of spiritual wisdom, nothing upon the earth will be able to fascinate thee; but everything, yea even riches, and glory, and honor, and whatever else there be of that kind, will appear insignificant when thou regards heavenly things. According to Paul all the glories of the present life appeared trifling, and more unprofitable than dead things. Hence his exclamation, "The world is crucified unto me." Hence also his admonition, "Set your affections on things above." Above? What kinds of things do you speak of pray? Where the sun is, where the moon is? Nay, says he. But where then? Where angels are? Where archangels? Where the cherubim? Where the seraphim are? Nay, says he. But where then? "Where Christ sits at the right hand of God."

9. Let us obey then, and let us think of this continually, that even as to the bird caught in the snare, wings are of no service, but he beats them about vainly, and to no purpose; so also to thee there is no utility in thy reasoning, when once thou art powerfully captivated by wicked lust, but struggle as much as thou may, thou art

captured! For this reason wings are given to birds; that they may avoid snares. For this reason men have the power of thinking; that they may avoid sin. What pardon then, or what excuse will be ours, when we become more senseless than the brutes? For the bird which has once been captured by the snare, yet afterwards escaped, and the deer which has fallen into the net, but has broken through it, are hard to be captured again with the like; since experience becomes a teacher of caution to everyone. But we, though often snared in the same nets, fall into the same again; and though honored with reason, we do not imitate the forethought and care of the irrational animals! Hence how often do we, from beholding a woman, suffer a thousand evils; returning home, and entertaining an inordinate desire, and experiencing anguish for many days; yet, nevertheless, we are not made discreet; but when we have scarcely cured one wound, we again fall into the same mischief, and are caught by the same means; and for the sake of the brief pleasure of a glance, we sustain a kind of lengthened and continual torment. But if we learn constantly to repeat to ourselves this saying, we shall be kept from all these grievous evils.

10. The beauty of woman is the greatest snare. Or rather, not the beauty of woman, but unchastened gazing! For we should not accuse the objects, but ourselves, and our own carelessness. Nor should we say, Let there be no women, but Let there be no adulteries. We should not say, Let there be no beauty, but Let there be no fornication. We should not say, Let there be no belly, but let there be no gluttony; for the belly makes not the gluttony, but our negligence. We should not say, that it is because of eating and drinking that all these evils exist; for it is not because

of this, but because of our carelessness and insatiableness. Thus the devil neither ate nor drank, and yet he fell! Paul ate and drank, and ascended up to heaven! How many do I hear say, Let there be no poverty! Therefore let us stop the mouths of those who murmur at such things. For it is blasphemy to utter such complaints. To such then, let us say, Let there be no meanness of spirit. For poverty brings innumerable good things into our state of life, and without poverty riches would be unprofitable. Hence we should accuse neither the one nor the other of these; for poverty and riches are both alike weapons which will tend to virtue, if we are willing. As then the courageous soldier, whichever weapon he takes, displays his own virtue, so the unmanly and cowardly one is encumbered by either. And that thou may learn that this is true, remember, I pray, the case of Job; who became both rich, and likewise poor, and handled both these weapons alike, and conquered in both. When he was rich, he said, "My door was open to every comer." But when he had become poor, "The Lord gave, and the Lord hath taken away. As it seemed good unto the Lord, so hath it come to pass." When he was rich, he shewed much hospitality; when he was poor, much patience. And thou, then,—art thou rich? Display much bountifulness! Hast thou become poor? Shew much endurance and patience! For neither is wealth an evil, nor poverty in itself; but these things, either of them, become so according to the free choice of those who make use of them. Let us school ourselves then to entertain no such opinions on these subjects; nor let us accuse the works of God, but the wicked choice of men. Riches are not able to profit the little-minded: nor is poverty able ever to injure the magnanimous.

11. Let us then discern the snares, and walk far off from them! Let us discern the precipices, and not even approach them! This will be the foundation of our greatest safety not only to avoid things sinful, but those things which seem indeed to be indifferent, and yet are apt to make us stumble towards sin. For example; to laugh, to speak jocosely, does not seem an acknowledged sin, but it leads to acknowledged sin. Thus laughter often gives birth to foul discourse, and foul discourse to actions still more foul. Often from words and laughter proceed railing and insult; and from railing and insult, blows and wounds; and from blows and wounds, slaughter and murder. If, then, thou would take good counsel for thyself, avoid not merely foul words, and foul deeds, or blows, and wounds, and murders, but unseasonable laughter, itself, and the very language of banter; since these things have proved the root of subsequent evils. Therefore Paul says, "Let no foolish talking nor jesting proceed out of thy mouth." For although this seems to be a small thing in itself, it becomes, however, the cause of much mischief to us. Again, to live in luxury does not seem to be a manifest and admitted crime; but then it brings forth in us great evils,—drunkenness, violence, extortion, and rapine. For the prodigal and sumptuous liver, bestowing extravagant service upon the belly, is often compelled to steal, and to seize the property of others, and to use extortion and violence. If, then, thou avoids luxurious living, thou removes the foundation of extortion, and rapine, and drunkenness, and a thousand other evils; cutting away the root of iniquity from its extremity. Hence Paul says, that "she who lives in pleasure is dead while she lives." Again, to go to the theatres, or to survey the horserace, or to play at dice, does not seem, to most men, to be an admitted

crime; but it introduces into our life an infinite host of miseries. For spending time in the theatres produces fornication, intemperance, and every kind of impurity. The spectacle of the horse-race also brings about fighting, railings, blows, insults, and lasting enmities. And a passion for dice-playing hath often caused blasphemies, injuries, anger, reproaches, and a thousand other things more fearful still.

12. Therefore, let us not only avoid sins, but those things too which seem to be indifferent, yet by degrees lead us into these misdeeds. He, indeed, who walks by the side of a precipice, even though he may not fall over, trembles; and very often he is overset by this same trembling, and falls to the bottom. So also he who does not avoid sins from afar, but walks near them, will live in fear, and will often fall into them. Besides, he who eagerly looks at strange beauties, although he may not commit adultery, hath in so doing entertained lust; and hath become already an adulterer according to the declaration of Christ; and often by this very lust he is carried on to the actual sin. Let us then withdraw ourselves far from sins. Do you wish to live soberly? Avoid not only adultery, but also the licentious glance! Do you wish to be far removed from foul words? Avoid not only foul words, but also inordinate laughter, and every kind of lust. Do you wish to keep far from committing murders? Avoid railing too. Do you wish to keep aloof from drunkenness? Avoid luxury and sumptuous tables, and pluck up the vice by the roots.

13. The licentiousness of the tongue is a great snare, and needs a strong bridle. Therefore also someone says. "His own lips are a powerful snare to a man, and he is snared by the words of his own mouth." Above all the

other members, then, let us control this; let us bridle it; and let us expel from the mouth railings, and contumelies, and foul and slanderous language, and the evil habit of oaths. For again our discourse hath brought us to the same exhortation. But I had arranged with your charity, yesterday, that I would say no more concerning this precept, forasmuch as enough has been said upon it on all the foregoing days. But what is to become of me? I cannot bear to desist from this counsel, until I see that ye have put it in practice; since Paul also, when he says to the Galatians, "Henceforth let no man trouble me," appears again to have met and addressed them. Such are the paternal bowels; although they say they will depart, yet they depart not, until they see that their sons are chastened. Have ye heard to-day what the prophet speaks to us concerning oaths; "I lifted up mine eyes, and I saw," says he, "and, behold, a flying sickle, the length thereof twenty cubits, and the breadth thereof ten cubits; and he said to me, What sees thou? And I said, I see a flying sickle, twenty cubits in length, and ten cubits in breadth. It shall also enter into the house," says he, "of every one that swears in my name, and shall remain in the midst, and shall pull down the stones and the wood." What, forsooth, is this which is here spoken? And for what reason is it in the form of a "sickle," and that a "flying sickle," that vengeance is seen to pursue the swearers? In order that thou may see that the judgment is inevitable, and the punishment not to be eluded. For from a flying sword someone might perchance be able to escape, but from a sickle, falling upon the neck, and acting in the place of a cord, no one can escape. And when wings too are added, what further hope is there of safety? But on what account doth it pull down the stones and the wood of the swearer's house? In order that the ruin may be a correction to all. For since it is necessary that the earth must hide the swearer when dead; the very sight of his ruined house, now become a heap, will be an admonition to all who pass by and observe it, not to venture on the like, lest they suffer the like; and it will be a lasting witness against the sin of the departed. The sword is not so piercing as the nature of an oath! The sabre is not so destructive as the stroke of an oath! The swearer, although he seems to live, is already dead, and hath received the fatal blow. And as the man who hath received the halter, before he hath gone out of the city and come to the pit, and seen the executioner standing over him, is dead from the time he passed the doors of the hall of justice: so also the swearer.

14. All this let us consider, and let us not put our brethren on oath. What dost thou, O man? At the sacred table thou exacts an oath, and where Christ lies slain, there thou slays thine own brother. Robbers, indeed, murder on the highways; but thou slays the son in the presence of the mother: committing a murder more accursed than Cain himself; for he slew his brother in solitude and only with present death; but thou slays thy brother in the midst of the church, and that with the deathless death that is to come! For think you that the church was made for this purpose, that we might swear? Yea, for this it was made, that we might pray! Is the Table placed there, that we may make adjurations? It is placed there to this end, that we may loose sins, not that we may bind them. But thou, if thou heeds nothing else, reverence at least that book, which thou reaches forth in putting the oath; and open the Gospel, which thou takes in hand when thou bids swear; and when thou hears what Christ there

declares concerning oaths, shudder and desist! What then does He there say concerning oaths? "But I say unto you, Swear not at all." And dost thou convert the Law which forbids swearing into an oath. Oh, what contempt! Oh, what outrage! For thou does just the same thing as if anyone should bid the lawgiver, who prohibits murder, become himself a party to the murder. Not so much do I lament and weep, when I hear that some persons are slain upon the highway, as I groan, and shed tears, and am horrified, when I see any one coming near this Table, placing his hands upon it, and touching the Gospels, and swearing! Art thou in doubt, I ask, concerning money, and would you slay a soul? What gains thou to match the injury thou does to thine own soul, and to thy neighbor? If thou believes that the man is true, do not impose the obligation of the oath; but if thou knows him to be a liar, do not force him to commit perjury. "But that I may have a full assurance:" says one. Verily, when thou hast not sworn him, then thou wilt receive a good and full assurance.

15. For now, when thou hast returned home, thou wilt be continually the prey of conscience, whilst reasoning thus with thyself; "Was it to no purpose, then, that I put him upon his oath? Was he not really perjured? Have I not become the cause of the sin?" But if thou dost not put him upon his oath, thou wilt receive much consolation on returning home, rendering thanks to God, and saying, "Blessed be God, that I restrained myself, and did not compel him to swear vainly, and to no purpose. Away with gold! Perish the money!" for that which specially gives us assurance is, that we did not transgress the law, nor compel another to do it. Consider, for Whose sake thou didst not put any one on his oath; and this will

suffice thee for refreshment and consolation. Often, indeed, when a fight takes place, we bear being insulted with fortitude, and we say to the insulter, "What shall I do with thee? Such a one hinders me, who is thy patron; he keeps back my hands." And this is sufficient to console us. So when thou art about to put any one on his oath, restrain thyself; and stop; and say to him who is about to swear, "What shall I do with thee? God hath forbidden me to put any one on oath. He now holds me back." This suffices both for the honor of the Lawgiver, and for thy safety, and for keeping him in fear who is ready to swear. For when he sees that we are thus afraid to put others on oath, much more will he himself be afraid to swear rashly. Would you say thus, thy return to thine own home would be with much fullness of assurance. Hear God, therefore, in His Commandments, that He may Himself hear thee in thy prayers! This word shall be written in heaven, and shall stand by thee on the Day of Judgment, and shall discharge many sins.

16. This also let us consider not only with respect to an oath, but to everything. And when we are about to do any good action for God's sake, and it is found to bring loss with it, let us look not merely at the loss connected with the matter, but at the gain which we shall reap by doing it for God. That is to say, Hath any one insulted thee? Bear it nobly! And thou wilt do so, if thou thinks not of the insult merely, but of the dignity of Him who commands thee to bear it, and thou bears it meekly. Hast thou given an alms? Think not of the outlay, but of the produce which arises from the outlay. Hast thou been mulcted of money? Give thanks, and regard not only the pain which is the result of the loss, but the gain which comes of thanksgiving. If we thus regulate ourselves,

none of those heavy events which may befall us will give us pain; but from those things which may seem to be grievous, we shall be even gainers, and loss will be sweeter and more desired than wealth, pain than pleasure, and mirth and insult than honor. Thus all things adverse will turn to our gain. And here we shall enjoy much tranquility, and there we shall attain the kingdom of heaven; which God grant that we may all be deemed worthy to obtain, by the grace and lovingkindness of our Lord Jesus Christ, through Whom and with Whom, to the Father with the Holy Spirit, be glory, dominion, and honor, now and ever, and world without end. Amen.

Homily XVI.

This Homily was delivered on the occasion of the Prefect entering the Church, for the purpose of pacifying the minds of the people, in consequence of a rumor of an intended sack having been announced to him, when all were meditating flight. It treats also on the subject of avoiding oaths, and on the words of the Apostle, "Paul, a prisoner of Jesus Christ."

1. I commend the Prefect's consideration, that seeing the city agitated, and everyone purposing a flight, he hath come here and afforded you consolation, and hath led you to entertain favorable hopes. But for you I blushed, and was ashamed, that after these long and frequent discourses ye should have needed consolation from without. I longed that the earth would open and swallow me up, when I heard him discoursing with you, alternately administering comfort, or blaming such ill-timed and senseless cowardice. For it was not becoming, that you should be instructed by him; but you ought yourselves to be teachers to all the unbelievers. Paul did not permit even going to law before the unbelievers; but thou, after so much admonition of our Fathers, hast needed teachers from without; and certain vagabonds and miscreants have again unsettled this great city, and set it upon flight. With what eyes shall we hereafter look upon the unbelievers, we who were so timid and cowardly? With what tongue shall we speak to them, and persuade them to exercise courage as to approaching evils, when we became through this alarm more timid than any hare? "But what could we do," says someone, "we are but men!" This is indeed the very reason why we ought not to

be terrified, because we are men, and not brutes. For these are scared by all manner of sounds and noises; because they have not reasoning power, which is adequate to dispel fear. But thou who hast been honored with the gift of speech and reason, how is it that thou sinks to their ignoble condition? Hath someone entered the city, and announced the march of soldiers against it? Be not terrified, but leaving him, bend the knee: call upon thy Lord: groan bitterly, and He will keep off the dreaded event.

2. Thou has heard indeed a false report of the march, and wert in danger of being severed from the present life. But that blessed Job, when the messengers came one after another, and he had heard them announcing their dreadful news, and adding thereto the insupportable destruction of his children, neither cried nor groaned, but turned to prayer, and gave thanks to the Lord. Him do thou too imitate; and when any comer announces that soldiers have encircled the city, and are about to plunder its wealth, flee to thy Lord and say, "The Lord gave, the Lord hath taken away; as it seemed good to the Lord, so is it done. Blessed be the name of the Lord forever." The experience of the actual events did not terrify him; yet the mere report frightens thee. And how are we to be accounted of, who when we are commanded boldly to encounter death itself, are thus affrighted by a false rumor! The man who is bewildered constructs fear which is unreal; and trouble which is not visible; but he who abides in a settled and tranquil condition of soul, breaks in pieces even that which is real. Sees not pilots; when the sea is raging, and the clouds are rushing together, and the thunders are bursting forth, and all on board are in confusion, they seat themselves at the helm

without tumult or disturbance; giving earnest heed to their own art, and considering how they may ward off the effects of the approaching storm. Be these thy example; and laying hold of the sacred anchor, the hope that is in God, remain unshaken and immoveable. "Whosoever hears these sayings of mine, and doeth them not, shall be likened unto a foolish man, which built his house upon the sand; and the rain descended, and the floods came, and the winds blew, and beat upon that house; and it fell, and great was the fall of it." See that it is the character of folly to fall down headlong, and to be overthrown? Or rather, we were not only reduced to the condition of that foolish man, but our fall was still more wretched. For the house of that man fell down after the rivers and rains had descended, and the winds had beaten upon it; but we, when there were no winds striking, nor floods invading, nor blasts assaulting, before the experience of disaster, were overturned by a mere rumor, and dropped at once all the philosophy we were meditating.

3. What think ye are now my thoughts? How should I conceal,—yea, bury myself? How must I blush with shame? If I had not been forcibly urged by our Fathers, I would not have arisen, I would not have spoken, whilst my mind was darkened with sadness because of your pusillanimity. But neither now have I been able to recover myself; since anger and sorrow have laid such siege to my soul. For who would not feel provoked and indignant, that after so much teaching ye should need the instructions of Gentiles, that ye might be comforted and persuaded to bear in a manly way the present alarm. Pray ye therefore that free utterance may be given us in opening our mouth; and that we may be able to shake off this sadness, and to hold up again a little;

for indeed this shame on account of your pusillanimity hath greatly depressed our spirits.

4. Lately, I addressed to your Charity many things concerning the snares lying on all sides of us; and concerning fear and sadness, sorrow and pleasure; and also concerning the sickle that flies down upon the houses of swearers. Now, out of all these many matters, I would have you especially to remember what I said respecting the "winged sickle," and its settling in the swearer's house; and pulling down the stones and the wood, and consuming the whole mass. And withal, take heed to this; that it is the extreme of folly to swear by taking the Gospels, and to turn the very Law which forbids swearing into an oath; and that it is better to suffer loss of property than to impose an oath on our neighbors; since this is a great honor to be done to God. For when thou says to God, "For thy sake I have not put such a one, who hath robbed and injured me, on his oath," God will pay thee back a great recompense on account of this honor, both here and hereafter. Say these things to others, and observe them also yourselves. I know that in this place we become more reverent, and lay aside every evil habit. But what is to be aimed at is, not that we be lovers of wisdom here only, but that when we depart, we may take this reverence out with us, where we especially need it. For those who carry water do not merely have their vessels full when near the fountain, and empty them when they reach home, but there they put them away with especial caution, that they may not be overturned, and their labors rendered useless. Let us all imitate these persons; and when we come home, let us strictly retain what has been spoken; since if ye here have gotten full, but return home empty, having the vessels of your understandings destitute of

what ye have heard, there will be no advantage from your replenishment here. Shew me not the wrestler in the place of exercise, but of actual contest; and religion not at the season of hearing, but at the season of practice.

5. Thou applauds what is said now. When thou art required to swear, then remember all these things. If ye quickly accomplish this law, we will advance our teaching to other and greater things. Lo! This is the second year that I am discoursing to your Charity; and I have not yet been able to explain a hundred lines of the Scriptures. And the reason is, that ye need to learn of us what ye might reduce to practice at home, and of yourselves; and thus the greater part of our exhortation is consumed on ethical discourse. But this ought not to have been so; the regulation of manners you ought to have learnt at home, and of yourselves; but the sense of the Scriptures, and the speculations upon them, you might commit to us. If, however, it were necessary that you should hear such things of us, there was no need of more than one day: for what there is to be said is of no diversified or difficult character, or such as requires any elaboration. For when God declares His sentence, subtle arguments are unseasonable. God hath said, "Thou shalt not swear." Do not then demand of me the reasons of this. It is a royal law. He who established it, knows the reason of the law. If it had not been profitable, He would not have forbidden it. Kings bring in laws, and not all perchance profitable; for they are men, and cannot be competent to discover what is useful, like God. Nevertheless, we obey them. Whether we marry, or make wills, or are about to purchase servants, or houses, or fields, or to do any other act, we do these things not according to our own mind, but according to the laws

which they ordain; and we are not entirely at liberty to dispose of the things which concern ourselves according to our own minds; but in many cases we are subject to their will; and should we do anything that is contrary to their judgment, it becomes invalid and useless. So then tell me, are we to pay so much respect to the laws of men, and trample underfoot the law of God? What defense, or what pardon can such conduct be worthy of? He hath said, "Thou shalt not swear." In order that thou may do and speak all things with safety, do not in practice lay down a law contrary to His.

6. But enough of these matters. Let us now proceed to lay before you one sentence of those which have been read to-day, and thus end this discourse. "Paul, a prisoner of Jesus Christ," says he, "and Timothy the brother." Great is the designation of Paul: no title of principality and power, but he speaks of bonds and chains! Truly great indeed! Although many other things made him illustrious; his being caught up into the third heaven, his being transported to Paradise, his hearing unutterable words; yet he sets down none of these, but mentions the chain instead of all, for this made him more conspicuous and illustrious than these. And why so? Because the one were the free gifts of the Lord's lovingkindness; and the other the marks of the constancy and patience of the servant. But it is customary with those who love, to glory more in the things which they suffer for those who are beloved, than in the benefits they receive from them. A king is not so proud of his diadem, as Paul gloried in his chains. And very justly. For a diadem affords but an ornament to the crowned head; but the chain is a much greater ornament as well as a security. The kingly crown often betrays the head it encircles, and

allures innumerable traitors, and invites them to the lust of empire. And in battles this ornament is so dangerous, that it must be hidden and laid aside. Hence kings in battle, change the outward dress, and so mingle in the crowd of combatants; so much betrayal does there result from the crown; but the chain will bring nothing of this kind upon those who have it, but altogether the contrary; since if there be a war, and an engagement with demons, and the hostile powers; the man who is thus encompassed, by holding forth his chain, repels their assaults. And many of the secular magistrates not only bear the name of office while they are in authority, but when they have given up their authority. Such a one is called an ex-consul, such a one an ex-prætor. But he, instead of all such titles, says, "Paul the prisoner." And very rightly. For those magisterial offices are no complete evidences of virtue in respect to the soul; for they are to be purchased by money, and obtained by the solicitations of friends; but this distinction that is obtained by bonds is a proof of the soul's love of wisdom, and the strongest sign of a longing for Christ. And the former are soon gone, but this distinction has none to succeed to it. Behold at least from that time to the present day how long a time has passed, and yet the name of this Prisoner has become increasingly illustrious. As to all the consuls, whoever they were, of former times, they are passed into silence; and not even their names are known to the generality of mankind. But the name of this Prisoner, the blessed Paul, is still great here, great in the land of the barbarians, great also among the Scythians and Indians; and were you to go even to the very bounds of the habitable world, you would hear of this appellation, and whithersoever anyone could come, he would perceive that the name of Paul was borne in the mouths of all men. And what marvel is it, if it be so by land and sea, when even in the heavens the name of Paul is great; with angels and archangels and the powers above, and with the King of these, even God! "But what were the chains," says someone, "that brought glory to him who was thus fettered? Were they not formed of iron?" Of iron, indeed, they were formed; but they contained the grace of the Spirit, abundantly flourishing in them; since he wore them for Christ's sake. Oh, wonder! The servants were bound, the Master was crucified, and yet the preaching of the Gospel every day increases! And through the means by which it was supposed that it would be extinguished, by these very means it was kindled; and the Cross and bonds, which were thought to be an abomination, these are now become the symbols of salvation; and that iron was to us more precious than all gold, not by its intrinsic nature, but for this cause and ground!

7. But here I see an enquiry arising out of this point; and if you give me your attention, I will both state the question exactly, and will add the solution. What then is the subject of enquiry? This same Paul once having come before Festus, whilst discoursing to him, and defending himself concerning the charges which the Jews had alleged against him, and telling how he had seen Jesus, how he had heard that blessed voice; how he had been struck with blindness and recovered sight, and had fallen down and risen up again; how he had come a captive into Damascus, bound without chains; after speaking likewise of the Law and of the Prophets, and shewing that they had foretold all these things, he captured the judge, and almost persuaded him to come over to himself. For such are the souls of holy men: when

they have fallen into dangers, they do not consider how they may be delivered from dangers, but strive every way how they may capture their persecutors. Just so did it then happen. He came in to defend himself, and he departed taking the judge with him! And to this the judge bore witness, saying, "Almost thou persuades me to be a Christian." And this ought to have happened to-day; and this Prefect, on coming among you, ought to have admired your magnanimity, your fortitude, your perfect tranquility; and to have gone away, taking with him a lesson from your good order, admiring your assembly, praising your congress, and learning from the actual fact, how great a difference there is between Gentiles and Christians!

8. But as I was saying:—When Paul had caught him, and he said, "Almost thou persuades me to be a Christian," Paul answered thus, "I would to God that not only thou, but also all that hear me this day, were both almost and altogether such as I am, except these bonds." What say you, O Paul? When thou writes to the Ephesians, thou says, "I therefore, the prisoner of the Lord, beseech you, that ye walk worthy of the vocation wherewith ye are called." And when thou speaks to Timothy, "Wherein I suffer trouble as an evil-doer, even unto bonds." And again, when to Philemon, thus; "Paul, a prisoner of Jesus Christ." And again, when debating with the Jews, thou says, "For the hope of Israel I am bound with this chain." And writing to the Philippians, thou says, "Many of the brethren in the Lord, waxing confident by my bonds, are much more bold to speak the word without fear." Everywhere thou bears about the chain, everywhere thou puts forward thy bonds, and boasts in the thing. But when thou comes to the tribunal, thou betrays

thy philosophy, where it were right to have spoken the most boldly, and says to the judge, "I would to God that thou might become a Christian 'without' these bonds!" Yet surely if the bonds were good, and so good, that they could be the means of making others to grow bold in the cause of true religion; (for this very thing thou didst declare before, when thou says, "Many of the brethren, waxing confident by my bonds, did speak the word without fear"); for what reason dost thou not glory in this thing in the presence of the judge, but does even the reverse?

9. Does not what I say appear a question? The solution of it, however, I will bring forward at once. For Paul acted thus, not from distress or fear, but from an abundance of wisdom and spiritual understanding. And how this was, I proceed to explain. He was addressing a Gentile, and an unbeliever, who knew nothing of our matters. Hence he was unwilling to introduce him by way of disagreeable things, but as he said, "I became to them that are without law, as without law;" so he acted in the present instance. His meaning is, "If the Gentile hear of bonds and tribulations, he will straightway be taking flight; since he knows not the power of bonds. First, let him become a believer; let him taste of the word preached, and then he will even of himself hasten towards these bonds. I have heard the Lord saying, "No man puts a piece of new cloth into an old garment, for that which is put in to fill it up taketh from the garment, and the rent is made worse. Neither do men put new wine into old wine-skins; else the wine-skins burst." The soul of this man is an old garment: an old wine-skin. It is not renewed by the faith, nor renovated by the grace of the Spirit. It is yet weak and earthly. It affects the things of this life. It

flutters eagerly after worldly show. It loves a glory that is present. Should he hear at once, even from the first, that if he becomes a Christian he will become immediately a prisoner, and will be encompassed with a chain; feeling ashamed and indignant, he will recoil from the word preached. Therefore, says he, "Except these bonds." Not as deprecating the bonds themselves, God forbid! But condescending to the other's infirmity; for he himself loved and welcomed his bonds, even as a woman fond of ornament doth her jewels of gold. Whence is this apparent? "I rejoice," says he, "in my sufferings for you, and fill up that which is behind of the afflictions of Christ in my flesh." And again; "Unto you it is given in the behalf of Christ, not only to believe on Him, but to suffer for His sake." And again; "And not only so, but we also glory in tribulations." Wherefore, if he rejoices and glories in this, and calls it a gift of grace, it is manifest that when he was addressing the judge, he spoke to him as he did, for the reason assigned. Moreover, also in a different passage, when he happened to find a necessity for glorying, he shews the very same by saying, "Most gladly, therefore, will I glory in my infirmities......in reproaches, in necessities, in persecutions, in distresses, that the power of Christ may rest upon me." And again; "If I must needs glory, I will glory of the things which concern mine infirmities."1679 And elsewhere, comparing himself with others, and exhibiting to us his superiority in the comparison, he thus speaks; "Are they ministers of Christ? (I speak as a fool), I am more." And wishing to shew this superiority, he did not say that he had raised the dead, nor that he had expelled demons, nor that he had cleansed lepers, nor that he had done any other thing of the sort, but that he had suffered those innumerable hardships. Hence when he said," I am more," he presently cites the multitude of his trials; "In stripes, above measure, in deaths oft, in prisons more frequent…..of the Jews five times received I forty stripes save one, once was I stoned, thrice I suffered shipwreck, a night and a day I have been in the deep;" and all the rest. Thus Paul everywhere glories in tribulations; and prides himself upon this circumstance exceedingly. And very justly. For this it is which especially shews the power of Christ, viz. that the Apostles conquered by such means; by bonds, by tribulations, by scourging, and the worst of ills.

10. For these two things Christ had announced, tribulation and remission, labors and crowns, toils and rewards, things pleasant and sad. Nevertheless, to the present life he assigns the sorrowful things; but for the life to come, he has stored up those which are pleasant; at once shewing that He did not mean to deceive men, and wishing by this arrangement to diminish the burden of human woes. For the imposter first holds out the things which are pleasant, and afterwards brings forward those which are disagreeable. Thus for example:—Kidnappers, when they intend to steal and carry off little children, do not promise them blows and stripes, or any other thing of that kind, but offer them cakes, and sweetmeats, and such like, by which the age of childhood is usually gratified; in order that, enticed by these things, they may sell their liberty, and may fall into the utmost peril. Moreover, bird-catchers, and fishermen, thus entice the prey which they pursue, offering first their usual food, and such as is agreeable to them, and by this means concealing the snare. So that this is especially the work of imposters, first to hold out things which are agreeable, but afterwards to

introduce the things which are disagreeable. But the case is altogether the reverse with those who are really careful and provident for others. Fathers at least act quite in a contrary manner to kidnappers. When they send their children to school, they set masters over them, threaten them with stripes, and encompass them with fear on all sides. But when they have thus spent the first portion of their lives, and their habits are formed, they then put them in possession of honor, and power, and luxury, and all the wealth that is theirs.

11. And thus God has acted. After the manner of provident fathers, and not after that of kidnappers, He has first involved us in things that are grievous; handing us over to present tribulation, as it were to schoolmasters and teachers; in order that being chastened and sobered by these things, after shewing forth all patience, and learning all right discipline, we may afterwards, when formed into due habits, inherit the kingdom of heaven. He first prepares and fits us for the management of the wealth He is to give, and then puts us into the actual possession of riches. For if He had not acted thus, the giving of riches would have been no boon, but a punishment and a vengeance. For even as a son that is senseless and prodigal, when he has succeeded to a paternal inheritance, is precipitated headlong by this very thing, having none of the practical wisdom requisite for the economy of wealth; but if he be intelligent, and gentle, and sober, and moderate, managing his paternal estate as is befitting, he becomes by this means more illustrious and distinguished: so must it also necessarily happen in our case. When we have acquired spiritual understanding, when we have all attained to "perfect manhood," and the measure of full stature;" then He puts us in possession of all that He has

promised: but now as little children He chastens us, together with consolation and soothing. And this is not the only advantage of receiving the tribulation beforehand, but there is also another, not less than this. For the man who first of all lives luxuriously, and then has to expect punishment after his luxurious living, has not even a sense of his present luxury, merely by reason of the expectation of impending woes; but he who is first in a sorrowful state, if he is anticipating the enjoyment of good things afterwards, overlooks present difficulties, in the hope of the good things which are to come. Not only, then, on account of our security, but also for our pleasure and consolation hath He ordained that the things which are grievous should be first; in order that being lightened with the hope of futurity, we should be rendered insensible to what is present. And this Paul would shew and make plain, when he said, "Our light affliction, which is but for a moment, worked for us a far more exceeding and eternal weight of glory. While we look not at the things which are seen, but at the things which are not seen." He calls tribulation light, not because of the intrinsic nature of things that are grievous, but because of the expectation of good things to come. For even as the merchant is indifferent to the labor that attends navigation, being buoyed up with the hope of a cargo; and as the boxer bravely sustains the blows on his head, looking to the crown beyond; so also indeed do we, earnestly gazing towards heaven, and the good things that are in the heavens, whatever evils come on us, sustain them all with fortitude, being nerved with the good hope of the things to come.

12. Therefore let us go home, taking with us this saying; for though it be simple and short, it nevertheless

contains much of the doctrine of spiritual wisdom. He who is in a state of grief and tribulation, hath a sufficient consolation; he who lives in luxury and abundance, hath that which may greatly sober him. For when as thou sits at the table thou art reminded of this saying, thou wilt speedily shrink from drunkenness and gluttony; learning through this sentence, how needful it is for us to be striving; and thou wilt say with thyself, "Paul lived in bonds and in dungeons, but I in drunkenness and at a luxurious table! What pardon then shall I obtain?" This also is a fit saying for women; since those who are fond of ornament, and expensive dresses, and bind themselves about with gold on every side, when they remember this chain, will hate, I feel assured, and abominate that adorning of themselves; and will hasten to such bonds as these. For those ornaments have often been the cause of manifold evils, and introduced a thousand quarrels into a family, and have bred envy, and jealousy, and hatred. But these loosed the sins of the wide world, affrighted demons, and drove away the devil. With these, while tarrying in prison, he persuaded the jailor; with these he attracted Agrippa himself; with these he procured many disciples. Therefore he said, "Wherein I suffer trouble as an evil-doer unto bonds, but the word of God is not bound." For just as it is not possible to bind a sunbeam, or to shut it up within the house, so neither the preaching of the word; and what was much more, the teacher was bound, and yet the word flew abroad; he inhabited the prison, and yet his doctrine rapidly winged its way everywhere throughout the world!

Knowing these things then, let us not be depressed, when adverse affairs meet us, but then let us be more strong, then more powerful; "for tribulation worked patience." Let us not grieve for the calamities which befall us, but let us in all things give thanks unto God!

13. We have completed the second week of the fast, but this we should not consider; for going through the fast does not consist in merely going through the time, but in going through it with amendment of manners. Let us consider this; whether we have become more diligent; whether we have corrected any of our defects; whether we have washed away our sins? It is common for everyone to ask in Lent, how many weeks each has fasted; and some may be heard saying that they have fasted two, others three, and others that they have fasted the whole of the weeks. But what advantage is it, if we have gone through the fast devoid of good works? If another says, "I have fasted the whole of Lent," do thou say, "I had an enemy, but I was reconciled; I had a custom of evil-speaking, but I put a stop to it; I had a custom of swearing, but I have broken through this evil practice." It is of no advantage to merchants, to have gone over a great extent of ocean, but to have sailed with a freight and much merchandise. The fast will profit us nothing, if we pass through it as a mere matter of course, without any result. If we practice a mere abstinence from meats, when the forty days are past, the fast is over too. But if we abstain from sins, this still remains, even when the fast has gone by, and will be from this time a continual advantage to us; and will here render us no small recompense, before we attain unto the kingdom of heaven. For as he who is living in iniquity, even before hell, hath punishment, being stung by his conscience; so the man who is rich in good works, even before the kingdom, will have the benefit of exceeding joy, in that he is nourished with blessed hopes.

14. Therefore Christ says, "I will see you again, and your heart shall rejoice, and your joy no man taketh from you." A brief saying, but one that hath in it much consolation. What then is this, "your joy no man taketh?" if thou hast money, many are able to take away the joy that comes of thy wealth; as, for instance, a thief, by digging through the wall; a servant by carrying off what was entrusted to him; an emperor by confiscation; and the envious man by contumely. Should you possess power, there are many who are able to deprive you of the joy of it. For when the conditions of office are at an end, the conditions of pleasure will also be ended. And in the exercise of office itself too, there are many accidents occurring, which by bringing difficulty and care, strike at the root of thy satisfaction. If thou hast bodily strength, the assaults of disease put a stop to joy from that source. If thou hast beauty and bloom, the approach of old age withers it, and takes away that joy. Or if thou enjoys a sumptuous table, when evening comes on the joy of the banquet is at an end; for everything belonging to this life is liable to damage, and is unable to afford us a lasting pleasure; but piety and the virtue of the soul is altogether the reverse of this. If thou hast done an alms, no one is able to take away this good work. Though an army, or kings, or myriads of calumniators and conspirators, were to beset thee on all sides, they could not take away the possession, once deposited in heaven; but the joy thereof continually abides; for it is said, "He hath dispersed, he hath given to the poor, his righteousness endures forever." And very justly; for in the storehouses of heaven it is laid up, where no thief breaks in, nor robber seizes, nor moth devours. If thou pours out continued and fervent prayers, no man will be able to spoil thee of the fruit of them; for

this fruit too is rooted in the heavens; it is out of the way of all injury, and remains beyond mortal reach. If when evil-treated thou has done a kind action; if thou hast borne with patience to hear thyself evil spoken of; if thou hast returned blessings for reproaches; these are good works that abide continually, and the joy of them no man taketh away; but as often as thou remembers these, thou art glad and rejoices, and reaps large fruits of pleasure. So also, indeed, if we succeed in avoiding oaths; and persuade our tongue to abstain from this pernicious practice, the good work will be finished in a short time, but the delight arising from it will be continuous and unfailing.

15. And now, it is time that you should be teachers and guides of others; that friends should undertake to instruct and lead on their neighbors; servants their fellow-servants; and youths those of their own age. What if anyone had promised thee a single piece of gold for every man who was reformed, would you not then have used every exertion, and been all day long sitting by them, persuading and exhorting. Yet now God promises thee not one piece of gold, nor ten, or twenty, or a hundred, or a thousand; no, nor the whole earth, for thy labors, but He gives thee that which is greater than all the world, the kingdom of heaven; and not only this, but also another thing besides it. And what kind of thing is that? "He who taketh forth the precious from the vile," says He, "shall be as my mouth." What can be equal to this in point of honor or security? What kind of excuse or pardon can be left to those, who after so great a promise neglect their neighbor's safety? Now if you see a blind man falling into a pit, you stretch forth a hand, and think it a disgraceful thing to overlook one who is about to perish? But daily beholding all thy brethren precipitated into the wicked

custom of oaths, dost thou not dare even to utter a word? Thou hast spoken once, perhaps, and he hath not heard. Speak therefore twice, and thrice, and as often as it may be, till thou hast persuaded him. Every day God is addressing us, and we do not hear; and yet He does not leave off speaking. Do thou, therefore, imitate this tender care towards thy neighbor. For this reason it is that we are placed with one another; that we inhabit cities, and that we meet together in churches, in order that we may bear one another's burdens, that we may correct one another's sins. And in the same manner as persons inhabiting the same shop, carry on a separate traffic, yet put all afterwards into the common fund, so also let us act. Whatever advantages each man is able to confer upon his neighbor, let him not grudge, nor shrink from doing it, but let there be some such kind of spiritual commerce, and reciprocity; in order that having deposited everything in the common store, and obtained great riches, and procured a large treasure, we may be all together partakers of the kingdom of heaven; through the grace and loving-kindness of our Lord Jesus Christ, by Whom and with Whom, to the Father, with the Holy Ghost, be glory, both now and ever, and world without end. Amen.

Homily XVII.

Of the Commissioners (Hellebichus Commander of the Troops, and Cæsarius Master of the Offices) sent by the Emperor Theodosius for the inquisition of the offenders, on account of the overturning of the Statues.

1. Most opportunely have we all this day sung together, "Blessed be the Lord God of Israel, who only doeth wondrous things." For marvelous, and beyond all expectation, are the things which have happened? A whole city, and so great a population, when just about to be overwhelmed—to sink under the waves, and to be utterly and instantly destroyed— He hath entirely rescued from shipwreck in a single moment of time! Let us give thanks then, not only that God hath calmed the tempest, but that He suffered it to take place; not only that He rescued us from shipwreck, but that He allowed us to fall into such distress; and such an extreme peril to hang over us. Thus also Paul bids us "in everything give thanks." But when he says, "In everything give thanks," he means not only in our deliverance from evils, but also at the time when we suffer those evils. "For all things work together for good to them that love God." Let us be thankful to Him for this deliverance from trials; and let us never forget them. Let us devote ourselves to prayer, to continual supplications, and to much piety.

2. When the sad conflagration of these calamities was first kindled, I said, that it was a season not for doctrine, but for prayer. The very same thing I now repeat, when the fire has been extinguished—that it is now especially, and more than before, a time for prayer; that now is the season especially for tears and

compunction, for an anxious soul, for much diligence, and for much caution. For at that time the very nature of our tribulation restrained us, however unwillingly, and disposed us to sobriety; and led us to become more religious; but now when the bridle is removed, and the cloud has passed away, there is fear lest we should fall back again into sloth, or become relaxed by this respite; and lest one should have reason to say of us too, "When He slew them, then they sought Him, and returned, and enquired early after God." Wherefore also Moses admonished the Jews, saying, "When thou shalt have eaten, and drunk, and art full, remember the Lord thy God." The goodness of your disposition will now be rendered manifest, if you continue in the practice of the same piety. For at that time, many imputed your earnestness to fear, and the approach of calamity; but now, it will be purely your own achievement, if you still persevere in maintaining this earnestness. Since with a boy too, as long as he is guided by some tutor whom he fears, if he lives with sobriety and meekness, there is nothing to admire, for all persons ascribe the sobriety of the stripling to his fear of the tutor. But when he remains in the same seemly behavior, after the restraint from that quarter is done away with, all persons give him credit too for the sobriety that was seen in his earlier age. Thus also let us act; let us continue in the same state of godly fear, in order that for our former diligence too we may gain much praise from God.

3. We had expected innumerable woes; that our property would be plundered, that the houses would have been burnt together with their inmates, that the city would have been plucked up from the midst of the world, that its very fragments would have been utterly destroyed, and

that its soil would have been placed under the plough! But, lo! All these things existed only in expectation, and did not come into operation. And this is not the only wonder, that God hath removed so great a danger, but that He hath also greatly blessed us, and adorned our city; and by this trial and calamity hath made us more approved! But how, I will state. When those who were sent by the Emperor erected that fearful tribunal for making inquisition into the events which had taken place, and summoned everyone to give account of the deeds which they had perpetrated, and various anticipations of death pervaded the minds of all, then the monks who dwelt on the mountain-tops shewed their own true philosophy. For although they had been shut up so many years in their cells, yet at no one's entreaty, by no one's counsel, when they beheld such a cloud overhanging the city, they left their caves and huts, and flocked together in every direction, as if they had been so many angels arriving from heaven. Then might one see the city likened to heaven, while these saints appeared everywhere; by their mere aspect consoling the mourners, and leading them to an utter disregard of the calamity. For who on beholding these would not deride death, would not despise life. And not only was this wonderful, but that when they drew nigh to the magistrates themselves, they spoke to them with boldness on behalf of the accused, and were all ready to shed their blood, and to lay down their heads, so that they might snatch the captured from the terrible events which they expected. They also declared that they would not depart until the judges should spare the population of the city, or send them themselves together with the accused to the Emperor. "He," said they, "who rules over our portion of the world is a godly man, a believer, one who lives in the practice of piety. We therefore shall assuredly reconcile him. We will not give you leave, nor permit you to embrue the sword, or take off a head. But if ye do not desist, we also are quite resolved to die with them. We confess that the crimes committed are very heinous; but the iniquity of those deeds does not surpass the humanity of the Emperor." One of them is also reported to have uttered another saying, full of wisdom, to this effect: "The Statues which have been thrown down are again set up, and have resumed their proper appearance; and the mischief was speedily rectified; but if ye put to death the image of God, how will ye be again able to revoke the deed! Or how to reanimate those who are deprived of life, and to restore their souls to their bodies?" Many things too they said to them of the Judgment.

4. Who could but be astonished? Who could but admire the moral wisdom of these men? When the mother of one of the accused, uncovering her head, and exposing her grey hairs, laid hold of the horse of the judge by the bridle, and running beside him through the forum, thus entered with him the place of justice, we were all struck with astonishment, we all admired that exceeding tenderness and magnanimity. Ought we not, then, to have been much more impressed with wonder at the conduct of these men? For if she had even died for her son, it would have been nothing strange, since great is the tyranny of nature, and irresistible is the obligation arising from the maternal pangs! But these men so loved those whom they had not begotten, whom they had not brought up, yea rather, whom they had never seen, whom they had not heard of, whom they had never met, whom they knew only from their calamity, that if they had possessed a thousand lives, they would have chosen to deliver them

all up for their safety. Tell me not that they were not slaughtered, that they did not pour forth their blood, but that they used as much boldness with their judges as it was likely that no other men would do, but such as had already renounced their own lives; and that with this sentiment they ran from the mountains to the tribunal. For, indeed, if they had not before prepared themselves against every sort of slaughter, they would not have been able to speak thus freely to the judges, or to have manifested such magnanimity. For they remained all day long sitting before the doors of the place of justice, being prepared to snatch from the hands of the executioners those who were about to be led off to punishment!

5. Where now are those who are clad in threadbare cloaks, and display a long beard, and carry staves in the right hand; the philosophers of the world, who are more abject in disposition than the dogs under the table; and do everything for the sake of the belly? All these men then forsook the city, they all hasted away, and hid themselves in caves! But they only, who truly by works manifest the love of wisdom, appeared as fearlessly in the forum, as if no evil had overtaken the city. And the inhabitants of the city fled away to the mountains and to the deserts, but the citizens of the desert hastened into the city; demonstrating by deeds what, on the preceding days, I have not desisted from saying, that the very furnace will not be able to harm the man who leads a virtuous life. Such a thing is philosophy of soul, rising superior to all things, and to all prosperous or adverse events; for neither is it enfeebled by the former, nor beaten down and debased by the latter, but abides on the same level through the whole course of things, shewing its own native force and power! Who, indeed, was not convicted of weakness by the difficulty of

the present crisis? Those who had held the first offices in our city, who were in places of power, who were surrounded with immense wealth, and who were in high favor with the Emperor, leaving their houses utterly deserted, all consulted their own safety, and all friendship and kindred were found worthless, and those whom they formerly knew, at this season of calamity, they desired not to know, and prayed to be unknown of them! But the monks, poor as they were, having nothing more than a mean garment, who had lived in the coarsest manner, who seemed formerly to be nobodies, men habituated to mountains and forests; as if they had been so many lions, with a great and lofty soul, whilst all were fearing and quaking, stood forth and relieved the danger, and that, not in the course of many days, but in a brief moment of time! And as distinguished warriors without coming into close conflict with their adversaries, but merely by making their appearance in the ranks, and shouting, put the foe to rout, so also these in one day descended, and said their say, and removed the calamity, and returned to their own tabernacles. So great is the moral wisdom that was brought among men by Christ.

6. And why do I speak of the rich, and of those in authority? When those very persons who had been invested with power to judge the criminals; who acted with the highest authority, were entreated by these selfsame monks to grant a sentence of pardon, they said, they had no power over the result; for that it was unsafe and dangerous, not only to insult the Emperor, but even to dismiss those who had insulted him, when taken, without punishment. But these men were too powerful for anyone to resist; and besieging them by magnanimity and perseverance, they induced these officers by their

importunity to exercise a power which they had not received from the Emperor; and even succeeded in persuading the judges, when men had been manifestly convicted of the guilt, not to declare the sentence of condemnation, but to defer the final result to the decision of the Emperor; and they promised certainly to persuade him to grant a pardon to those who had transgressed against him; and they were about to set out on a journey to him. But the judges, reverencing the moral wisdom of these men, and being struck with their loftiness of spirit, did not permit them to undertake this long journey, but promised that if they should only receive their words in writing, they would themselves depart and successfully importune the Emperor to dismiss all anger (which, indeed, we are now expecting that he will). For when sentence should have been given, they, on being admitted into court, uttered words of the highest wisdom, and besought the Emperor by letters to shew mercy; and they reminded him of the Judgment, and said that they would lay down their own heads, if his mercy was not granted. And the judges took down these words in writing, and departed. This, more than the brightest crown, will adorn our city. And what has here taken place, the Emperor will now hear; yea, the great City will hear, and the whole world will hear, that the monks who dwell at the city of Antioch, are men who have displayed an apostolic boldness; and now when their letters are read at court, all men will admire their magnanimity; all men will call our city blessed; and we shall shake off our evil reputation; and it will be known everywhere, that what has happened was not the work of the inhabitants of the city, but of strangers and corrupt-minded men; and that this testimony of the monks will be a sufficient evidence of the character of the city.

7. Therefore, beloved, let us not be distressed, but let us entertain favorable hopes; for if their boldness toward men has been able to prevent such a danger, then what will not their boldness toward God effect? These things also let us tell the Greeks, when they dare to dispute with us respecting their philosophers! From hence it is manifest that their stories of former days are false, but that the things of old reported among us are true; that is, the things concerning John, and Paul, and Peter, and all the rest. For inasmuch as these monks have succeeded to the piety of those men, they have consequently exhibited their boldness. Inasmuch as they were brought up in the same laws, they have consequently imitated their virtues. So that we stand in no need of writings for the purpose of shewing the apostolical virtues, whilst the very facts cry aloud, and the masters are shewn forth by the scholars. We have no need of disputation to display the trifling of the Greeks, and the little-mindedness of their philosophers, whilst their deeds now loudly proclaim, as they did aforetime, that all with them is a fable, a stage-play, a piece of acting.

8. And the same magnanimity was displayed by the priests too, as well as the monks, and they shared among them the charge of our safety. One of them, indeed, proceeded to court, esteeming all things as secondary to the love of you; and being himself ready, if he could not persuade the Emperor, to lay down his own life. And these, who remained here, have displayed the same virtues as the monks themselves; and holding fast the judges with their own hands, they would not let them enter into the court, before they gave a promise respecting

the result of the trial. And when they saw them making signs of refusal, they again exerted themselves with much boldness; and as soon as they saw that they did consent, embracing their feet and knees, and kissing their hands, they gave an exceeding proof of either virtue, of liberty and meekness. For that theirs was not the boldness of presumption, they plainly signified by their kissing the knees, and embracing the feet of the judges. Again, in proof that this was not flattery, nor a kind of fawning servility, nor the fruit of a slavish spirit, their former acts attested their boldness. And these are not the only good results we have reaped from the trial, but also an abundance of sobriety and meekness; and our city has become all at once a monastery. Not thus would anyone have adorned it, had he erected golden statues in the forum, as it has now been adorned and distinguished, in producing those beautiful images of virtue, and displaying its true riches!

9. But it may be that the things which the Emperor hath decreed are painful. No! Not even these are really burdensome, but have brought much advantage with them. For what is there, I ask, which is oppressive in any of them? That the Emperor hath shut up the Orchestra, that he hath forbidden the Hippodrome, that he hath closed and stopped up these fountains of iniquity. May they never again be opened! From thence did the roots of wickedness shoot forth to the injury of the city! From thence sprung those who blast its character; men who sell their voices to the dancers, and who for the sake of three obols prostitute their salvation to them, turning all things upside down! Art thou distressed, O beloved! For these things? Truly it were fitting that for these you should be glad, and rejoice, and express thy thanks to the Emperor,

since his castigation hath proved a correction, his punishment a discipline, his wrath a means of instruction! But that the Baths are shut up? Neither is this an intolerable hardship, that those who lead a soft, effeminate, and dissolute life, should be brought back, though unwillingly, to the love of true wisdom.

10. But is it complained of, that the Emperor hath taken away the dignity of the city, and hath no more permitted it to be called a metropolis? But what was he to do? Could he praise what had been done, and acknowledge it as a favor? Then who would not have blamed him, for not shewing even the outward form of indignation? See not that fathers do many things of a similar nature towards their children? They turn away from them, and forbid them the table. This also hath the Emperor done by imposing such punishments as have nothing in them hurtful, but carry with them much correction. Think what we expected, and what has taken place, and then we shall especially discern the favor of God! Do you grieve that the dignity of the city is taken away? Learn what the dignity of a city is; and then thou wilt know clearly, that if the inhabitants do not betray it, no one else will be able to take away the dignity of a city! Not the fact that it is a metropolis; nor that it contains large and beautiful buildings; nor that it has many columns, and spacious porticoes and walks, nor that it is named in proclamations before other cities, but the virtue and piety of its inhabitants; this is a city's dignity, and ornament, and defense; since if these things are not found in it, it is the most insignificant in the world, though it may enjoy unlimited honor from Emperors! Do you wish to learn the dignity of thy city? Do you wish to know its ancestry? I will tell it exactly; not only that thou may

know, but that thou may also emulate. What then is after all the dignity of this city of ours? "It came to pass, that the disciples were first called Christians at Antioch." This dignity, none of the cities throughout the world possesses, not even the city of Romulus herself! For this it can look the whole world in the face; on account of that love toward Christ, that boldness and virtue. Do you wish farther to hear of a different dignity and commendation belonging to this city? A grievous famine was once approaching, and the inhabitants of Antioch determined, as far as each person had the means, to send relief to the Saints dwelling at Jerusalem. Behold a second dignity, charity in a time of famine! The season did not make them niggardly, nor the expectation of the calamity backward in helping; but when all are apt to be scraping up what is not their own, then they distributed their own, not merely to those who were near, but also to those who were living afar off! See here the faith towards God, and the love towards their neighbor? Would you learn another dignity of this city? Certain men came down from Judæa to Antioch, defiling the doctrine preached, and introducing Jewish observances. The men of Antioch did not bear this novelty in silence. They did not hold their peace, but having come together, and made an assembly, they sent Paul and Barnabas to Jerusalem, and caused the Apostles to provide that pure doctrines, cleared from all Jewish imperfection, might be distributed throughout all parts of the world! This is the dignity of the city! This is its precedence! This makes it a metropolis, not in the earth, but in heaven; forasmuch as that all other honors are corruptible, and fleeting, and perish with the present life, and often come to their end before the close of it, as they have done in the present instance! To me, a city that hath not pious citizens is meaner than any village, and more ignoble than any cave.

11. And why do I speak of a city? For that thou may exactly understand that virtue alone is the ornament of the inhabitants, I will not speak to thee of a city, but I will endeavor to demonstrate this by bringing forward what is more venerable than any city—the Temple of God which was in Jerusalem. For this was the Temple in which were sacrifices and prayers and services; where was the Holy of Holies, and the Cherubim, the Covenant, and the golden pot; the great symbols of God's providence towards that people; where oracles from heaven were constantly being received, where prophets became inspired, where the fashioning was not the work of human art, but proceeded from the wisdom of God, where the walls were on every side resplendent with much gold, and where, in surpassing excellence, costliness of material and perfection of art met together, and demonstrated that there was no other temple like this upon earth! Yea rather, not only the perfection of art, but also the wisdom of God assisted in that building. For Solomon had learned all, not intuitively and from himself, but from God; and having received the design of it from the heavens, he then marked it out and erected it. Nevertheless, this Temple, thus beautiful and marvelous and sacred, when those who used it were corrupted, was so dishonored, despised, and profaned, that even before the captivity it was called "a den of robbers, a cave of hyænas;" and afterwards it was delivered over to hands that were barbarous, polluted, and profane!

12. Would you learn the same truth respecting cities? What could be more illustrious than the cities of Sodom? For the houses and the buildings were splendid,

and so were their walls; and the country was fat and fertile, and "like the Paradise of God." But the tent of Abraham was mean and small, and had no fortification. Yet when a foreign war took place, the strangers broke down and took the walled cities, and departed, carrying away their inhabitants captives. Abraham, however, the citizen of the desert, they could not resist when he attacked them! And so it was likely to be. For he had true piety: a power much greater than numbers and the defense of walls. If thou art a Christian, no earthly city is thine. Of our City "the Builder and Maker is God." Though we may gain possession of the whole world, we are withal but strangers and sojourners in it all! We are enrolled in heaven: our citizenship is there! Let us not, after the manner of little children, despise things that are great, and admire those which are little! Not our city's greatness, but virtue of soul is our ornament and defense. If you suppose dignity to belong to a city, think how many persons must partake in this dignity, who are whoremongers, effeminate, depraved and full of ten thousand evil things, and at last despise such honor! But that City above is not of this kind; for it is impossible that he can be a partaker of it, who has not exhibited every virtue.

13. Let us not therefore be senseless; but then let us grieve when any one deprives us of our dignity of soul, when we commit sin, when we have offended the common Lord of all; since as regards the things that have now befallen us, so far are they from injuring the city, that if we are watchful, they will greatly benefit us. For even already our city seems to be like a decorous, noble, sober-minded matron. Fear hath made her gentler and more dignified, and hath delivered her from those miscreants who were concerned in the late audacious deeds. Let us

therefore not give way to womanish lamentations. For I have heard many about the forum saying, "Alas! For thee, Antioch! What hath befallen thee! How art thou dishonored!" Truly when I heard, I smiled at the puerile mind which could give vent to these words! Such words were not becoming now; but when thou sees men dancing, drunken, singing, blaspheming, swearing, perjuring themselves, and lying, then apply such a saying as this: "Alas! For thee, O city, what hath befallen thee!" But if thou sees the forum containing a few meek, modest, and temperate persons, then pronounce the city, "Blessed!" For the fewness will never be able to injure it in any respect, if there be virtue withal; as on the other hand, numbers will never profit it at all, whilst iniquity is there. "If," says the prophet, "the number of the sons of Israel be as the sand of the sea, the remnant shall be saved;" that is to say, "Multitude will never prevail with Me." So also Christ spoke. He called cities wretched; not because of their littleness, nor because they were not of metropolitan rank. And Jerusalem itself again, He calls wretched for the very same reason, speaking thus; "O Jerusalem, Jerusalem; thou that kills the prophets, and stones them which are sent unto thee!" For what advantage, I ask, does a multitude bring, if their system of living be vicious? Nay, on the contrary, even injury results from it. What else, indeed, hath wrought the evils which have lately sprung up? Was it not the sloth, the recklessness, and the depravity of the inhabitants? Did the dignity of the city, did the magnificence of its architecture, or the circumstance that it was a metropolis, do it any service? If with the king who is on earth, nothing could protect it when it had done thus amiss, but all these privileges are taken away; much more with the

Lord of angels will its dignity fail to protect it? For at that Day, it will naught avail us, that we have dwelt in a metropolis, that has many spacious porticoes, and other dignities of this kind! And why do I say, at That Day? For as regards the present life, what can it benefit thee that this thy city is a metropolis? Pray, has any one restored a distressed family by means of this? Or received any revenue from this dignity? Or dispelled sadness? Or got rid of any bodily infirmity? Or put away a vice of the soul? Beloved! Let us not trifle, nor regard the opinions of the multitude, but understand what is indeed the dignity of a city; what it is that makes a city truly a metropolis?

14. I say all this, though I expect that the city will again regain even this outward distinction, and appear in its own proper place of precedence. For the Emperor is both philanthropic and godly. But I am desirous that if it should be restored, ye may not think too much of this; nor be boastful of it; nor place the honor of our city to that account. When you wish to pronounce an encomium on the city, tell me not of the suburb of Daphne, nor of the height and multitude of its cypresses, nor of its fountains of waters, nor of the great population who inhabit the city, nor of the great freedom with which its market-place is frequented even to midnight, nor of the abundance of its wares! All these are things of the outward sense, and remain only as long as the present life. But if you are able to mention virtue, meekness, alms-giving, nocturnal vigils, prayers, sobriety, true wisdom of soul; commend the city for these things! To those who inhabit the desert, the presence of these things makes it more illustrious than any city; and again the vilest of all places, should these things not be found with its citizens. Let us make this estimate not in the case of cities only, but also of men.

And if you see a big man, who has been brought into good condition, tall, and surpassing others in length of limb, do not admire him, until you have ascertained what the man's soul is. Not from the outward comeliness, but from the beauty that appertains to the soul, should we pronounce any persons blessed! David was little, and short of stature; nevertheless, one so short and little, and bare of all arms, brought down at one blow so large an army, and that tower of flesh; and this without hurling spear, or letting fly arrow, or unsheathing sword, but doing all with a small pebble! For this reason a certain one exhorts, saying, "Commend not a man for his beauty, neither abhor a man for his outward appearance. The bee is little among such as fly, but her fruit is the chief of sweet things."

15. Thus also let us speak both of a city, and of men, and utter such wisdom one to another, and be continually thankful to God, as well for present as for past mercies; and call upon Him in common with all our might, that those who now dwell in prison may be discharged, and that those who are about to be sent into exile may return back again. They too are our members. With us they have buffeted the waves, with us they have withstood the storm! Let us, then, beseech the merciful God, that with us they may enjoy the calm! Let no one say, "What farther concerns me? I am freed from danger; such an one may perish; such another may be destroyed!" Let us not provoke God by this indifference; but lament, as if we ourselves were in the same peril. So let us supplicate God with intense earnestness, fulfilling that saying of Paul, "Remember them that are in bonds, as bound with them; and them which suffer adversity, as being yourselves also in the body. Weeping also with

them that weep; condescending to men of low estate." This will also be of the greatest advantage to ourselves; for nothing uses so much to delight God, as that we should be very ready to mourn for our own members. Him therefore let us supplicate in common, both for things present, and for things to come; in order that He may deliver us from punishment hereafter. For the things present, whatever they are, are endurable, and have an end; but the torments there are immortal, and interminable! And while we are consoled, let us also ourselves endeavor to fall no more into such sins, knowing that hereafter we shall enjoy no pardon! Let us, then, all in common prostrate ourselves before God; and both while we are here, and when we are at home, let us say, "Thou, O Lord, art righteous in all things which Thou hast done towards us; for Thou hast brought upon us by a just judgment whatever Thou hast brought." If "our sins rise up against us, undertake for us, for thy Name's sake;" and do not permit us any more to experience such grievous troubles. "Lead us not into temptation, but deliver us from evil, for Thine is the kingdom, the Power, and the Glory, for ever and ever. Amen.

Homily XVIII.

The former subject of the Sedition continued; also of fasting; and upon the Apostolic saying, "Rejoice in the Lord always."

1. I have observed many persons rejoicing, and saying one to another, "We have conquered; we have prevailed; the half of the fast is spent." But I exhort such persons not to rejoice on this account, that the half of the fast is gone, but to consider whether the half of their sins be gone; and if so, then to exult. For this is a fit subject of gratification. This is what is to be sought after, and for which all things are done, that we may correct our defects; and that we may not quit the fast the same persons as we entered upon it, but in a cleansed state; and that having laid aside all that belongs to evil habits, we may thus keep the sacred feast, since if the case be otherwise, we shall be so far from obtaining any advantage, that the completion of the fast will be the greatest injury to us. Let us, therefore, not rejoice that we have gone through the length of the fast, for this is nothing great; but let us rejoice, if we have got through it with fresh attainments, so that when this is over, the fruit of it may shine forth. For the gain of winter is more especially manifested after the season is gone by. Then, the flourishing corn, and the trees teeming with leaves and fruit, proclaim, by their appearance, the benefit that has accrued to them from the winter! Let the same thing also take place with us. For during the winter, we have enjoyed divers and frequent showers, having been during the fast partakers of a continued course of instruction, and

have received spiritual seeds, and cut away the thorns of luxury.

2. Wherefore let us persevere, retaining with all diligence what we have heard; that when the fast is over, the fruit of the fast may abound, and that by the good things we gathered from the fast, we may remember the fast itself. If thus we fashion ourselves, we shall, when the fast returns, welcome it again with pleasure. For I see many who are so feebleminded, that at the present season they are anxious about the following Lent; and I have heard many saying, that after their liberation from the fast, they are insensible to any pleasure from this remission, on account of their anxiety about the coming year. What can be more feeble-minded than this? I ask; and what is the cause of this? It is, that when the fast is arrived, we do not take pains that the concerns of the soul may be well ordered, but we limit the fast solely to an abstinence from food. Since, were we to reap the full benefit of it in a reformation of conduct, we should wish the fast to come round every day, receiving in very deed an experience of its good effects; and we should never cast away the desire of it, or be dejected and anxious whilst expecting it.

3. For there is nothing whatever that will be able to afflict one who is well ordered in mind, and careful about his own soul; but he will enjoy a pure and continued pleasure. And that this is true ye have to-day heard from Paul, who exhorts us, saying, "Rejoice in the Lord always, and again I say, rejoice." I know indeed that to many this saying seems impossible. "For how is it possible," says someone, "that he who is but a man, can continually rejoice? To rejoice is no hard matter, but to rejoice continually, this seems to me to be impossible."

For many are the causes of sadness, which surround us on all sides. A man has lost either a son, or a wife, or a beloved friend, more necessary to him than all kindred; or he has to sustain the loss of wealth; or he has fallen into sickness; or he has to bear some other change of fortune; or to grieve for contemptuous treatment which he did not deserve; or famine, or pestilence, or some intolerable exaction, or circumstances in his family trouble him;—nay, there is no saying how many circumstances of a public or private nature are accustomed to occasion us grief. How then, he may say, is it possible to "rejoice always?" Yea, O man! It is possible; and if it were not so, Paul would not have given the exhortation; nor would a man endowed with spiritual wisdom have offered such counsel; and for this reason I have constantly said to you, and will not cease to say, that what ye could nowhere have learnt from any other, that wisdom ye may here meditate. For mankind are universally desirous of pleasure, and of rejoicing; and for this, they do all, say all, and undertake all things. Therefore it is, that the merchant goes on a voyage, in order that he may amass wealth; and he amasses wealth, to the end that he may rejoice over what he has treasured up. The soldier also for this reason exercises his warfare, and the husbandman his husbandry; for this each man plies his art. Those also who love dominion, love it for this end, that they may obtain glory; and they desire to obtain glory, that they may rejoice; and any one may perceive that each of our undertakings is directed to this point, and that every man looking to this makes haste to go towards it through a variety of means.

4. For as I said, all love gladness, but all are not able to attain it, since they know not the way which leads to it; but many suppose that the source of it is in being

rich. But if this were its source, no one possessed of wealth would ever be sad. But in fact many of the rich think life not worth living, and would infinitely prefer death when they experience any hardship; and of all men these are the most liable to excessive sadness. For you should not look to their tables, or their flatterers, and parasites, but to the trouble that comes of such things, the insults, the calumnies, the dangers, and the distresses, and what is far worse, that they meet these reverses unpracticed, and know not how to take them philosophically, or to bear with fortitude what befalls them; whence it happens that calamities do not appear to them such as they are in their own nature, but even things which are really light come to seem intolerable; whereas, with regard to the poor, the contrary takes place; things that are irremediable seem easy to be borne, since they are familiar with many such. For it is not so much the nature of the events as the disposition of the sufferers, that makes the evils which come upon us seem great or small. And that I may not go a long way off for examples of both these facts, I will speak to you of what has lately befallen ourselves. Behold then how all the poor escaped, and the populace are delivered from the danger, and enjoy an entire freedom! but those who manage the affairs of the city, the men who keep their studs of horses, and preside over the public games, and such as have borne other public charges, they are now the inmates of the prison, and fear the worst; and they alone pay the penalty of the deeds that have been perpetrated by all, and are in a state of constant terror; and they are now the most wretched of men, not because of the greatness of the danger, but on account of the luxury in which hitherto they have lived! Many, at least when exhorted by us, and counselled to sustain these adverse affairs with fortitude, said this, "We never practiced anything of the kind, and do not know how to exercise such philosophy; this is why we need so much consolation."

5. Others again suppose, that to enjoy good health is the source of pleasure. But it is not so. For many of those who enjoy good health have a thousand times wished themselves dead, not being able to bear the insults inflicted on them. Others again affirm, that to enjoy glory, and to have attained to power, and to administer the highest offices, and to be flattered by multitudes, is productive of continual gladness. But neither is this the case. And why do I speak of other offices of power? For although we were to mount up in thought to royalty itself, and to him who lives in that station, we should find it encompassed with a diversity of troubles, and having so many necessary causes the more of sadness, in proportion as it is surrounded with a greater weight of affairs. And what need is there to speak of wars, and battles, and the insurrections of barbarians? Oftentimes he has reason to fear those by whom he is surrounded at home. For many of those monarchs who have escaped from the hands of their enemies, have not escaped the conspiracies of their own body-guards. And kings have of necessity as many causes of sadness as there are waves on the ocean. But if monarchy is unable to render life devoid of grief, then what else can possibly achieve this? Nothing, indeed, of this life; but this saying of Paul alone, brief and simple as it is, will of itself open to us this treasure.

6. For many words are not needed, nor a long round of argument, but if we only consider his expression, we shall find the way that leads to it. He does not simply say, "Rejoice always;" but he adds the cause of the

continual pleasure, saying, "Rejoice in the Lord always." He who rejoices "in the Lord," cannot be deprived of the pleasure by anything that may happen. For all other things in which we rejoice are mutable and changeable, and subject to variation. And not only does this grievous circumstance attend them, but moreover while they remain they do not afford us a pleasure sufficient to repel and veil the sadness that comes upon us from other quarters. But the fear of God contains both these requisites. It is steadfast and immoveable, and sheds so much gladness that we can admit no sense of other evils. For the man who fears God as he ought, and trusts in Him, gathers from the very root of pleasure, and has possession of the whole fountain of cheerfulness. And as a spark falling upon a wide ocean quickly disappears, so whatever events happen to the man who fears God, these, falling as it were upon an immense ocean of joy, are quenched and destroyed! This indeed is most to be wondered at, that whilst things which minister sadness are present, the man should remain joyful. For if there was nothing to produce grief, it would be no great matter to him that he was able continually to rejoice. But that at a time when he is urged to sadness by the pressure of many things, he is superior to all these, and is blithe in the midst of sorrow, this is truly a matter for astonishment! And as no one would have wondered that the three Children were not burnt, if they had remained far off from the furnace of Babylon! (for the circumstance that astonished all was, that having been so long in such close contact with the fire, they left it more free from hurt than those who had not been in contact with it); so also we are able to say of the saints, that if no temptation had fastened itself upon them, we should not have wondered at their continual rejoicing. But the point worthy of admiration, and that which surpasses human nature, is this, that being encircled on all sides with innumerable waves, their condition is easier than that of those who enjoy an entire calm!

7. From what has been said, it is evident that amongst those who are outside the church it is impossible to find any situation in life, encircled with continual gladness from the things without. But that the believer cannot possibly be deprived of the enjoyment of a continued pleasure is what I will now proceed to prove, to the end that ye may not only learn, but also emulate this painless condition of life. For suppose a man having nothing for which to condemn himself, but cherishing a good conscience, and yearning after the future state, and the fulfilment of those good hopes; what, I ask, will be able to throw such a person into sadness? Does not death seem the most insupportable of all things? Yet the expectation of this is so far from grieving him, that it makes him the more joyful; for he knows that the arrival of death is a release from labor, and a speeding toward the crowns and rewards laid up for those who have contended in the race of piety and virtue. But is it the untimely end of his children? Nay, he will also bear this nobly, and will take up the words of Job, "The Lord gave, the Lord hath taken away; as it seemed good unto the Lord, so is it come to pass. Blessed be the name of the Lord forever." But if death and loss of children cannot grieve, much less can the loss of money, or dishonor, or reproaches, or false accusations, at any time affect a soul so great and noble; no, nor anguish of body, since the Apostles were scourged, yet they were not made sad. This, indeed, was a great thing; but what is much more, instead of being made

sad, they considered their very scourging, as a ground of additional pleasure. "And they departed from the presence of the council, rejoicing that they were counted worthy to suffer shame for the name of Christ." Did any person insult and revile such a one? Well, he was taught by Christ to rejoice in these revilings. "Rejoice," Says He, "and be exceeding glad, when they shall say all manner of evil against you falsely for my sake; for great is your reward in heaven." But suppose a man hath fallen into disease? Well, he hath heard another admonishing, and saying, "In disease and poverty trust thou in Him; for as gold is tried in the fire, so are acceptable men in the furnace of humiliation." Since, therefore, neither death, nor loss of money, nor bodily disease, nor dishonor, nor reproach, nor any other thing of that nature, will be able to grieve him, but makes him even the more joyful, what foundation for sadness will he have at any time?

8. "What then," says someone, "used not the Saint to be in sadness? Do you not hear Paul saying, "I have great heaviness, and continual sorrow in my heart?" This, indeed, is the thing to wonder at, that sorrow brought a gain, and a pleasure that resulted from the gain; for as the scourge did not procure them anguish, but gladness; so also again the sorrow procured them those great crowns. And this is the paradox; that not only the sadness of the world, but also its joy, contains extreme loss; but in the case of spiritual things, it is exactly the reverse; and not the joy only, but the sadness too contains a rich treasure of good things! But how, I proceed to explain. In the world, a person often rejoices, on beholding an enemy in trouble; and by this joy he draws on himself a great punishment. Again, another person mourns, on seeing a brother fall; and because of this sadness he will procure

for himself much favor with God. See how godly sorrow is better and more profitable than the joy of the world? Thus also Paul sorrowed for sinners, and for those who disbelieved in God; and this sorrow was the means of laying up a great reward for him. But that I may make what I say more clear, and that ye may know that although what I assert is very strange, it is nevertheless true, viz. that grief is often capable of refreshing distressed souls, and of rendering a burdened conscience light: consider how often women, when they have lost their most beloved children, break their hearts, and perish, if they are forbidden to mourn, and to shed tears. But if they do all which those who are sad, are wont to do, they are relieved, and receive consolation. And what wonder that this should be the case with women, when you may even see a prophet affected in a similar manner? Therefore he was continually saying, "Suffer me—I will weep bitterly—labor not to comfort me, because of the spoiling of the daughter of my people." So that, oftentimes, sadness is the bearer of consolation; and if it is so with regard to this world. Much more with regard to spiritual things. Therefore he says, "Godly sorrow worked repentance unto salvation, not to be repented of." This indeed seems to be obscure; but what he says is to this effect: "If thou grieves over wealth, thou art nothing profited. If for sickness, thou hast gained nothing, but hast increased thy affliction."

    9. And I have heard many, after such experience, blame themselves, and say, What advantage is it that I have grieved? I have not recovered my money, and I have injured myself. But if thou hast grieved on account of sin, thou hast blotted it out, and hast reaped the greatest pleasure. If thou hast grieved for thy brethren who have

fallen, thou hast both encouraged and comforted thyself, and hast also restored them; and even if thou wert not to profit them, thou hast an abundant recompense. And that thou may learn that this grieving for those who have fallen, though we should not at all benefit them, still brings us a large reward, hear what Ezekiel says; or rather, what God Himself speaks through him. For when He had sent certain messengers to overturn the city, and to consume all the dwellings with sword and fire, along with their inhabitants, He thus charges one of them: "Set a mark upon the forehead of the men that groan, and are in anguish." And after charging the others, and saying, "Begin ye from mine holy ones," He goes on to add, "But upon whomsoever the sign is, touch them not." For what reason, tell me? Because although they avail nothing, they nevertheless lament the things which are done, and deplore them. And again, He accuses others, saying, That in their luxury, and gluttony, and enjoyment of great security, when they beheld the Jews carried away into captivity, they did not grieve, nor partake of their sadness. And hear what He says, reproaching them: "They suffered nothing in the affliction of Joseph:" meaning by Joseph the whole people. And again: "The inhabitants of Ænan went not forth to bewail the house next unto them. For although they are justly punished, God wills that we should condole with them, and not rejoice or insult. "For if I that punish," says He, "do not this rejoicingly; nor take pleasure in their punishment; for "I do not at all will the death of the sinner;" it is right that you should imitate thy Lord; and should mourn for this very thing, that the sinner hath provided matter and occasion for a just punishment." So that if anyone entertains a godly sorrow, he will thence reap a great advantage.

10. Since therefore those who are scourged are more blessed than the scourgers, and those in tribulation among us than those who are free from it outside the Christian pale; and those who are sad are more blessed than those in pleasure; what further source of tribulation shall we have? On this account we should call no man happy, save him only who lives according to God. These only the Scripture terms blessed. For "blessed," it is said, "is the man who hath not walked in the counsel of the ungodly. Blessed is he whom Thou chastens, and teaches him out of Thy law. Blessed are the undefiled in the way. Blessed are all they who trust in Him. Blessed is the people whose God is the Lord. Blessed is he whom his soul condemns not. Blessed is the man that fears the Lord." And again, Christ speaks thus: "Blessed are they that mourn; blessed are the humble; blessed are the meek; blessed are the peacemakers; blessed are they who are persecuted for righteousness' sake." See how the divine laws everywhere pronounce blessed none of the rich, or of the well-born, or of the possessors of glory, but the man who has gotten hold of virtue. For what is required of us is, that in everything we do or suffer, the fear of God should be the foundation; and if you implant this as the root, not merely will ease, and honor, and glory, and attention, produce fruits that shall be pleasurable to thee; but hostilities also, and calumnies, and contempt, and disgrace, and torments, and all things without exception. And just as the roots of trees are bitter in themselves, and yet produce our sweetest fruits, so, verily, godly sorrow will bring us an abundant pleasure. They know, who have often prayed with anguish, and shed tears, what gladness they have reaped; how they purged the conscience; how they rose up with favorable hopes! For as I am always

saying, it is not the nature of the things, but our disposition, which is wont to make us sad or joyful. If then we can render the latter such as it ought to be, we shall have a pledge for all gladness. And just as, with the body, it is not so much the nature of the air, or the things it meets from without, as its own internal condition, that either injures or assists it, so also it is in the case of the soul; and much more so; for in the one case, there is the necessity of nature; in the other, the whole is seated in the power of choice. Therefore Paul, when he had endured innumerable evils—shipwrecks, wars, persecutions, plots, the assaults of robbers, and things too numerous to be recounted, dying also daily deaths—was so far from grieving or being discontented, that he gloried, and rejoiced, and said, "I now rejoice in my sufferings, and fill up that which is behind of the afflictions of Christ in my flesh." And again: "And not only so, but we glory in tribulations." Now, glorying signifies an extension of pleasure.

11. If then thou desires joy, seek not after riches, nor bodily health, nor glory, nor power, nor luxury, nor sumptuous tables, nor vestures of silk, nor costly lands, nor houses splendid and conspicuous, nor anything else of that kind; but pursue that spiritual wisdom which is according to God, and take hold of virtue; and then naught of the things which are present, or which are expected, will be able to sadden thee. Why do I say to sadden? Verily, the things that make others sad, will prove to thee an accession of pleasure. For scourges, and death, and losses, and slanders, and the being evil entreated, and all such things, when they are brought upon us for God's sake, and spring from this root, will bring into our souls much pleasure. For no one will be able to

make us miserable, if we do not make ourselves such; nor, on the other hand, blessed, if we do not make ourselves such, following up the grace of God.

12. And that ye may learn that he only is blessed, who fears the Lord, I will now demonstrate this to you, not by what has happened in past times, but by what has befallen ourselves. Our city was in danger of being utterly effaced; and no man among the rich, or eminent, or illustrious, dared to appear in public, but all fled, and hurried out of the way. But they who feared God, the men who passed their time in monasteries, hastened down with much boldness, and set all free from this terror; and the terrible events that had taken place, and the threats which had been expected to be put into execution, were so far from causing them to fear, or from throwing them into anxiety, that although they were placed far off from the calamity, and had no share in it, they cast themselves willingly into the midst of the fire, and rescued all; and as for death, which seems universally terrible and awful, they awaited it with the utmost readiness, and ran to meet it with more pleasure than others do towards principalities and honors. And why, but because they knew, that this is the greatest principality and honor? And they shewed in very deed that he only is blessed who lays hold of the wisdom which is from above, that he undergoes no change and sustains no adversity, but enjoys a continued tranquility, and laughs to scorn all things which seem to be sorrowful. At the present time at least, those who were once in power are oppressed by much sadness, inhabiting the prison, and loaded with chains, and daily expecting to be put to death. But these men on the contrary enjoy the purest pleasure; and if it be their lot to suffer anything terrible, this, and the very things which seem formidable

to others, are welcome to them, for they know well towards what point they are running, and what lot will await them when they depart hence. But whilst they live with so much exactness, and smile at death, they nevertheless grieve for others, and reap therefrom, in turn, the greatest advantage. Let us then be in earnest to take care of our souls, and nothing which may come unlooked for can make us sad. And on behalf of those who are in prison, let us beseech God that He will deliver them from their present calamity. For it was in God's power at once to release us from this dire evil, and not to suffer even the smallest part of it to remain; but in order that we may not again go back to our former negligence, He hath provided that the torrent of these evils should subside gently and by little and little, holding us fast to the same pious resolutions.

13. And that this is true, and that many would have gone back to their former supineness, if we had been released from the whole difficulty at once, is manifest from this circumstance; that whilst yet the remnants of the calamity are left, whilst the sentence of the Emperor is yet doubtful, and those who conducted the affairs of the city are all in prison, many of our fellow inhabitants, through their inordinate desire of bathing, run to the river, there making endless merriment, behaving wantonly, leaping, dancing, and dragging women after them. What pardon can such be worthy of? What kind of excuse can they offer? Or rather, what kind of punishment and vengeance do they not deserve? The head of the city is in the public prison; our members are in exile; the sentence concerning them is doubtful; and dost thou, I ask, dance, sport, and laugh? "Why, we could not endure," says someone, "to remain without the bath?" O shameless disposition, sordid

and perverted! How many months, I ask, how many years, have past? Thou hast not been as yet shut out from the bath for twenty days; and thou art as much distressed and discontented, as if thou has continued without washing for a whole year! Tell me, was this thy state, when thou wert expecting an attack from the military, when thou wert daily anticipating bring put to death, when thou fled to the deserts, and was hurrying to the mountain tops? If anyone had then proposed to thee to remain "a year" without the bath, so that thou might be rescued from the impending distress, would you not readily have accepted the proposal, and submitted to it? When, therefore, it were becoming that you should give thanks to God, Who hath freed thee from all these things without any loss, dost thou again grow wanton and contemptuous; and when the fear has passed away, turn back afresh to a worse state of negligence? Have these dire events really touched thee, and yet art thou so desirous of the baths? Why, if the bath had been permitted, would not the calamity of those who are yet in confinement have been sufficient to persuade those who are not in the same grievous condition to be forgetful of every luxury? Life itself is at stake, and dost thou remember the baths, and desire to be luxurious? Do you despise the danger because thou hast now escaped it? Take heed lest thou entangle thyself in the necessity of a greater punishment, and call back in larger measure the wrath which is removed, and experience the very thing which Christ declared concerning the devils. For He says, that "when the unclean spirit is gone out, and afterwards finds the house void and swept, he taketh seven other spirits more wicked than himself, and entered into the soul, and the last state of that man is worse than the first." Therefore let us also fear, lest now we are liberated from our former evils, we afterwards by our listlessness draw upon us those which are greater! I know that ye yourselves are free from this folly; but ye should restrain, punish, and sober those who walk disorderly, that ye may always rejoice even as Paul commanded, that both for our own good works, and for our forethought for others, we may enjoy both here and in the life to come an abundant recompense; through the grace and lovingkindness of our Lord Jesus Christ, by Whom, and with Whom, to the Father, with the Holy Ghost, be glory, honor, and adoration, now and ever, and world without end. Amen.

Homily XIX.

On the Sunday called "Episozomenes," to those who had come to Antioch from the country— also on the subject of avoiding oaths.

1. Ye have reveled during the last few days in the Holy Martyrs! Ye have taken your fill of the spiritual feast! Ye have all exulted with honest exultation! Ye have beheld their ribs laid bare, and their loins lacerated; the blood flowing forth all around; ten thousand forms of torture! Ye have seen human nature exhibiting that which is above nature, and crowns woven with blood! Ye have danced a goodly dance throughout the whole city; this, your noble captain leading you on; but sickness compelled me to remain at home, although against my will. But if I did not take a part in the festival, I partook of the pleasure of it. If I could not have the enjoyment of your public assembly, yet did I share in your gladness. For such is the power of love, that it makes those who are not actually in the enjoyment to rejoice equally with those who are; persuading them to think the good things of their neighbor common to themselves. Therefore even whilst I sat at home, I was rejoicing with you; and now whilst I am not yet entirely freed from my sickness, I have risen up, and run to meet you, that I may see your much desired faces, and take a part in the present festival.

2. For I think the present day to be a very great festival indeed on account of our brethren, who by their presence beautify our city, and adorn the Church; a people foreign to us in language, but in harmony with us concerning the faith, a people passing their time in tranquility, and leading an honest and sober life. For

among these men there are no spectacles of iniquity—no horse racings, nor harlots, nor any of that riot which pertains to a city, but every kind of licentiousness is banished, and great sobriety flourishes everywhere. And the reason is, that their life is a laborious one; and they have, in the culture of the soil, a school of virtue and sobriety, and follow that art which God introduced before all others into our life. For before the sin of Adam, when he enjoyed much freedom, a certain tillage of the ground was enjoined upon him; not indeed a laborious or a troublesome one, but one which afforded him much good discipline, for he was appointed, it is said, "to till the garden, and to keep it." Each of these men you may see at one time employed in yoking the laboring oxen, and guiding the plough, and cutting the deep furrow; and at another ascending the sacred pulpit, and cultivating the souls of those under their authority; at one time cutting away the thorns from the soil with a bill-hook, at another purging out the sins of the soul by the Word. For they are not ashamed of work like the inhabitants of our city, but they are ashamed of idleness, knowing that this has taught every kind of wickedness; and that to those who love it, it has proved a teacher of iniquity from the beginning.

3. These are our philosophers, and theirs the best philosophy, exhibiting their virtue not by their outward appearance, but by their mind. The pagan philosophers are in character no wise better than those who are engaged on the stage, and in the sports of actors; and they have nothing to shew beyond the threadbare cloak, the beard, and the long robe! But these, quite on the contrary, bidding farewell to staff and beard, and the other accoutrements, have their souls adorned with the doctrines of the true philosophy, and not only with the

doctrines, but also with the real practice. And were you to question any one of these, who live a rustic life at the spade and plough, as to the dogmas respecting which the pagan philosophers have discoursed an infinite deal, and have expended a multitude of words, without being able to say anything sound; one of these would give you an accurate reply from his store of wisdom. And not only is this to be wondered at, but that they confirm the credibility of these doctrines by their actions. For of the fact that we have an immortal soul, and that we shall hereafter render an account of what we have done here, and stand before a fearful Tribunal, their minds are at once thoroughly persuaded, and they have also regulated their whole course of life by such hopes as these; and have become superior to all worldly show, instructed as they have been by the sacred Scriptures, that "all is vanity, yea, vanity of vanities," and they do not greedily long for any of those things which seem to be so splendid.

4. These too know how to philosophize concerning God, even as God hath determined; and if, taking one of them, you were now to bring forward some pagan philosopher;—or rather, now you could not find one!—But if you were to take one of these, and then open the books of their ancient philosophers, and go through them, and institute an enquiry by way of parallel as to what these now answer, and the others in their day philosophically advanced; you would see how much wisdom belonged to the former, and how much folly to the latter. For whilst some of those would aver, that the things existing were destitute of a providence, and that the creation had not its origin from God; that virtue was not sufficient for itself, but stood in need of wealth, and nobility, and external splendor, and other things still more

ridiculous; and whilst these, on the other hand, would discourse wisely respecting Providence, respecting the future Tribunals of judgment, respecting the creative power of God, bringing forth all things out of nothing, as well as respecting all other points, although at the same time they were entirely destitute of worldly schooling; who could but learn from hence the power of Christ, which hath proved these unlearned and simple persons to be as much wiser than those, who make so much boast of their wisdom, as men of discretion are seen to be in comparison of little children? For what harm can result to them from their simplicity in regard to learning, when their thoughts are full of much wisdom? And what advantage have those philosophers from this learning, when the understanding is devoid of right thoughts? It were just as if one should have a sword that had its hilt of silver, whilst the blade was weaker than the vilest lead. For truly these philosophers have their tongue decked out with words and names, but their understanding is full of mere weakness and good for nothing. Not so with these philosophers, but quite the reverse. Their understanding is full of spiritual wisdom and their mode of life is a transcript of their doctrines. Amongst these there are no luxurious women; there are no ornaments of dress, nor colors, nor paints; but all such corruption of manners is discountenanced. Hence the population under their charge are the more readily trained to sobriety, and the law which Paul gave, when he directed that food and covering should be had, and nothing more be sought after, they most rigidly observe. Amongst them, there are no perfumed unguents to fascinate the senses; but the earth bringing forth herbs, prepares for them a varied fragrance of flowers, above all the skill of perfumers. For this reason, their bodies as well as souls enjoy a sound state of health, inasmuch as they have banished all luxury of diet, and driven off all the evil floods of drunkenness; and they eat just as much as suffices for subsistence. Let us then not despise them because of their outward appearance, but let us admire their mind. For of what advantage is the external habit, when the soul is more wretchedly clad than any beggar! The man ought to be praised and admired, not for dress, nay more, not for his bodily form, but for his soul. Lay bare the soul of these men, and you will see its beauty and the wealth it possesses, in their words, in their doctrines, and in the whole system of their manners!

5. Let the Gentiles then be ashamed, let them hide their heads, and slink away on account of their philosophers, and their wisdom, wretched as it is beyond all folly! For the philosophers that have been amongst them in their lifetime have hardly been able to teach their doctrines to a very few, who can easily be numbered; and when any trifling peril overtook them, they lost even these. But the disciples of Christ, the fishermen, the publicans, and the tentmakers, in a few years brought over the whole world to the truth; and when from that time, ten thousand perils have been constantly arising, the preaching of the Gospel was so far from being put down, that it still flourishes and increases; and they taught simple people, tillers of the ground, and occupied with cattle, to be lovers of wisdom. Such are the persons, who beside all the rest having deeply rooted in them that love which is the source of all good things, have hastened to us, undertaking so long a journey, that they might come and embrace their fellow-members.

6. Come then, and in return for these favors, (I speak of their love and kind feeling), let us give them a

provision, and so send them home; and let us again raise the question concerning oaths; that from the minds of all we may pluck up by the roots this evil custom. But first, I desire to put you a little in mind to-day of the things we spoke of lately. When the Jews, having been released from Persia, and set free from that tyranny, were returned back to their own county, "I saw," says one, "a flying sickle, twenty cubits in length, and ten cubits broad." They heard also the Prophet giving them this instruction, "This is the curse, that goes forth over the face of the whole land, and entered into the house of him that swears falsely; and it shall rest in the midst thereof, and throw down the timber and all the stones." When we had read this passage, we also enquired then why it was, that it should destroy not the swearer only, but also his house, and we stated this to be the reason; that God will have the punishments of the most grievous sins to remain continually visible; that all may afterwards learn prudence. Inasmuch then as it was necessary that the perjurer when dead should be buried, and committed to the bosom of the earth; in order that his wickedness might not be buried along with him, his house was made a heap, so that all who passed by, beholding it, and learning the reason of the overthrow, might avoid imitating the sin.

7. This also happened at Sodom. For when they burned in their lust one towards another, then too the very earth itself was burned up, being kindled by the fire from above. For He designed, that the vengeance of this sin should permanently remain.

And observe the mercy of God! Those who had sinned, He caused not to continue burning to the present day, but when they had been for once in flames, He buried them; and burning up the face of the ground, He placed it visibly before all who after should desire to look at these things; and now the sight of the land, through all the generations since, hath given an admonition beyond all powers of speech, crying out as it were, and saying, "Dare not to do the deeds of Sodom, lest ye suffer the lot of Sodom!" For precept commonly makes not so deep an impression upon the mind as a fearful spectacle does, which bears upon it the vestiges of calamity though all time. And persons that have visited these places bear witness, who often, when they hear the Scripture discoursing of these things, are not much terrified; but when they have gone and stood upon the site, and see the whole surface of it disfigured, and have witnessed the effects of the fire, with soil nowhere visible, but everything dust and ashes, they come away astonished with the sight, and taking with them a strong lesson of chastity. For truly, the very nature of the punishment was a pattern of the nature of the sin! Even as they devised a barren intercourse, not having for its end the procreation of children, so did God bring on them such a punishment, as made the womb of the land ever barren, and destitute of all fruits! For this reason also He threatened to destroy the dwellings of the swearers, in order that by their punishments, they may make others to be more self-controlled.

8. But I am ready to shew to-day, not the destruction of one, two, or three houses in consequence of oaths, but that of a whole city and of a people beloved of God; of a nation that had always enjoyed much of the divine care; and of a race that had escaped many dangers. For Jerusalem herself, the city of God, which had the holy ark, and all that divine service;—where there were once prophets, and the grace of the Spirit, and the ark; and the

tables of the covenant, and the golden pot;—where angels were frequent visitors;—this city, I say, when a multitude of wars took place, and many foreign nations made attacks upon it, as if girt by a wall of adamant, ever laughed them all to scorn, and whilst the land was utterly destroyed, sustained no injury! And not only is this to be wondered at, but that frequently in driving out its enemies, it inflicted upon them a heavy blow, and enjoyed so much of the providential care of God, that God Himself said, "I found Israel as a bunch of grapes in the desert; and I beheld your fathers as the earliest fruit on the fig tree." And again, of the city itself: "As olive berries on the extremity of the highest bough, and they shall say, Do them no harm." Nevertheless, the city beloved of God; that had escaped so many perils; that had been favored with pardon, amidst the multitude of its sins; that alone had been able to avoid captivity, whilst all the rest were carried away, not once or twice, but very often; was ruined solely by an oath. But how, I proceed to state.

9. One of their kings was Zedekiah. This Zedekiah took an oath to Nebuchadnezzar, king of the barbarians, that he would remain in alliance with him. Afterwards he revolted, and went over to the king of Egypt, disdaining the obligation of his oath, and suffered the things of which ye shall hear presently. But first, it is necessary to mention the parable of the prophet, in which he enigmatically represented all these matters: "The word of the Lord," says he, "came to me, saying, Son of man, put forth a riddle, and speak a parable, and say, Thus says the Lord God: A great eagle, with great wings, and long extended, full of claws." Here he calls the king of the Babylonians an eagle, and speaks of him as being "great, and long-winged;" and he calls him long-extended and

"full of claws," on account of the multitude of his army, and the greatness of his power, and the swiftness of his invasion. For just as the wings and claws of the eagle are his armor, so are horses and soldiers to kings. This eagle, he goes on to say, "hath the leading to enter into Lebanon." What is meant by the "leading?" Counsel—design. And Judæa is called Lebanon, because of its situation near that mountain. Afterwards, intending to speak of the oaths and treaties, "He took," says he, "of the seed of the land, and planted it in a fruitful field, that it might take root by great waters. He placed it to be looked upon; and it grew, and became a weak vine, and of small stature, and it stretched out its branches towards him, and its roots were under him." Here he calls the city of Jerusalem a vine; but in saying that it stretched out its branches towards the eagle, and that its roots were under him, he refers to the treaties and alliances made with him; and that it cast itself upon him. Next, purposing to declare the iniquity of this, he says, "And there was another great eagle," (speaking of the Egyptian king), "with great wings, and having many claws; and the vine did bend itself toward him, and its tendril toward him, and shot out its branches, that it might be watered. Therefore, I said, Thus says the Lord God: Shall it prosper?" That is to say, "after having broken the oath, and the treaties, shall it be able to remain, or to be safe, or to avoid falling?" Presently, for the purpose of shewing that this is not to happen, but that it is certainly to be destroyed on account of the oath, he discourses concerning its punishment, and alleges the cause. "For its tender roots and its fruits shall become corrupt, and all which springs therefrom shall be withered." And for the purpose of shewing that it will not be destroyed by human strength, but because it hath made

God its enemy by means of these oaths, he subjoins, "Not by a mighty arm, nor by much people, to pluck it up by its roots." Such indeed is the parable, but the prophet again explains it, when he says, "Behold, the king of Babylon cometh against Jerusalem." And then, after saying some other things between, he mentions the oaths and the treaties. "For" says he, "he shall make a covenant with him;" and presently, speaking of the departure from it, he goes on to say, "And he will depart from him, by sending messengers into Egypt, that they might give him horses and much people." And then he proceeds to shew that it is on account of the oath that all this destruction is to take place. "Surely in the place where the king dwelled that made him king, he who hath despised My curse, and hath transgressed My covenant, in the midst of Babylon he shall die; and not by great power nor by multitude, because he despised the oath in transgressing this My covenant; I will surely recompense upon his own head this My oath which he hath dishonored, and My covenant which he hath broken; and I will spread My net upon him." See that not once, or twice, but repeatedly, it is said that because of the oath he was to suffer all these things. For God is inexorable when oaths are treated contemptuously. Nor merely from the punishment which was brought upon the city by the oath, but also from the delay, and the postponement, may it be seen how much God is concerned for the inviolability of oaths. "For it came to pass," we are told, "in the ninth year of the reign of Zedekiah, on the tenth day of the month, that Nebuchadnezzar the king of Babylon came, and all his host, against Jerusalem, and pitched against it, and built a wall against it round about, and the city was besieged until the eleventh year of king Zedekiah, and the ninth day of the month, and there was no bread for the people to eat, and the city was broken up." He might indeed, at once from the first day, have delivered them up, and have given them into the hands of their enemies; but He permitted that they should first be wasted for the space of three years, and experience a most distressing siege; to the end that during this interval, being humbled by the terror of the forces without, or the famine that oppressed the city within, they might compel the king, however unwillingly, to submit to the barbarian; and some alleviation might be obtained for the sin committed. And to prove that this is true, and no conjecture of my own, hear what He says to him by the prophet: "If thou shalt go forth to the king of Babylon's princes, then thy soul shall live, and this city shall not be burned with fire; and thou shalt live, and thine house. But if thou wilt not go forth to the king of Babylon's princes, then shall this city be given into the hand of the Chaldeans; and they shall burn it with fire, and thou shalt not escape out of their hand. And the king said, I am afraid of the Jews that are fallen to the Chaldeans, lest they deliver me into their hands and they mock me. But Jeremiah said, They shall not deliver thee. Obey, I beseech thee, the word of the Lord, which I speak unto thee; so shall it be better for thee, and thy soul shall live. But if thou refuse to go forth, this is the word that the Lord hath shewed me. All the women that are left in the king of Judah's house, shall be brought forth to the king of Babylon's princes; and those shall say, The men who are at peace with thee have deceived thee, and have prevailed over thee; they shall prevail when thy feet slip; they are turned away from thee, and they shall bring out all thy wives, and thy children to the Chaldeans, and thou shalt not escape out of their hand, for thou shalt be taken by the hand of the king of Babylon, and this city shall be burned with fire."

10. But when He did not prevail with him by this address, but he remained in his sin and transgression, after three years, God delivered up the city, displaying at once His own clemency and the ingratitude of that king. And entering in with the utmost ease, they "burnt the house of the Lord, and the king's house, and the houses of Jerusalem, and every great house, the captain of the guard burnt, and overthrew the wall of Jerusalem;" and everywhere there was the fire of the barbarian, the oath being the conductor of the conflagration, and carrying about the flame in all directions. "And the captain of the guard carried away the rest of the people that were left in the city, and the fugitives that fell away to the king of Babylon. And the pillars of brass that were in the house of the Lord the Chaldeans brake up, and the bases, and the brazen sea that was in the house of the Lord, did the Chaldees break in pieces. And the pots, and the flesh-hooks, and the bowls, and the censers, and all the vessels of brass wherewith they ministered, took they away. And the firepans, and all the golden and silver bowls they took away. Moreover, Nebuzaradan, the captain of the guard, took away the two pillars, and the bases, and the sea which Solomon had made in the house of the Lord. And they took away Seraiah the chief priest, and Zephaniah the second priest, and the three keepers of the door; and out of the city one eunuch that was set over the men of war; and five men that were in the king's presence; and Shaphan the chief captain, and the principal scribe, and threescore men. And he took these, and brought them to the king of Babylon, and the king smote them, and slew them."

11. Be mindful therefore, I pray, now of the "flying sickle" that "rested in the swearer's house;" and "destroyed the walls and the timber and the stones." Be mindful, I pray, how this oath entered into the city, and overturned houses, and temple, and walls, and splendid buildings, and made the city an heap; and that neither the Holy of Holies, nor the sacred vessels, nor anything else could ward off that punishment and vengeance, for that the oath had been transgressed! The city, indeed, was thus miserably destroyed. But the king endured what was still more wretched and deplorable. And as the flying sickle overthrew the buildings, so did it also cut him down in his flight. For "the king," it says, "went forth by night, by way of the gate, and the Chaldeans encompassed the city, and the army of the Chaldeans pursued after the king and overtook him, and they took the king, and brought him to the king of Babylon, and the king of Babylon gave judgment upon Zedekiah, and slew his sons before his face, and put out the eyes of Zedekiah, and bound him with fetters, and carried him to Babylon." What is meant by the expression, "he spoke judgment with him?" He demanded of him an account of his conduct, he pleaded against him; and first he slew his two sons, that he might be a spectator of the calamity of his house, and might behold that deplorable tragedy; and then he put out his own eyes. For what reason, I ask again, did this occur? In order that he might go as a teacher to the barbarians, and too the Jews who dwelt among them; and that they who had eyes might discern by him who was bereft of sight, how great an evil is an oath! Nor only these; but all who dwelt by the way, beholding the man fettered and blinded, might learn by his calamity the greatness of his sin. Therefore one of the prophets declares, "He shall not see

Babylon." And another, "He shall be carried away to Babylon." And the prophecy seems, indeed, to be contradictory. But it is not so; for both of these are true. For he saw not Babylon, though he was carried away to Babylon. How then did he not see Babylon? Because it was in Judæa he had his eyes put out; for where the oath had been set at naught, there also was it vindicated, and he himself subjected to punishment. And how was he carried away to Babylon? In a state of captivity. For since the punishment was twofold, deprivation of sight and captivity, the prophets took them severally. The one says, "He shall not see Babylon," speaking of the loss of his eyes; the other says, "He shall be carried away to Babylon," signifying his captivity.

12. Knowing these things, then, brethren, and gathering up what has been now advanced, as well as what has been said before; let us at last desist from this evil custom, yea, I pray and beseech you all! For if in the old dispensation, when the Jews had not the strictest moral wisdom required of them, but much condescension was extended to them, such wrath was the effect of one oath; such capture and captivity; what punishment is it likely that those who swear should now be subjected to, after an express law forbidding the practice, and so large an addition of precepts. Is it, indeed, all that is required, that we come to the assembly, and hear what is spoken? Why truly it is a reason for greater condemnation, and for more inevitable punishment, that we are continually hearing, and yet do not what is bidden! What excuse shall we have, or what pardon, if assembling here from earliest youth to latest old age, and enjoying the advantage of so much instruction, we remain just like them, and do not take pains to correct a single defect. Let no one

henceforth allege custom. For this is the very thing at which I am indignant and provoked, that we are not able to get the better of custom. And, pray, if we do not get the better of custom, how can we get the better of concupiscence, which hath its root even in the principles of our nature; for it is natural to feel desire; but to desire wickedly, comes after of choice. But this practice of swearing takes not even its first principle from nature, but from mere negligence.

13. And that thou may learn that not from the difficulty of the thing, but through our inattention, this sin has advanced to such a pitch, let us call to mind how many things far more difficult than these, men accomplish; and that too without expecting any recompense therefrom. Let us think what services the Devil imposes; how laborious, how troublesome they are; and yet, the difficulty has not become an obstacle to these services. For what can be more difficult, I ask, than when any young person delivering himself up to those, who undertake to make his limbs supple and pliant, uses his most strenuous exertion to bend his whole body into the exact shape of a wheel, and to turn over upon the pavement; his powers being tasked at the same time through the eyes, and through the movement of the hands, as well as other convolutions for the purpose of being transformed into the likeness of woman-kind. Yet neither the difficulty of these feats, nor the degradation arising from them, are thought of. And again, those who are dragged upon the dancing-stage, and use the members of the body as though they were wings, who that beholds them can help being struck with wonder? So too they who toss knives aloft in the air one after another, and catch them all by the handle, whom might they not put to shame

of those who refuse to undergo any labor for the sake of virtue? And what can anyone say of those men, who balancing a pole on the forehead, keep it just as steady as a tree rooted in the ground? And this is not the only marvelous part of the affair but that they set little children to wrestle with one another on the top of the tree; and neither the hands, nor any other part of the body assisting, the forehead alone sustains the pole unshaken, and with more steadiness than any kind of fastening. Again: another walks on the slenderest rope, with the same fearlessness as men do when they run over level plains. Nevertheless these things, which even in thought seem impracticable, have become possible by art. What like this have we, I ask, to allege concerning oaths? What kind of difficulty? What toil? What art? What danger? There is only needed on our part a little earnestness, and the whole of our task will be quickly performed.

14. And do not tell me, "I have accomplished the greater part of it;" but if thou hast not accomplished the whole, consider that thou hast not as yet done anything; for this little, if neglected, is destruction to all the rest. Often indeed when men have built a house, and put on the roof, they have destroyed the whole fabric, by not making any concern of a single tile that has been shaken off from it. And one may see the same thing occur with respect to garments; for there too if a small hole is made, and not repaired, a large rent is the consequence. And this also is frequently the case in regard to floods; for these, if they find but a small entrance, let in the whole torrent. Thou also, then, even if thou hast fortified thyself all around, and but a small part be left still unfortified, yet block up this also against the devil, that thou may be made strong on all sides! Thou hast seen the sickle! Thou hast seen the

head of John! Thou hast heard the history pertaining to Saul! Thou hast heard the manner of the Jewish captivity! And beside all these, thou hast heard the sentence of Christ declaring, that not only to commit perjury, but to swear in any way, is a diabolical thing, and the whole a device of the evil one. Thou hast heard that everywhere perjuries follow oaths. Putting all these things then together, write them upon thy understanding. Do you not see how women and little children suspend Gospels from their necks as a powerful amulet, and carry them about in all places wherever they go. Thus do thou write the commands of the Gospel and its laws upon thy mind. Here there is no need of gold or property, or of buying a book; but of the will only, and the affections of the soul awakened, and the Gospel will be thy surer guardian, carrying it as thou wilt then do, not outside, but treasured up within; yea, in the soul's secret chambers. When thou rises up then from thy bed, and when thou goes out of thine house, repeat this law: "I say unto you, Swear not at all." And the saying will be to thee a discipline; for there is no need of much labor, but only of a moderate degree of attention. And that this is true, may thus be proved. Call thy son, and frighten him, and threaten to lay a few stripes upon him, if he does not duly observe this law; and thou wilt see, how he will forthwith abstain from this custom. Is it not therefore truly absurd, that little children, out of the fear we inspire, should perform this commandment, and that we should not fear God as our sons fear us?

15. What then I said before this, I now again repeat. Let us lay down a law for ourselves in this matter; not to meddle either with public or private affairs until we have fulfilled this law; and then surely under the pressure

of this obligation we shall easily conquer, and we shall at once adorn ourselves, and decorate our city. For consider what a thing it would be to have it said everywhere throughout the world, "A practice becoming Christians is established at Antioch, and you will hear no one giving utterance to an oath, even though the greatest necessity is laid upon him!" This is what the neighboring cities will certainly hear; nay, not the neighboring cities only, but even to the ends of the earth will the report be conveyed. For it is indeed probable that both the merchants who mix with you, and others who arrive from this place, will report all these matters. When, therefore, many persons in the way of encomium mention the harbors of other cities, or the markets, or the abundance of wares, enable those who come from hence to say, that there is that at Antioch, which is to be seen in no other city; for that the men who dwell there would sooner have their tongues cut out, than suffer an oath to proceed from their mouths! This will be your ornament and defense, and not only so, but it will bring an abundant reward. For others also will certainly emulate, and imitate you. But if, when a person has gained but one or two, he shall receive so great a reward from God; what recompense shall ye not receive when ye are the instructors of the whole world. It is your duty then to bestir yourselves, to be watchful, and to be sober; knowing that not only from our own personal good works, but from those we have also wrought in others, shall we receive the best recompense, and enjoy much favor with God, which may He grant us all continually to enjoy, and hereafter to obtain the kingdom of heaven, in Christ Jesus our Lord; to Whom with the Father, and the Holy Ghost, be glory and power both now and ever, and world without end. Amen.

Homily XX.

That the fast of Lent is not sufficient to make us competent to partake of the Communion, but that holiness is the first thing required. How it is possible not to entertain resentment, and that God takes much account of this law; and that the entertaining of resentment punishes those who are guilty of it even before they reach the place of torment.—Also concerning abstinence from oaths, and those who have not succeeded in abstaining from swearing.

1. At length the season is verging towards the end of the Fast, and therefore we ought the more earnestly to devote ourselves to holiness. For as in the case of those who run a race, all their circuits will be of no avail if they miss the prize; so neither will any advantage result from these manifold labors and toils with regard to the fast, if we are not able to enjoy the sacred Table with a good conscience. For this end are fasting and Lent appointed, and so many days of solemn assemblies, auditories, prayers, and teachings, in order that by this earnestness being cleansed in every possible way from the sins which we had contracted during the whole year, we may with spiritual boldness religiously partake of that unbloody Sacrifice; so that should this not be the result, we shall have sustained so much labor entirely in vain, and without any profit. Let everyone, therefore, consider with himself what defect he hath corrected, what good work he hath attained to; what sin he hath cast off, what stain he hath purged away; in what respect he has become better. And should he discover that in this good traffic he has made any gain by the fast, and be conscious in himself of much

care taken of his wounds, let him draw near! But if he hath remained negligent, having nothing to shew but mere fasting, and hath done nothing which is right besides, let him remain outside; and then let him enter, when he hath purged out all these offences. Let no one rest on the fast merely; whilst continuing unreformed in evil practices. For it is probable, that he who omits fasting may obtain pardon, having infirmity of body to plead; but it is impossible that he can have an excuse who hath not amended his faults. Thou hast not fasted, it may be, on account of bodily weakness. Tell me for what reason thou art not reconciled to thine enemies? Hast thou, indeed, here to allege bodily infirmity? Again; if thou retains envy and hatred, what apology hast thou then I ask? For no one in offences of this kind is able to take refuge in the plea of bodily infirmity. And this was a work of Christ's love toward man, viz. that the chief of the precepts, and those which maintain our life, should not be impaired in any degree through the weakness of the body.

2. But since we need to practice all the divine laws alike, and more especially that which bids us consider no man as an enemy, nor retain resentment long, but forthwith to be reconciled; suffer us to-day to discourse to you concerning this commandment. For as it is not to be imagined that the fornicator and the blasphemer can partake of the sacred Table, so it is impossible that he who hath an enemy, and bears malice, can enjoy the holy Communion. And this with good reason. For a man when he has committed fornication, or adultery, at the same time that he hath accomplished his lust, hath also completed the sin; and should he be willing by watchful living to recover from that fall, he may afterwards, by manifesting great penitence, obtain some relief. But he

who is resentful worked the same iniquity every day, and never brings it to an end. In the former case the deed is over, and the sin completed; but here the sin is perpetrated every day. What excuse can we then have, I ask, for delivering ourselves willingly to such an evil monster? How canst thou ask thy Lord to be mild and merciful to thee, when thou hast been so hard and unforgiving to thy fellow-servant?

3. But thy fellow-servant hath treated thee with contempt perhaps? Yes! And thou hast treated God with contempt oftentimes. And what comparison is there between a fellow servant and the Lord? As to the former, when he was perchance in some way injured, he insulted thee, and thou wert exasperated. But thou insults the Lord, when thou art neither treated with injustice nor ill-will by Him, but receiving blessing of Him day by day. Consider, then, that if God chose to search out rigorously what is done against Him, we should not live a single day. For the prophet says, "If Thou wilt be extreme to mark iniquity, O Lord, O Lord, who shall stand?" And, to pass by all those other things, of which the conscience of every sinner is aware, and of which he has no human witness, but God only; were we to be called to account for those which are open and admitted, what allowance could we expect for such sins? What if He were to scrutinize our listlessness and negligence in our prayers; and how, whilst standing before God and supplicating Him, we do not exhibit even so much fear and reverence for Him as servants do toward their masters, as soldiers do toward their officers, as friends do toward friends? When thou discourses with a friend, thou gives heed to what thou art doing, but when waiting on God on account of thy sins, and asking pardon for so many offences, and thinking that thou shalt obtain

forgiveness, thou art often listless; and whilst thy knees are lying on the ground, thou suffers thy mind to wander everywhere, in the market, or in the house, babbling the while with thy mouth vainly and to no purpose! And this we experience, not once or twice, but frequently! Did God then choose to scrutinize this alone, do you think that we could obtain pardon, or be able to find any excuse? Truly, I think not!

4. But what if the evil-speaking which we unkindly utter every day one against another, were brought forward against us; as well as the rash judgments with which we condemn our neighbor; and that for no reason, but because we are fond of blaming, and given to find fault; what, I say, should we be able to allege in defense? Again, should He scrutinize those roving glances of ours, and those evil desires which we carry in the mind, so frequently admitting disgraceful and impure thoughts from the unlicensed wandering of the eyes, what punishment must we not sustain? And should He demand a reason for our reviling, (for He says, "Whosoever shall say to his brother, Thou fool, shall be in danger of hell fire,") how could we, forsooth, open our mouths, or move our lips at all, or say anything great or small in reply? Moreover, as to the vainglorious feelings we allow in our prayers, our fasting, our almsgiving, were we to scrutinize, them,—I do not say, were God, but were we ourselves, who are the sinners, to do this,—should we be able to lift up our eyes toward heaven? Then, as to the deceits which we devise one against another—praising a brother now, whilst he is present, and discoursing as with a friend; and when he is absent, reviling him; can we endure the punishments of all these? Then what of the oaths? Or what of the lying? What of the perjuries? What

of the unjust anger, and of the envy with which we too often regard men when honored, not enemies only, but also friends? Furthermore, what of the fact, that we are pleased when others suffer evil, and account the misfortunes of others a consolation for our own distress?

5. But suppose the penalty were exacted for our listlessness in our solemn assemblies what would our condition be? For this ye cannot but know, that often whilst God Himself is addressing us all by His prophet, we are holding frequent and long conversations with those near us, about matters which in no way concern us. Passing by, then, all the rest, should He choose to exact of us the penalty due for this sin only, what hope of salvation will there be? For do not suppose that this offence is a small one, but if you would be aware of its magnitude, examine how this very thing is regarded among men, and then thou wilt perceive the enormity of the sin. Just venture, when some magistrate is talking to thee, or rather some friend who is of somewhat superior dignity, to turn from him, and enter into conversation with thy servant; and thou wilt then perceive, what thou ventures on in dealing thus with God! For if he be any one of the more distinguished classes, he will even demand reparation of thee for such an insult. Yet God, whilst He is treated with as great, and still greater contempt than this, every day; and that not by one, or two, or three persons, but by almost all of us; is still forbearing and longsuffering, not in regard to this alone, but to other things which are far more grievous. For these things are what must be admitted, and what are obvious to all, and by almost all men they are daringly practiced. But there are yet others, which the conscience of those who commit them is privy to. Surely, if we were to think of all this; if we were to

reason with ourselves, supposing even that we were the cruelest and harshest of men, yet upon taking a survey of the multitude of our sins, we should for very fear and agony be unable to remember the injury done by others towards ourselves. Bear in mind the river of fire; the envenomed worm; the fearful Judgment, where all things shall be naked and open! Reflect, that what are now hidden things, are then to be brought to light! But should you pardon thy neighbor all these sins which till then await their disclosure are done away with here; and when thou shalt depart this life, thou wilt not drag after thee any of that chain of transgressions; so that thou receives greater things than thou gives. For many such transgressions, indeed, we have often committed, which no other person knows; and when we think, that on That Day these our sins shall lie exposed to the eyes of all, upon the public theatre of the universe, we are in pain beyond any punishment, being choked and strangled by our conscience. Yet this shame, great as it is; these sins, these punishments, great as they are; there is a possibility of purging away through forgiveness exercised toward our neighbor.

6. For indeed there is nothing equal to this virtue. Would you learn the power of this virtue? "Though Moses and Samuel stood before Me," says God, "my soul would not regard them." Nevertheless, those whom Moses and Samuel were not able to snatch away from God's wrath, this precept when observed was able to snatch away. Hence it is, that He continually exhorts those to whom He had spoken these things, saying, "Let none of you revengefully imagine evil against his brother in your heart," and "let none of you think of his neighbor's malice." It is not said merely, forego wrath;

but retain it not in thy mind; think not of it; part with all thy resentment; do away the sore. For thou supposes that thou art paying him back the injury; but thou art first tormenting thyself, and setting up thy rage as an executioner within thee in every part, and tearing up thine own bowels. For what can be more wretched than a man perpetually angry? And just as maniacs, who never enjoy tranquility, so also he who is resentful, and retains an enemy, will never have the enjoyment of any peace; incessantly raging, as he does, and daily increasing the tempest of his thoughts calling to mind his words and acts, and detesting the very name of him who has aggrieved him. Do you but mention his enemy, he becomes furious at once, and sustains much inward anguish; and should he chance to get only a bare sight of him, he fears and trembles, as if encountering the worst evils. Yea, if he perceives any of his relations, if but his garment, or his dwelling, or street, he is tormented by the sight of them. For as in the case of those who are beloved, their faces, their garments, their sandals, their houses, or streets, excite us, the instant we behold them; so also should we observe a servant, or friend, or house, or street, or anything else belonging to those we hate and hold our enemies, we are stung by all these things; and the strokes we endure from the sight of each one of them are frequent and continual.

    7. What is the need then of sustaining such a siege, such torment and such punishment? For if hell did not threaten the resentful; yet for the very torment resulting from the thing itself we ought to forgive the offences of those who have aggrieved us. But when deathless punishments remain behind, what can be more senseless than the man, who both here and there brings punishment

upon himself, while he thinks to be revenged upon his enemy! For suppose that we see him still prosperous, then we are ready to die of chagrin; but if in an adverse condition, we are in fear, lest some propitious turn of events should take place. But for both of these there is stored up for us an inevitable punishment. For, "Rejoice not," he says, "when thine enemy stumbles." And tell me not of the greatness of the injuries received; for it is not this which makes thy wrath to be retained; but this, that thou art unmindful of thine own offences; that thou hast not before thine eyes either hell or the fear of God! To convince thee that this is true, I will endeavor to make it manifest from the events which have happened in this city. For when the persons impeached of those flagrant crimes were dragged to the tribunal of justice;—when the fire was kindled within, and the executioners stood around, and were lacerating their ribs, if any one standing beside them had proclaimed, "If ye have any enemies, dismiss your resentment, and we shall be able to set you free from this punishment;"—would they not have kissed their very feet? And why do I say their feet? If one had bidden them take them for their masters, they would not then have refused. But if punishment that is human, and hath its bounds, would have triumphed over all anger, much more would the punishment to come, if it had continual possession of our thoughts, expel from the soul not only resentment, but every evil imagination? For what is easier, I ask, than to get rid of resentment against the injurer? Is there any long journey to be undertaken? Is there any expenditure of money? Is the aid of others to be invoked? It suffices only to resolve, and the good deed at once reaches the goal. What punishment, then, must we not deserve, if on account of worldly affairs we stoop to slavish occupations; and shew a servility unworthy of ourselves; and expend money; and enter into conversation with porters, that we may flatter impious men; and do and say all manner of things, so that we may perfectly attain the end we have in view; and yet cannot endure, for the sake of God's laws, to entreat a brother who hath injured us, but consider it a disgrace to be the first to make advances. Art thou ashamed, tell me, when thou art going to be the first to make gain? Rather, on the contrary, you ought to be ashamed of persisting in this passion; and waiting until the person who has committed the injury comes to you to be reconciled; for this is a disgrace, and a reproach, and the greatest loss.

8. For he who comes the first it is, who reaps all the fruit; and when at the entreaty of another thou lays aside thine anger, the good work is to be accounted his; for thou hast discharged the law as doing a favor to him, not as obeying God. But if, when no one entreats, when not even the man who has done the injury approaches, or solicits thee, thou thyself dismissing from thy thoughts all shame, and all delay, runs forward freely to the injurer, and dost quell anger entirely, the good deed becomes wholly thine own, and thou shalt receive all the reward. If I say, "Practice fasting," thy plea, perchance, is bodily weakness. If I say, "Give to the poor," it is poverty, and bringing up children. If I say, "Make time for the assembles of the Church," it is worldly cares. If I say, "Give heed to what is spoken, and consider the power of what is taught," it is want of learning. If I say, "Correct another," you say, "When counsel is given him, he takes no heed, for I have often spoken, and been scorned." Frigid, as such pretenses are, yet you have some pretenses to allege. But suppose I say, "Dismiss thine anger," which

of these wilt thou then allege? For neither infirmity of body, nor poverty, nor lack of culture, nor want of leisure, nor any other thing of that kind hast thou to advance; but this sin is above all other the most inexcusable. How wilt thou be able to stretch thine hands toward heaven, or how to move thy tongue, or to ask pardon? For although God be desirous to pardon thy sins, thou thyself dost not suffer Him, while thou retains that of thy fellow-servant! But suppose that he is cruel, fierce, and savage, and greedy of revenge and retaliation? Why for this reason thou oughtest especially to grant forgiveness. Hast thou been wronged much, and robbed, and slandered, and injured in matters of the first importance; and dost thou wish to see thine enemy punished? Yet even for this, it will be of use to thee to pardon him. For suppose that thou thyself takes vengeance, and prosecutes it, either by words, by deeds, or imprecation against the adversary; then God will not afterwards prosecute it too, inasmuch as thou hast taken thy revenge; and not only will He not prosecute the matter for thee, but will also demand a penalty of thee as a despiser of Himself. For if this same thing takes place amongst mankind, viz. that if we beat the servant of another, the master is indignant, and calls the act an insult (for although we be treated injuriously, whether by slaves, or by freemen, it is fitting that we should await the legal decisions of magistrates or masters); if then even amongst men, to avenge ourselves would not be safe, how much more so when God is the avenger!

9. Hath thy neighbor wronged and grieved thee, and involved thee in a thousand ills? Be it so, yet do not prosecute vengeance on thine own part, lest thou do desire to thy Lord! Yield the matter to God, and He will dispose of it much better than thou canst desire. To thee He has

given charge simply to pray for the injurer; but how to deal with him, He hath ordered thee to leave to Himself. Never canst thou so avenge thyself, as He is prepared to avenge thee, if thou gives place to Him alone, and dost not utter imprecations on him who has aggrieved thee; but suffers God to be sole arbiter of the sentence. For although we may pardon those who have aggrieved us; although we may be reconciled; although we may pray for them; yet God does not pardon, unless they themselves are converted, and become better. And He withholds pardon, with a view to their own advantage. For He praises thee, and approves thee for thy spiritual wisdom; but visits him, in order that he may not grow worse by thy wisdom. So that the common saying on this subject is not to the point. For many there are, who when I reproach them because after being exhorted to be reconciled to their enemies, they will not be persuaded to it, think fit to proffer this apology, which is nothing less than a cloak for their iniquity. "I am unwilling," says one, "to be reconciled, lest I should make the man worse, more ill-tempered, and more disposed to treat me contemptuously hereafter." Besides this, they also make this plea: "Many people," say they, "think it is weakness in me to come first to a reconciliation, and to entreat my enemy." All these things are foolish; for the Eye that slumbers not has seen thy good intention; wherefore, it behooved thee to make no account of the opinion of thy fellow-servants, when thou hast gained the opinion of the Judge, Who is about to try thy cause.

10. But if thy concern be, lest thine enemy should become worse by thy clemency learn this,—that it is not thus he is made worse; but far rather if thou art unreconciled. For although he were the vilest of men;

although he might neither confess nor publish it openly; yet he will silently approve thy Christian wisdom, and in his own conscience will respect thy gentleness. Should he, however, persist in the same iniquity, whilst thou art endeavoring to soften and conciliate, he will have to abide the heaviest punishment from God. And that ye may know, that although we should pray for our enemies, and for those who have injured us, God does not pardon, if they are likely to become worse by our forbearance, I will mention to you an ancient piece of history. Miriam once spoke against Moses. What then did God do? He sent a leprosy upon her, and made her unclean; notwithstanding that in other respects she had been meek and modest. Afterwards, when Moses himself, the party injured, besought that the wrath might be removed, God consented not: but what did He say? "If her father had but spit in her face, should she not be ashamed? Let her remain," says He, "without the camp seven days." But what He means is to this effect. "If," says He, "she had a father, and he had put her away from his presence, would she not have undergone the rebuke? I approve thee indeed for thy fraternal piety, and thy meekness and clemency; but I know when is the due time to remit her punishment." Do thou then shew all humanity towards thy brother; and do not pardon his offences in the desire of a greater punishment for him, but of thy tenderness and good will; yet understand this very plainly, that the more he shall slight thee, whilst thou art laboring to conciliate, so much the greater punishment will he draw down upon himself.

11. What says thou? Tell me, Is he the worse for thy attentions? This is blame to him, but thy praise. Thy praise, that, whilst seeing him thus behave himself, thou didst not desist from doing God's will in conciliating him.

But to him it is blame, because he has not been made better by thy clemency. But "it is far more desirable that others should be blamed because of us, than we because of them." Make me not this frigid reply, of saying, "I am afraid of its being thought that I made an overture to him out of fear; and that he will therefore despise me the more." Such a reply indicates a childish and foolish mind, agitated about human approbation. Let him suppose, that it was out of fear you made the first advance to him; your reward will be so much the greater; since, being aware of this beforehand, you still consented to endure all for the fear of God. For he who is in chase of human approbation, and seeks reconciliation for that end, curtails the recompense of reward; but he who is quite sure of the fact, that many will vilify and ridicule him, and even then does not desist, from the attempt at reconciliation, will have a twofold, yea, a threefold crown. And this is indeed the man who does it for the sake of God. Nor tell me, that the man has wronged thee in this, or in that particular; for if he hath displayed, in his conduct towards thee, every kind of iniquity that is in man, yet even so God hath enjoined thee to forgive him all!

12. Lo! I forewarn, and testify, and proclaim this with a voice that all may hear! "Let no one who hath an enemy draw near the sacred Table, or receive the Lord's Body! Let no one who draws near have an enemy! Hast thou an enemy? Draw not near! Wilt thou draw near? Be reconciled, and then draw near, and touch the Holy Thing!" Nor, indeed, is this my declaration. Rather it is that of the Lord Himself, Who was crucified for us. That He might reconcile thee to the Father, He refused not to be sacrificed, and to shed His blood! And art thou unwilling to utter a word, or to make the first advance,

that thou may be reconciled to thy fellow-servant? Hear what the Lord says, concerning those who are in this disposition; "If thou bring thy gift to the altar, and there remembers that thy brother hath aught against thee"—He does not say, "wait for him to come to thee," nor "speak with another as mediator," nor "entreat some other," but "do thou thyself make the advance towards him." For the exhortation is, "Go thy way, first be reconciled to thy brother." O transcendent wonder! Does He Himself account it no dishonor, that the gift should be left unoffered, and dost thou think it a mark of disgrace to go first and be reconciled? And how can such a case, I ask, be deemed worthy of pardon? Were you to see a member of yours cut off, would you not use every exertion so that it might be reunited to the body? This do with regard to thy brethren; when thou sees them cut off from thy friendship, make all haste to recover them! Do not wait for them to make the first advance, but press onward, that thou may be foremost to receive the prize.

13. We are commanded to have only one enemy, the devil. With him be thou never reconciled! But with a brother, never be at enmity in thy heart. And if there should be any narrowness of soul, let it be only an ephemeral thing, and never last beyond a day's space. For, "let not the sun," he says, "go down upon your wrath." For if, before evening, you are reconciled, you will obtain some pardon from God. But if you remain longer at enmity, that enmity is no longer the result of your being suddenly carried away by anger and resentment, but of wickedness, and of a foul spirit, and one which makes a practice of malice! And this is not the only terrible thing, that you deprive yourself of pardon, but that the right course becomes still more difficult. For

when one day is past, the shame becomes greater; and when the second has arrived, it is still further increased; and if it reach a third, and a fourth day, it will add a fifth. Thus the five become ten; the ten, twenty; the twenty an hundred; and thenceforth the wound will become incurable; for as time goes on, the breach becomes wider. But do thou, O man, give way to none of these irrational passions; nor be ashamed, nor blush, nor say within yourself, "A short time ago we called each other such names, and said a vast number of things fit or not fit to be spoken; and shall I now hurry at once to a reconciliation? Who then will not blame my excessive easiness?" I answer, no one who has sense will blame thy easiness; but when thou remains implacable, then, all persons will deride thee. Then thou wilt give to the devil the advantage of this wide breach. For the enmity becomes then more difficult to be got rid of, not by mere lapse of time, but from the circumstances too that take place in the meanwhile. For as "charity covers a multitude of sins," so enmity gives a being to sins that do not exist, and all persons henceforth, are deemed worthy of credit who turn accusers; who rejoice in the ills of others, and blaze abroad what is disgraceful in their conduct.

14. Knowing all these things then, make the first advance to a brother; lay hold of him before he has entirely shrunk away from thee; and should it be necessary, to run through all the city on the same day; should it be necessary to go beyond the walls, or to take a long journey; still leaving all other things that may be in hand, attend only to this one work of reconciling thy brother. For if the work be laborious, reflect that it is for God's sake thou undergoes all this, and thou shalt receive sufficient consolation. Stir up thy soul also when it is

shrinking, and backward, and bashful, and ashamed, by perpetually harping on this theme and saying, Why art thou delaying? Why art thou shrinking and holding back? Our concern is not for money, nor for any other of these fleeting things, but for our salvation. God bids us do all these things, and all things should be secondary to His commands. This matter is a sort of spiritual merchandise. Let us not neglect it, let us not be slothful. Let our enemy too understand that we have taken much pains, in order to do what is well-pleasing unto God. And though he may again insult, or strike us, or do any other such thing of a still more grievous kind, let us sustain all things courageously, since we are not so much benefitting him thereby, as ourselves. Of all good works, this shall most especially befriend us on That Day. We have sinned and offended in many and great matters, and have provoked our Lord. Through His lovingkindness He hath given us this way of reconciliation. Let us, then, not betray this good treasure. For had He not power to charge us simply to make reconciliation, and not have any reward assigned to it? For whom hath He to gainsay or rectify His appointment? Nevertheless, through His great lovingkindness, He hath promised us a large and unspeakable reward, and one which we must be especially desirous to obtain, the pardon of our sins; thus also making this our obedience more easy of performance.

15. What allowance then can be made for us, if even when we might receive so great a reward we still do not obey the Lawgiver, but persist in our contempt; for that this is a contempt is plain from hence. If the Emperor had laid down a law, that all those who were enemies should be reconciled to one another, or have their heads cut off, should we not everyone make haste to a

reconciliation with his neighbor? Yes! Truly, I think so! What excuse then have we, in not ascribing the same honor to the Lord, that we should do to those who are our fellow-servants? For this reason we are commanded to say, "Forgive us our debts, as we forgive our debtors." What can be more mild, what more merciful, than this precept! He hath made thee a judge of the pardon of thine own offences! If thou forgives few things, He forgives thee few! If thou forgives many things, He forgives thee many! If thou pardons from the heart, and sincerely, God in like manner also pardons thee! If besides pardoning him thou accounts him a friend, God will also thus deal with thee; so that the more he has sinned, so much the more is it necessary that we should hasten to a reconciliation; since it becomes a cause of greater offences being forgiven us. Art thou willing to learn that there is no pardon for us, if we are mindful of injuries, and that there is no one who can deliver us? I will make what I assert plain by an example. Suppose that a neighbor has done you a certain injury, that he has seized your goods; has confiscated or embezzled them; and not to confine myself to such a case, let me add to it more things and worse beside, and whatever you will; he has longed to destroy you; he has exposed you to a thousand perils; he has manifested every sort of malice towards you; and left nothing undone that human wickedness can do? For not to go over everything separately, suppose that he has injured you to such an extent as no one ever injured any before;—why, even in this case, if you are resentful, you will not be worthy of pardon. And I will explain how it is so.

16. If one of your servants owed you an hundred pieces of gold; and someone again was indebted to him in

a few pieces of silver; and if the servants' debtor were to come, and entreat and supplicate you that he might obtain indulgence, and you were to call in your own servant, and charge him, saying, "Forgive this man the debt, and from the sum thou owes me I will deduct this debt;" should that servant afterwards be wicked and shameless enough to seize on his debtor, could anyone then rescue him out of your hands? Would you not most assuredly inflict a thousand stripes upon him, as having been insulted to the last extremity? And very justly too. This also God will do: for He will say to thee on That Day, "O wicked and villainous servant, yea, was it of thine own thou forgives him? Out of what thou wert indebted to Me, thou wert ordered to account to him. For "Remit," He says, "and I will remit unto thee! Although, to speak truly, if I had not added this condition, it would have been even then thy duty to have remitted at the instance of thy Lord. But in this case, I did not command thee as a master, but I asked it as a favor from a friend; and I asked it out of My own property; and I promised to give greater things in return; and yet with all this, thou wert not made a better man." Moreover men, when they act in this manner, put down as much to their own servants' accounts, as the measure of the debt is. Thus, for example, suppose the servant owes his master a hundred pieces of gold; and the debtor of the servant owes ten pieces, should the latter remit his debt, the master does not remit him his hundred pieces, but these ten only; and all the rest he still demands. But it is not so with God; if you remit a few things to your fellow-servant, He remits all your debt.

17. Whence does this appear? From the very Prayer itself. "For if," says He, "ye forgive men their debts, your heavenly Father will forgive your debts." And

as much as the difference is between "a hundred pence" and "ten thousand talents," so great is it between the debts on the one side, and those on the other!

What punishment then must he not deserve, who when he would receive ten thousand talents, in the room of a hundred pence, yet will not even so remit this small sum, but offers up the Prayer against himself. For when thou says, "Forgive us, as we forgive," and afterwards dost not forgive, thou art supplicating of God nothing else than that He would entirely deprive thee of all excuse or indulgence. "But I do not presume to say," replies someone, "Forgive me as I forgive" but only, "Forgive me." But what matters this? For if thou say it not thyself, yet God so doeth; as thou forgives, He forgives. And this He hath made quite evident from what follows; for there it is said, "If ye forgive not men, neither doth your heavenly Father forgive you." Think not, therefore, that it is a pious caution, not to repeat the whole sentence; nor offer up the Prayer by halves, but as He bade thee so pray thou, in order that the very obligation of that expression, putting thee daily in fear, may compel thee to the exercise of forgiveness towards thy neighbors.

18. Do not tell me, "I have besought him many times, I have entreated, I have supplicated, but I have not effected a reconciliation." Never desist till you have reconciled him. For He said not, "Leave thy gift, and go thy way." Entreat thy brother. But, "Go thy way. Be reconciled." So that, although you may have made many entreaties, yet you must not desist until you have persuaded. God entreats us every day, and we do not hear; and yet He does not cease entreating. And dost thou then disdain to entreat thy fellow-servant. How is it then possible for thee ever to be saved? Suppose that thou hast

often pleaded and been repulsed; for this, however, thou wilt obtain a larger reward. For in proportion as he is contentious, and thou perseveres in entreating, so much the more is thy recompense increased. In proportion as the good work is accomplished with greater difficulty, and the reconciliation is one of much labor, so much the greater will be the judgment on him, and so much the brighter will be the crowns of victory for thy forbearance. Let us not merely applaud all this, but exemplify it too in our deeds; and never recede from the work, until we are restored to our former state of friendship. For it is not enough merely to avoid grieving an enemy, or doing him an injury, or being in our minds unkindly disposed towards him; but it is necessary that we should prepare him to be kindly affected towards ourselves. For I hear many saying, "I have no hostility; I am not annoyed; neither have I anything to do with him." But this is not what God commands, that you should have nothing to do with him; but that you should have much to do with him. For this reason he is thy "brother." For this reason He said not, "Forgive thy brother what thou hast against him. But what then? "Go thy way. First be reconciled to him;" and should he have "anything against thee," yet desist not, before thou hast reunited the member in friendly concord." But thou, who in order that thou may obtain a useful servant, tells out the gold, and discourses with many merchants, and often undertakes long journeys, tell me, art thou not up and doing to the utmost, in order that thou may convert an enemy into a friend? And how then wilt thou be able to call upon God, whilst thou art thus neglecting His laws? Assuredly, the possession of a servant will be of no great profit to us; but the making an enemy a friend, will render God propitious and favorable toward us; and will easily set us free from our sins; and gain us praise with men, as well as great security in our life; for nothing can be more unsafe than he who has even only a single enemy. For our earthly reputation is injured, whilst such a man is saying a thousand evil things of us to everybody. Our minds are also in a state of fermentation, and our conscience disturbed; and we are exposed to a continual tempest of anxious thoughts.

19. Now since we are conscious of the truth of all this, let us set ourselves free from chastisement and vengeance; and let us shew our reverence for the present feast, by doing all that has been said; and those same favors which we think to obtain from the Emperor on account of the feast, let us ourselves enable others to enjoy. For I hear, indeed, many saying, that the Emperor, out of his reverence for the Holy Passover, will be reconciled to the city and will pardon all its offences. How absurd then is it, that when we have to depend for our safety upon others, we bring forward the feast, and its claims; but that when we are commanded to be reconciled one with another, we treat this same feast with disdain, and think nothing of it. No one, truly, so pollutes this holy feast, as he does, who, whilst he is keeping it, cherishes malignity. Or rather, I might say, that such a person cannot possibly keep it, though he should remain without food ten days successively. For where there is enmity and strife, there can be neither fast nor festival. You would not dare to touch the holy Sacrifice with unwashed hands, however pressing the necessity might be. Approach not then with an unwashed soul! For this is far worse than the other and brings a heavier punishment. For nothing so fills the mind with impurity, as anger remaining constantly within it. The spirit of meekness settles not

where wrath or passion exists; and when a man is destitute of the Holy Spirit, what hope of salvation shall he have, and how shall he walk aright? Do not then, O beloved, whilst thou art desirous to be revenged of thine enemy, cast thyself down headlong; nor cause thyself to be left alone without the guardianship of God! For, in truth, if the duty were a difficult one, yet the greatness of the punishment, which results from this action of disobedience, were sufficient to arouse the most slothful and supine, and to persuade them to undergo every degree of labor. But now our argument has shown that the duty is most easy, if we are willing.

20. Let us not then be negligent of what is our life, but let us be in earnest; and do everything, in order that we may be without an enemy, and so present ourselves at the sacred Table. For nothing,—nothing, I repeat, of what God commands will be difficult, if we give heed: and this is evident from the case of those who are already reformed. How many used to be cheated by the habit of using oaths, and to fancy this practice extremely difficult of reformation. Nevertheless, through the grace of God, when ye put forth but a little effort, ye for the most part washed yourselves clean of this vice. For this reason I beseech you to lay aside also what remains, and to become teachers of others. And to those who have not yet achieved it, but allege to us the length of time during which they were before swearers, and say that it is impossible for them to pluck up in a short time that which has been rooted for many years; I would make this answer, that where any precept among those commanded by God requires to be put in due practice, there is no need of length of time, nor of a multitude of days, nor an interval of years; but of fear only, and reverence of soul;

and then we shall be sure to accomplish it, and that in a short time. But lest you should suppose that I speak these things at random, take a man whom you think much addicted to swearing; one that swears more times than he speaks; hand this man over to me for only ten days, and if I do not rid him of all his habit in these few days, pass the severest sentence on me.

21. And that these words are not a vain boast, shall be made manifest to you from things that have already happened. What could be more stupid than the Ninevites? What more devoid of understanding? Yet, nevertheless, these barbarian, foolish people, who had never yet heard anyone teaching them wisdom, who had never received such precepts from others, when they heard the prophet saying, "Yet three days, and Nineveh shall be overthrown," laid aside, within three days, the whole of their evil customs. The fornicator became chaste; the bold man meek; the grasping and extortionate moderate and kind; the slothful industrious. They did not, indeed, reform one, or two, or three, or four vices by way of remedy, but the whole of their iniquity. But whence does this appear, says someone? From the words of the prophet; for the same who had been their accuser, and who had said, that "the cry of their wickedness hath ascended up even to heaven:" himself again bears testimony of an opposite kind, by saying, "God saw that everyone departed from their own evil ways." He does not say, from fornication, or adultery, or theft, but from their "own evil ways." And how did they depart? As God knew, not as man judged of the matter. After this are we not ashamed, must we not blush, if it turns out that in three days only the barbarians laid aside all their wickedness, but that we, who have been urged and taught

during so many days, have not got the better of one bad habit? These men had, moreover, gone to the extreme of wickedness before; for when you hear it said, "The cry of their wickedness is come up before me;" you can understand nothing else than the excess of their wickedness. Nevertheless, within three days they were capable of being transformed to a state of complete virtue. For where the fear of God is, there is no need of days, or of an interval of time; as likewise, on the contrary, days are of no service where there is a want of this fear. For just as in the case of rusted implements, he that rubs them only with water, though he spend a long time on them, will not rid them of all that foulness; but he that puts them in a furnace, will make them presently brighter than even those newly fabricated: so too a soul, stained with the rust of sin, if it cleanse itself slightly, and in a negligent way, and be every day repenting, will gain no further advantage. But if it cast itself into the furnace, as it were, of the fear of God, it will in a very short time purge all away.

22. Let us not then be procrastinating till to-morrow. For we "know not what the next day may bring forth;" nor let us say, "we shall conquer this habit by little and little;" since this little and little will never come to an end. Wherefore, dismissing that excuse, we should say, "If we do not reform the practice of swearing to-day, we will not leave off till we do, though ten thousand things were to press us; though it were necessary to die, or to be punished, or to lose all we have; we will not give the devil the advantage of slackness, nor the pretext of delay." Should God perceive thy soul inflamed, and thy diligence quickened, then He also Himself will lend His assistance to thy reformation! Yea, I pray and beseech you, let us be

in earnest, lest we also hear it said of us, "The men of Nineveh shall rise up, and shall condemn this generation;" for these, when they had once heard, reformed themselves; but we are not converted after frequent hearing. These were proficient in every part of virtue, but we in no part. They when they heard that their city would be overthrown were affrighted; but we, though we have heard of Hell, are not affrighted: these, men who did not partake of the instructions of the prophets; we, enjoying the advantage of perpetual teaching, and of much grace.

23. These things I now speak to you, not as if reproving you for your own sins, but for the sake of others; for I know full well that by you (as I have already observed), this law concerning swearing has been accomplished. But this does not suffice for our safety, unless by teaching we amend others, since he who produced the one talent, restoring as he did the whole portion committed to him, was punished, because he had not enriched that with which he was entrusted. Wherefore, let us not regard this point, that we ourselves have been set free from this sin; but until we have delivered others from it, let us not desist; and let everyone offer to God ten friends whom he has corrected; whether thou hast servants, or apprentices: or if you have neither servants, nor apprentices, you have friends; these do thou reform. Further, do not make me this reply; "We have banished oaths for the most part, and we are rarely caught in that snare;" but let even this rarity of offending be got rid of. If you had lost one piece of gold, would you not go about to all persons, searching and making enquiry, in order to find it? This do also with regard to oaths. If you perceive that you have been cheated out of one oath, weep, lament, as though your whole substance were lost. Again I say

what I did before. Shut up thyself at home; make it a subject of practice and exercise along with thy wife, thy children, and domestics. Say to thyself in the first instance, "I must not put a finger to private or public matters until I have rectified this soul of mine." If you will thus school your own sons, they too will instruct their children in turn, and thus this discipline, reaching even to the consummation and appearing of Christ, will bring all that great reward to those who go to the root of the matter. If your son has learnt to say, "Believe me;" he will not be able to go up to the theatre, or to enter a tavern, or to spend his time at dice; for that word, lying upon his mouth instead of a bridle, will make him however unwilling feel shame and blush. But if at any time he should appear in these places, it will quickly compel him to retreat. Suppose some persons laugh. Do thou on the other hand weep for their transgression! Many also once laughed at Noah whilst he was preparing the ark; but when the flood came, he laughed at them; or rather, the just man never laughed at them at all, but wept and bewailed! When therefore thou sees persons laughing, reflect that those teeth, that grin now, will one day have to sustain that most dreadful wailing and gnashing, and that they will remember this same laugh on That Day whilst they are grinding and gnashing! Then thou too shalt remember this laugh! How did the rich man laugh at Lazarus! But afterwards, when he beheld him in Abraham's bosom, he had nothing left to do but to bewail himself!

24. Being mindful then of all these things, be urgent with all, for the speedy fulfilment of this precept. And tell me not, that you will do this by little and little; nor put it off till the morrow, for this to-morrow never

finds an end. Forty days have already passed away. Should the Holy Easter pass away, I will thenceforward pardon no one, nor employ further admonition, but a commanding authority, and severity not to be despised. For this apology drawn from custom is of no force. Why may not the thief as well plead custom, and get free from punishment? Why may not the murderer and adulterer? Therefore I protest, and give warning to all, that if, when I have met you in private, and put the matter to the proof (and I will certainly put it to the proof), I detect any who have not corrected this vice, I will inflict punishment upon them, by ordering them to be excluded from the Holy Mysteries; not that they may remain always shut out, but that having reformed themselves, they may thus enter in, and with a pure conscience enjoy the Holy Table; for this is to be a partaker of the Communion! God grant that through the prayers of those who preside over us, as well as of all the saints, having corrected these and all other deficiencies, we may obtain the kingdom of heaven through the grace and lovingkindness of our Lord Jesus Christ, with Whom to the Father, together with the Holy Spirit, be glory, honor, and adoration, now and ever, world without end. Amen.

Homily XXI.

On the return of Flavian the Bishop, and the reconciliation of the Emperor with the city, and with those who had offended in overthrowing the Statues.

1. Today, I shall begin with that very same saying with which I have ever been used to open my address to you during the season of danger, and shall say together with you, "Blessed be God," Who hath granted us this day to celebrate this holy Feast with much joy and gladness; and hath restored the head to the body, the shepherd to the sheep, the master to the disciples, the general to the soldiers, the High Priest to the Priests! Blessed be God, "Who doeth exceeding abundantly above what we ask or think!" For to us it would have seemed sufficient, had we been but delivered from the hitherto impending evil; and for this we made all our supplication. But the God who loves man, and ever in His giving surpasses our prayers by an excess of bounty, hath brought back our Father too, sooner than we could at all have expected. Who would, indeed, have thought that in so few days, he would have gone, and have had audience with the Emperor, and set us free from the calamity, and again come back to us so quickly, as to be able to anticipate the Holy Passover, and to celebrate it with ourselves? Behold, however, this event, which was so contrary to expectation, hath been realized! We have received back our Father; and we enjoy so much the greater pleasure, inasmuch as we have received him back now beyond our hopes. For all these things, let us give thanks to the merciful God, and be amazed at the power, the lovingkindness, the wisdom, and the tender care which has been manifested on behalf of

the city. For the devil had attempted its entire subversion through the daring crimes committed; but God, by means of this same calamity, hath adorned the city, the Priest, and the Emperor; and hath made them all more illustrious.

2. The city hath won renown, because when such a danger had overtaken her, passing by at once all those who were in power, those who were surrounded with much wealth, those who possessed great influence with the Emperor, it fled for refuge to the Church, and to the Priest of God, and with much faith, rested itself entirely upon the hope which is from above! Many indeed, after the departure of the common Father, were ready to terrify those who lay in prison, by saying, "The Emperor does not lay aside his wrath, but is still more provoked, and is thinking of the utter ruin of the city." But whilst they were whispering all this, and much more, they who were then in bonds were not the least intimidated, but upon our saying, "These things are false, and they are a device of the devil, who desires to fill you with consternation;" they replied to us, "We need no consolation to be addressed to us; for we know where we have taken refuge from the first; and upon what hope we have rested ourselves. We have fixed our safety upon the sacred anchor! We have not entrusted this to man, but to the Almighty God; therefore we are most assuredly confident, that the result will be favorable; for it is impossible, truly impossible, that this hope can ever be confounded!" To how many crowns, how many encomiums, is this equivalent for our city? How much of God's favor will it draw down upon us too in our other affairs! For it is not, indeed it is not a thing belonging to a soul of mean order to be watchful against the attack of temptations, and to look to God; and scorning all that is human, to yearn after that Divine aid.

3. The city then hath thus won renown; and the Priest again not less than the city, for he exposed his life for all; and while there were many things to hinder him, as the winter, his age, the feast, and not less than these, his sister, then at her last breath, he raised himself above all these obstacles, and did not say to himself, "What a thing is this? Our only remaining sister, she who hath drawn the yoke of Christ along with me, and who hath been my domestic companion so long, is now at her last breath; and shall we desert her, and go hence, and not behold her expiring, and uttering her paring words? But she indeed was praying daily, that we might close her eyes, and shut and compose her mouth, and attend to all other things pertaining to the burial; but now in this case, as one deserted, and deprived of a protector, she will obtain none of these offices from her brother; of him whom she especially desired to obtain them; but when she gives up the ghost, she will not see him whom she loved more to have with her than all others? And will not this be heavier to her than dying many times over? Yes, although I were far away, would it not be right to come with speed, and do, and suffer any thing, for the purpose of shewing her this kindness? And now when I am near, shall I leave her, and taking my departure abandon her? And how then will she sustain the remainder of her days?"

4. Yet, so far was he from saying any of these things, that he did not even think of them; but esteeming the fear of God above all the ties of kindred, he recognized the fact, that as tempests display the pilot, and dangers the general, so also a time of trial makes the Priest to become manifest. "All men," says he, "are eagerly looking on us; the Jews as well as the Greeks; let us not confound the expectations which these have of us;

let us not overlook so great a shipwreck; but having committed to God all things that pertain to ourselves, let us venture our life itself too!" Consider, moreover, the magnanimity of the Priest, and the lovingkindness of God! All those things which he disregarded, all those he enjoyed; in order that he might both receive the reward of his readiness, and that he might obtain a greater pleasure by enjoying them contrary to expectation! He preferred to celebrate the festival in a foreign place, and far from his own people, for the sake of the city's safety. But God restored him to us before the Paschal feast, so as to take a common part with us in the conduct of the festival; in order that he might have the reward of his choice, and enjoy the greater gladness! He feared not the season of the year; and there was summer during the whole period he was travelling. He took not his age into account; and he dispatched this long journey with just as much ease as if he had been young and sprightly! He thought not of his sister's decease nor was enervated by it, and when he returned he found her still alive, and all things which were disregarded by him, were all obtained!

5. Thus, the priest hath indeed won renown both with God and man! This transaction hath also adorned the Emperor with a splendor beyond the diadem! First, in that it was then made apparent that he would grant that to the priests which he would not to any other; secondly, that he granted the favor without delay, and quelled his resentment. But that you may more clearly understand the magnanimity of the Emperor, and the wisdom of the priest, and more than both these, the lovingkindness of God; allow me to relate to you a few particulars of the conference which took place. But what I am now about to relate I learnt from one of those who were within the

palace; for the Father has told us neither much nor little on the affair; but ever imitating the magnanimity of Paul, he hides his own good deeds; and to those who on all sides were asking him questions as to what he said to the Emperor; and how he prevailed upon him; and how he turned away his wrath entirely, he replied, "We contributed nothing to the matter, but the Emperor himself (God having softened his heart), even before we had spoken, dismissed his anger, and quelled his resentment; and discoursing of the events that had taken place as if some other person had been insulted, he thus went over all the events that had happened without anger." But those things which he concealed from humility, God hath brought to light.

6. And what were these? I will proceed to relate them to you by going a little farther back in the story. When he went forth from the city, leaving all in such great despondency, he endured what was far more grievous than we ourselves suffered, who were in the midst of these calamities. For, in the first place, meeting in the midst of his journey with those who had been sent by the Emperor to make inquisition upon the events which had happened; and learning from them, on what terms they were sent; and reflecting upon the dreadful events that were in store for the city, the tumults, the confusion, the flight, the terror, the agony, the perils, he wept a flood of tears, and his bowels were rent with compassion; for with fathers, it is usual to grieve much more, when they are not able to be present with their suffering children; which was just what this most tender-hearted man now endured; not only lamenting the calamities which were in reserve for us, but that he was far away from us, whist we were enduring them. But this

was, however, for our safety. For as soon as he had learned these things from them; more warmly did the fountain of his tears then gush forth, and he betook himself to God with more fervent supplication; and spent his nights without sleep, beseeching Him that He would succor the city, while enduring these things, and make the mind of the Emperor more placable. And as soon as he came to that great city, and had entered the royal palace, he stood before the Emperor at a distance,—speechless,—weeping,—with downcast eyes,—covering his face as if he himself had been the doer of all the mischief; and this he did, wishing first to incline him to mercy by his posture, and aspect, and tears; and then to begin an apology on our behalf; since there is but one hope of pardon for those who have offended, which is to be silent, and to utter nothing in defense of what has been done. For he was desirous that one feeling should be got rid of, and that another should take its place; that anger should be expelled, and sadness introduced, in order that he might thus prepare the way for the words of his apology; which indeed actually took place. And just as Moses going up to the mount, when the people had offended, stood speechless himself, until God called him, saying, "Let me alone, and I will blot out this people;" so also did he now act: The Emperor therefore, when he saw him shedding tears, and bending toward the ground, himself drew near; and what he really felt on seeing the tears of the priest, he made evident by the words he addressed to him; for they were not those of a person provoked or inflamed, but of one in sorrow; not of one enraged, but rather dejected, and under constraint of extreme pain.

  7. And that this is true, ye will understand when ye hear what were his words. For he did not say, "What does

this mean? Hast thou come heading an embassy on behalf of impious and abominable men, such as ought not even to live; on behalf of rebels, of revolutionists, who deserve the utmost punishment?" But dismissing all words of that sort, he composed a defense of himself full of respectfulness and dignity; and he enumerated the benefits, which during the whole time of his reign he had conferred upon the city; and at each of these he said, "Was it thus I should have been treated in return for these things? What injuries had I done, that they should take such revenge? What complaint had they, great or small, that they must not insult me only, but the deceased also? Was it not sufficient to wreak their resentment against the living? Yet they thought they were doing nothing grand, unless they insulted those now in their graves. Granting that I had injured them, as they suppose; surely it would have been becoming to spare the dead, who had done them no wrong; for they could not have the same complaint against them. Did I not ever esteem this city above everything, and account it as dearer than my native place? And was it not a matter of my continual prayers to visit this city; and did I not make this my oath to all men?"

8. Upon this, the priest sobbing bitterly, and shedding warmer tears, no longer kept silence: for he saw that the defense of the Emperor was raising our crime to a still higher amount; but heaving from the bottom of his heart a deep and bitter sigh, he said, "We must confess, O Emperor, this love which you have shewn towards our country! We cannot deny it! On this account, especially, we mourn, that a city thus beloved has been bewitched by demons; and that we should have appeared ungrateful towards her benefactor, and have provoked her ardent

lover. And although you were to overthrow; although you were to burn; although you were to put to death; or whatever else you might do, you would never yet have taken on us the revenge we deserve. We ourselves have, by anticipation, inflicted on ourselves what is worse than a thousand deaths! For what can be more bitter, than when we are found to have unjustly provoked our benefactor, and one who loved us so much, and the whole world knows it, and condemns us for the most monstrous ingratitude! If Barbarians had made an incursion on our city, and razed its walls, and burnt its houses, and had taken and carried us away captive, the evil had been less. And why so? But because, whilst you live, and continue such a generous kindness towards us, there might be a hope that we might again be brought back to our former condition, and regain a more illustrious liberty. But now, having been deprived of your favor, and having quenched your love, which was a greater security to us than any wall, whom have we left to fly to? Where else shall we have to look, when we have provoked so benign a lord, so indulgent a father? So that while they seem to have committed offences of the most intolerable kind, they have on the other hand suffered the most terrible evils; not daring to look any man in the face; nor being able to look upon the sun with free eyes; shame everywhere weighing down their eyelids, and compelling them to hide their heads! Deprived of their confidence, they are now in a more miserable condition than any captives, and undergo the utmost dishonor; and whilst thinking of the magnitude of their evils, and the height of insolence to which they have rushed, they can scarce draw breath; inasmuch as they have drawn on their own heads severer reproaches from all the inhabitants of the world, than even from him who is seen to have been insulted.

9. But yet, O Emperor, if you are willing, there is a remedy for the wound, and a medicine for these evils, mighty as they are! Often, indeed, has it occurred amongst private individuals, that great and insufferable offences have become a foundation for great affection. Thus also did it happen in the case of our human race. For when God made man, and placed him in Paradise, and held him in much honor; the devil could not bear this his great prosperity, and envied him, and cast him out from that dignity which had been granted. But God was so far from forsaking him, that He even opened Heaven to us instead of Paradise; and in so doing, both shewed His own lovingkindness, and punished the devil the more severely. So do thou too now! The demons have lately used all their efforts, that they may effectually rend from your favor that city which was dearest of all to you. Knowing this then, demand what penalty you will, but let us not become outcasts from your former love! Nay, though it is a strange thing, I must say, display towards us now still greater kindness than ever; and again write this city's name among the foremost in your love;—if you are indeed desirous of being revenged upon the demons who were the instigators of these crimes! For if you pull down, and overturn, and raze the city, you will be doing those very things which they have long been desiring. But if you dismiss your anger, and again avow that you love it even as you did before, you have given them a deadly blow. You have taken the most perfect revenge upon them by shewing, not only that nothing whatever has come for them of their evil designs; but that all hath proved the very opposite of what they wished. And you would be just

in acting thus, and in shewing mercy to a city, which the demons envied on account of your affection; for if you had not so exceedingly loved her, they would not have envied her to such a degree! So that even if what I have asserted is extraordinary, it is nevertheless, true, that what the city hath suffered, hath been owing to thee, and thy love! What burning, what devastation, so bitter as those words, which you uttered in your own defense?

10. You say now, that you have been insulted, and sustained wrongs such as no Emperor ever yet did. But if you will, O most gracious, most wise, and most religious Sovereign, this contempt will procure you a crown, more honorable and splendid than the diadem you wear! For this diadem is a display of your princely virtue, but it is also a token of the munificence of him who gave it; but the crown woven from this your humanity will be entirely your own good work, and that of your own love of wisdom; and all men will admire you less for the sake of these precious stones, than they will applaud you for your superiority over this wrath. Were your Statues thrown down? You have it in your power again to set up others yet more splendid. For if you remit the offences of those who have done you injury, and take no revenge upon them, they will erect a statue to you, not one in the forum of brass, nor of gold, nor inlaid with gems; but one arrayed in that robe which is more precious than any material, that of humanity and tender mercy! Every man will thus set you up in his own soul; and you will have as many statues, as there are men who now inhabit, or shall hereafter inhabit, the whole world! For not only we, but all those who come after us, and their successors, will hear of these things, and will admire and love you, just as if they themselves had experienced this kindness!

11. And to shew that I do not speak this in a way of flattery, but that it will certainly be so, I will relate to you an ancient piece of history, that you may understand that no armies, nor warlike weapons, nor money, nor multitude of subjects, nor any other such things are wont to make sovereigns so illustrious, as wisdom of soul and gentleness. It is related of the blessed Constantine, that on one occasion, when a statue of himself had been pelted with stones, and many were instigating him to proceed against the perpetrators of the outrage; saying, that they had disfigured his whole face by battering it with stones, he stroked his face with his hand, and smiling gently, said, "I am quite unable to perceive any wound inflicted upon my face. The head appears sound, and the face also quite sound." Thus these persons, overwhelmed with shame, desisted from their unrighteous counsel.

This saying, even to the present day, all repeat; and length of time hath neither weakened nor extinguished the memory of such exalted wisdom. How much more illustrious is such an action, than any number of warlike trophies! Many and great titles did he build, and many barbarous tribes did he conquer; not one of which we now remember; but this saying is repeated over and over again, to the present day; and those who follow us, as well as those who come after them, will all hear of it. Nor indeed is this the only admirable thing; that they will hear of it; but that when men speak of it, they do so with approbation and applause; and those who hear of it, receive it with the like; and there is no one who, when he has heard it, is able to remain silent, but each at once cries out, and applauds the man who uttered it, and prays that innumerable blessings may be his lot even now deceased. But if amongst men, this saying has gained him so much honor, how many crowns will he obtain with the merciful God!

12. And why need I speak of Constantine, and other men's examples, when it were fitting that I should exhort you by considerations nearer home, and drawn from your own praiseworthy actions. You remember how but lately, when this feast was near at hand, you sent an epistle to every part of the world giving orders that the inmates of the prisons should be set free, and their crimes be pardoned. And as if this were not sufficient to give proof of your generosity, you said in your letters, "O that it were possible for me to recall and to restore those who are dead, and to bring them back to their former state of life!" Remember now these words. Behold the season of recalling and restoring the deceased, and bringing them back to former life! For these are indeed already dead, even before the sentence hath been pronounced; and the city hath now taken up its tabernacle at the very gates of Hades! Therefore raise it up again, which you can do without money, without expense, without loss of time or labor! It is sufficient merely for you to open your lips, and you will restore to life the city which at present lies in darkness. Grant now, that henceforth it may bear an appellation derived from your philanthropy; for it will not be so much indebted to the kindness of him who first founded it, as it will be to your sentence. And this is exceedingly reasonable; for he but gave it its beginning, and departed; but you, when it had grown up and become great; and when it was fallen, after all that great prosperity; will have been its restorer. There would have been nothing so wonderful in your having delivered it from danger, when enemies had captured, and barbarians overrun it, as in your now sparing it. That, many of the

Emperors have frequently done; but should you alone accomplish this, you will be first in doing it, and that beyond all expectation. And the former of these good deeds, the protection of your subjects, is not at all wonderful or extraordinary; but is one of those events which are of continual occurrence; but the latter, the dismissal of wrath after the endurance of such provocations, is something which surpasses human nature.

13. Reflect, that the matter now for your consideration is not respecting this city only, but is one that concerns your own glory; or rather, one that affects the cause of Christianity in general. Even now the Gentiles, and Jews, and the whole empire as well as the barbarians, (for these last have also heard of these events,) are eagerly looking to you, and waiting to see what sentence you will pronounce with regard to these transactions. And should you decree a humane and merciful one; all will applaud the decision, and glorify God, and say one to another, "Heavens! How great is the power of Christianity, that it restrains and bridles a man who has no equal upon earth; a sovereign, powerful enough to destroy and devastate all things; and teaches him to practice such philosophy as one in a private station had not been likely to display! Great indeed must be the God of the Christians, who makes angels out of men, and renders them superior to all the constraining force of our nature!"

14. Nor ought you, assuredly, to entertain that idle fear; nor to bear with those who say that other cites will become worse, and grow more contemptuous of authority, if this city goes unpunished. For if you were unable to take vengeance; and they, after doing these things, had

forcibly defied you; and the power on each side was equally matched; then reasonably enough might such suspicions be entertained. But if, terrified and half dead with fear, they run to cast themselves at your feet, through me; and expect daily nothing else but the pit of slaughter, and are engaged in common supplications; looking up to heaven and calling upon God to come to their aid, and to favor this our embassy; and have each given charge about his private affairs, as if they were at their last gasp; how can such a fear be otherwise than superfluous? If they had been ordered to be put to death, they would not have suffered as much as they do now, living as they have done so many days in fear and trembling; and when the evening approaches, not expecting to behold the morning; nor when the day arrives, hoping to reach the evening! Many too have fallen in with wild beasts, while pursuing their way through desert places, and removing to untrodden spots; and not men only, but also little children and women; free born, and of good condition; hiding themselves many days and nights in caves, and ravines, and holes of the desert! A new mode of captivity hath indeed befallen the city. Whilst the buildings and walls are standing, they suffer heavier calamities than when cities have been set on fire! Whilst no barbarian foe is present, whilst no enemy appears, they are more wretchedly situated than if actually taken; and the rustling only of a leaf scares them all every day! And these are matters which are universally known; so that if all men had seen the city razed to the ground, they would not have been taught such a lesson of sobriety, as by hearing of the calamities which have now befallen it. Suppose not, therefore, that other cities will be made worse in future! Not even if you had overturned other cities, would you have so effectually corrected them, as now, by this suspense concerning their fate, having chastised them more severely than by any punishment!

15. Do not, then, carry this calamity any farther; but allow them henceforth to take breath again. For to punish the guilty, and to exact the penalty for these deeds, were easy and open to anyone; but to spare those who have insulted you, and to pardon those who have committed offences undeserving of pardon, is an act of which only some one or two are capable; and especially so, where the person treated with indignity is the Emperor. It is an easy matter to place the city under the subjection of fear; but to dispose all to be loving subjects; and to persuade them to hold themselves well affected towards your government; and to offer not only their common, but individual prayers for your empire; is a work of difficulty. A monarch might expend his treasures, or put innumerable troops in motion, or do what else he pleased, but still he would not be able to draw the affections of so many men towards himself as may now very easily be done. For they who have been kindly dealt with, and those who hear of it too, will be well affected towards you, even as the recipients of the benefit. How much money, how many labors would you not have expended to win over to yourself the whole world in a short space of time; and to be able to persuade all those men who are now in existence, as well as all future generations, to invoke upon your head the same blessings which they pray for on behalf of their own children! And if you will receive such a reward from men, how much greater will you have from God! And this, not merely from the events which are now taking place, but from those good deeds which shall be performed by others in

time to come. For if ever it should be that an event similar to what has now occurred should take place, (which God forbid!) and any of those who have been treated with indignity, should then be consulting about prosecuting measures against the rioters; your gentleness and moral wisdom will serve them instead of all other teaching and admonition; and they will blush and be ashamed, having such an example of wisdom, to appear inferior. So that in this way you will be an instructor to all posterity; and you will obtain the palm amongst them, even although they should attain to the highest point of moral wisdom! For it is not the same thing for a person to set the first example of such meekness himself and by looking at others, to imitate the good actions they have performed. On this account, whatever philanthropy, or meekness, those who come after you may display, you will enjoy the reward along with them; for he who provides the root, must be considered the source of the fruits. For this reason, no one can possibly now share with you the reward that will follow your generosity, since the good deed hath been entirely your own. But you will share the reward of all those who shall come after, if any such persons should make their appearance; and it will be in your power to have an equal share in the merit of the good work along with them, and to carry off a portion as great as teachers have with scholars. And supposing that no such person should come into being, the tribute of commendation and applause will be accumulating to you throughout every age.

16. For consider, what it is for all posterity to hear it reported, that when so great a city had become obnoxious to punishment and vengeance, that when all were terrified, when its generals, its magistrates and

judges, were all in horror and alarm, and did not dare to utter a word on behalf of the wretched people; a single old man, invested with the priesthood of God, came and moved the heart of the Monarch by his mere aspect and intercourse; and that the favor which he bestowed upon no other of his subjects, he granted to this one old man, being actuated by a reverence for God's laws! For in this very thing, O Emperor, that I have been sent hither on this embassy, the city hath done you no small honor; for they have thus pronounced the best and the most honorable judgment on you, which is, that you respect the priests of God, however insignificant they may be, more than any office placed under your authority!

17. But at the present time I have come not from these only, but rather from One who is the common Lord of angels and men, to address these words to your most merciful and most gentle soul, "if ye forgive men their debts, your heavenly Father will forgive you your trespasses." Remember then that Day when we shall all give an account of our actions! Consider that if you have sinned in any respect, you will be able to wipe away all offences by this sentence and by this determination, and that without difficulty and without toil. Some when they go on an embassy, bring gold, and silver, and other gifts of that kind. But I am come into your royal presence with the sacred laws; and instead of all other gifts, I present these; and I exhort you to imitate your Lord, who whilst He is daily insulted by us, unceasingly ministers His blessings to all! And do not confound our hopes, nor defeat our promises. For I wish you withal to understand, that if it be your resolution to be reconciled, and to restore your former kindness to the city, and to remit this just displeasure, I shall go back with great confidence. But if

you determine to cast off the city, I shall not only never return to it, nor see its soil again, but I shall in future utterly disown it, and enroll myself a member of some other city; for God forbid that I should ever belong to that country, which you, the most mild and merciful of all men, refuse to admit to peace and reconciliation!

18. Having said this, and much more to the same effect, he so overcame the Emperor, that the same thing occurred which once happened to Joseph. For just as he, when he beheld his brethren, longed to shed tears, but restrained his feeling, in order that he might not spoil the part which he was playing; even so did the Emperor mentally weep, but did not let it be seen, for the sake of those who were present. He was not, however, able to conceal the feeling at the close of the conference; but betrayed himself, though against his will. For after this speech was finished, no further words were necessary, but he gave utterance to one only sentiment, which did him much more honor than the diadem. And what was that? "How, said he, "can it be anything wonderful or great, that we should remit our anger against those who have treated us with indignity; we, who ourselves are but men; when the Lord of the universe, having come as He did on earth, and having been made a servant for us, and crucified by those who had experienced His kindness, besought the Father on behalf of His crucifiers, saying, "Forgive them, for they know not what they do?" What marvel, then, if we also should forgive our fellow-servants! And that these words were not a presence was proved by all that followed. And not the least, that particular circumstance which I am now about to mention; for this our priest, when he would have remained there, and celebrated the feast together with himself, he urged,

though contrary to what he would have wished,—to use all speed, and diligence, to present himself to his fellow-citizens. "I know," said he, "that their souls are still agitated; and that there are many relics of the calamity left. Go, give them consolation! If they see the helmsman, they will no longer remember the storm that has passed away; but all recollection of these sorrowful events will be effaced!" And when the Priest was urgent, entreating him to send his own son, he, wishing to give the most satisfactory proof of his having entirely blotted out from his soul every wrathful feeling, answered; "Pray that these hindrances may be taken out of the way; that these wars may be put an end to; and then I will certainly come myself."

19. What could be gentler than such a soul? Let the Gentiles henceforward be ashamed; or rather, instead of being ashamed, let them be instructed; and leaving their native error, let them come back to the strength of Christianity, having learned what our philosophy is, from the example of the Emperor and of the Priest! For our most pious Emperor stayed not at this point; but when the Bishop had left the city, and come over the sea, he dispatched thither also certain persons, being most solicitous and painstaking to prevent any waste of time lest the city should be thus deprived of half its pleasure, whilst the bishop was celebrating the feast beyond its walls. Where is the gracious father that would have so busied himself on behalf of those who had insulted him? But I must mention another circumstance that redounds to the praise of the just man. For when he had accomplished this, he did not make it his endeavor, as anyone else might have done, who was fond of glory, to deliver those letters himself, which were to set us free from the state of

dejection in which we were; but since he was journeying at too slow a rate for this, he thought proper to send forward another person in his stead; one among those who were skilled in horsemanship, to be the bearer of the good news to the city; lest its sadness should be prolonged by the tardiness of his arrival. For the only thing he earnestly coveted was this; not that he might come himself, bringing these favorable tidings, so full of all that is delightful, but that our country might as soon as possible breathe freely again.

20. What therefore ye then did, in decking the forum with garlands; lighting lamps, spreading couches of green leaves before the shops, and keeping high festival, as if the city had just come into being, this do ye, although in another manner, throughout all time;—being crowned, not with flowers, but with virtue;—kindling in your souls the light which comes from good works; rejoicing with a spiritual gladness. And let us never fail to give God thanks continually for all these things, not only that he hath freed us from these calamities, but that he also permitted them to happen; and let us acknowledge his abundant goodness! For by both these has He adorned our city. Now all these things according to the prophetic saying, "Declare ye to your children; and let your children tell their children; and their children again another generation." So that all who shall be hereafter, even to the consummation, learning this act of God's lovingkindness towards the city, may call us blessed, in having enjoyed such a favor;—may marvel at our Sovereign, who raised up the city when it was so grievously falling;—and may themselves be profited, being stimulated to piety by means of all which has happened! For the history of what has lately happened to us, will have power to profit not

only ourselves, if we constantly remember it, but also those who shall come after us. All these things then being considered, let us always give thanks to God who loves man; not merely for our deliverance from these fearful evils, but for their being permitted to overtake us,— learning this from the divine Scriptures, as well as from the late events that have befallen us; that He ever disposes all things for our advantage, with that lovingkindness which is His attribute, which God grant, that we may continually enjoy, and so may obtain the kingdom of heaven, in Christ Jesus our Lord; to whom be glory and dominion for ever and ever. Amen.

Find this and other great works of the Early Church Fathers at lighthousechristianpublishing.com.

St. John Chrysostom

Our Father who art in heaven, hallowed be thy name.
Thy kingdom come, Thy will be done, on earth as it is in heaven.
Give us this day our daily bread and forgive us our trespasses as we forgive those who trespass against us.
And lead us not into temptation, but deliver us from evil, for Thine is the kingdom, the power and the glory. Forever and ever.

Amen

Hail Mary full of grace, the Lord is with thee. Blessed art thou amongst women and blessed is the fruit of thy womb Jesus. Holy Mary mother of God, pray for us sinners, now and the hour of our death.